Rosina Harrison (known as Rose) was born in Aldfield, North Yorkshire, in 1899. Her mother was a laundry maid and her father a stonemason. Rose went into service in 1914, and she was later a lady's maid to Lady Astor for thirty-five years. She later retired to Worthing, where she died in 1989.

# GENTLEMEN'S GENTLEMEN

## My Friends in Service

# ROSINA HARRISON

SPHERE

First published in Great Britain by Arlington Books (Publishers) Ltd 1976
First Sphere Books edition 1978

Reissued in 2015 by Sphere

1 3 5 7 9 10 8 4 6 2

A CIP catalogue record for this book
is available from the British Library.

ISBN 978-0-7515-6400-6

Printed and bound in Great Britain by
Clays Ltd, St Ives plc

Papers used by Sphere are from well-managed forests
and other responsible sources.

MIX
Paper from
responsible sources
FSC
www.fsc.org    FSC® C104740

Sphere
An imprint of
Little, Brown Book Group
Carmelite House
50 Victoria Embankment
London EC4Y 0DZ

An Hachette UK Company
www.hachette.co.uk

www.littlebrown.co.uk

To

*Gordon Grimmett*
*Edwin Lee*
*Charles Dean*
*George Washington*
*Peter Whiteley*

My Friends in Service

# CONTENTS

# CONTENTS

# FOREWORD

The title of this book may be a little misleading, it should perhaps be called, 'Some of My Friends in Service'.

I have heard people say that they can number their true friends on the fingers of one hand, I run out of toes when I am counting. Perhaps this is because in a lifetime in service I have had to rely on and depend on the others that worked with me to do their job in order that I could do mine. I quickly learnt those whom I could trust and I believe that trust is the basis of true and lasting friendships. I hope that this book will demonstrate what I mean. So while I am particularly grateful to the five men whose lives are contained herein and to whom I dedicate this book, I also appreciate the many others, some living, some dead, who have shared their lives with me during my forty-five years in service.

There are others whom I must thank for their help in the preparation of this book; my two sisters, Olive and Ann, and my brother-in-law Cyril Price, for their continued faith and support; Desmond Elliott, my agent and now my publisher who makes work such fun; my devoted typist and secretary Jenny Boreham; and finally Leigh 'Reggie' Crutchley, who has made it all possible.

# I

# PROLOGUE

When I began my book, *Rose, My Life in Service*, I thought it would be a story that primarily concerned me and a description of what my life was like as a lady's maid. Instead it became, almost unconsciously, a tale of the relationships of two women of completely different class and upbringing, Lady Astor and myself. I tried to tell the truth, hoping to show my deep affection for her, while at the same time explaining how difficult she often made it for that affection to be sustained; how we battled through life together, how as the years went by we became necessary to each other. I, with my humble background and lack of education, was no match for her sharp wit, but my native Yorkshire bluntness would take the wind out of her sails and exasperate her to a point of screaming heeby-jeebies. But this, it seemed, was what she wanted from me.

In order to verify my story, for I am a stickler for the truth, I set out on a journey visiting old friends who had worked for her ladyship. This book is largely a result of that journey, for as we talked I heard much more than I was able to include in *Rose, My Life in Service*. Our conversations took me back over domestic life during the whole of the twentieth century, indeed further, particularly in the case of Mr Lee who is ninety this year; he told of masters and servants who were an expression of mid-Victorian times and who lived and worked in areas of Britain where the relationship between the two had changed little since feudal times. So I like to think that this book is not just a series of the lives of servants but a bit of social history as well; that it shows the reliance that two sections of society placed on each other.

When I look at the world today, it frightens me. People, it seems, are jealous of each other and of each other's possessions. Knowing that they can never achieve either the positions or the things, the 'have-nots' have set out to destroy the 'haves'. Envy is eating us up. And what for? Happiness? I've known scullery maids who were happier than duchesses. Position and possession in my day brought with them responsibilities of the kind that I and others like me were unfitted to carry. The people I served felt that they had a duty towards society. They may have played hard but they also worked hard, and sometimes it was difficult to distinguish which was which, for many a dinner party secured a large cheque from one or more of the guests, which went to help humanity.

Much as people may dislike heredity, in my experience the sons and daughters of the so-called privileged classes were educated and brought up in the spirit of giving service to others. Today things have changed, Jack is as good as his master, so his master feels no responsibility towards Jack. 'Blow you Jack, I'm all right', has become the cry of the rich as well as the poor. Since Jack makes no secret of the fact that he's trying to overthrow his master, who's to blame them?

What I'm trying to say though goes deeper than the servant/ master relationship, it's reflected in all our lives. When I was a girl there was no social service run by the government, but there was a more human kind run out of good neighbourliness.

If people in my village were in trouble everyone did what they could to help, not just in their trouble, but to help them get out of it. People were of course expected to help themselves too. Spongers got short shrift.

My father was a stone mason on the Marquess of Ripon's estate. He never earned more than a pound a week and on that brought up a family of four children, yet when he died the entire village turned out to see him away, a sign of respect for a man who had done so much for other people. After his death my mother had little money, only what she earned from taking in laundry. We children followed the common fashion by sending her money and seeing that she was as well looked after as possible. Later I was able to buy a bungalow for her out of my earnings. I wasn't making a sacrifice, it gave me great pleasure.

Today if anyone falls on hard times, either through circumstances or their own fault, relatives and friends just give them a list of where they can get government grants, tell them it's their right and leave them to sort themselves out. To my mind rights should be earned. Things that come too easy aren't respected.

I think that this change in people's thinking is shown in the stories of this book, and I hope that it will prompt one or two questions. Are people with all the gadgets and entertainment that science has given us any happier today than we were? Are we now a better people? Is grabbing as good as getting?

Having got that sermonising off my Yorkshire chest, let me come down to earth. Because it suited me to make my life in service as a lady's maid I didn't marry. I thought about it but after an engagement lasting nine years I decided against it. However, as my mother would have said, 'I was always one for the boys.' I enjoyed their company and companionship, I loved dancing, I even flirted with them providing there was no 'hanky-panky'. I knew when and where to draw the line, and I saw to it that they knew as well. As I was, even at an early age, a career girl, putting my work first, my contact with men was reduced to those working with me and around me, and it was from amongst what might be called my own kind that I looked for and found friendship. I also made many women friends but in this book I'm limiting friendships to the men in my life, all of whom except one became butlers, but on their way up were lamp boys, page boys, hall boys, odd men, footmen, valets and under butlers.

I was in service for forty-five years; five years with Lady Ierne Tufton, five with Lady Cranborne (now the Dowager Marchioness of Salisbury), and finally thirty-five years with Lord and Lady Waldorf Astor. During my first ten years in service I was growing up and made no lasting relationships; even if I had there would have been no place for them in this book since none of the men I worked with then are now alive and would therefore have been unable to recall their lives to me; and being a stickler that the truth shall be told, and witnessed to be told, I have selected my friends from those who can verify what I have written of them. So it is that all the five story-tellers have at some time worked for the Astors.

When I retired from service in 1964 on Lady Astor's death, I found it wasn't something that I could put on one side. I continued to visit the friends that had served with me and on occasion I was ready to return to lend a hand at houses I had been to with my lady, if their servants were ill or on holiday. In this way I was able to keep in touch with the domestic scene, to watch the changes that were taking place and to make friends with some of the younger lot who had become servants under the new order of things.

So through the eyes and tongues of my five friends I am able to present a picture of the position of men servants over the whole of this century, and at second or third hand over a much longer period; to show the changes that have resulted from two world wars and the social attitudes of the British, and sometimes of the American, people. So far as I can I have tried to capture the personalities of those who seem to tell their own stories and to give them the language and mannerisms of speech which are very much their own.

This book though is not confined to servants. Where there is a downstairs there must be an upstairs, so that another picture will emerge, that of the way of life and behaviour of the aristocracy and the landed gentry. Because this picture is, as it were, painted by servants it may be thought that it's one-sided, particularly where conflict occurs, but if the masters or mistresses come in for criticism I think that it will be found that it is friendly and not malicious.

To a man my friends defend the system under which we worked and regret the passing of the privileged society which they served. They miss the glamour, the glitter, the manners and the style. Perhaps most of all they miss the business of 'knowing your place' and 'keeping your place', expressions which you will find they apply not only to themselves but to those whom they served.

Today such expressions, which were common in my life, may need explaining. When I first joined the Astor family Mr Lee, the butler, in describing Lady Astor said, 'She is not a lady as you would understand a lady, Miss Harrison.'

This remark spoke volumes to me; I knew that I would be serving a woman who couldn't or wouldn't conduct herself according to the rules and that because of this my life would be made precarious and unpredictable. If Lady Astor didn't know 'her place' it was going to be hard for me to keep mine. On the other hand when Mr Lee described Lord Astor as 'every inch a gentleman' I knew straight away that I would be able to serve him with ease.

The master/servant relationship which so many people now decry gave peace of mind and often social and financial security, providing it was conducted according to the rules. 'Playing the game' wasn't just something that was learnt and practised in English schools, it was a code of behaviour for life. Particularly is this seen to be true in the way stately homes were conducted.

Many people will say that this is a political book, that I'm an out and out Tory. It isn't, and I'm not. Perhaps in a way there's a touch of religion in it, though it would be impossible to pinpoint it. I'll try and show what I mean.

All my friends and I were born and brought up in country villages where church-going was a part of our lives. Consciously or unconsciously it influenced us, it gave us a set of values so that, at certain moments when later we were called upon to make decisions, we were able to make the right ones and to assume responsibilities that our schooling had not prepared us for.

But perhaps I'm stressing too much what I see as the serious side of the book. First and foremost it's a fun story. Domestic service was played to certain rules, but different people had different interpretations of rules and this led to conflict. Then of course rules are made to be broken and they were, on both sides, which adds to the fascination of the game, and to the writing about it.

The television series 'Upstairs, Downstairs' has given to the world a picture of what domestic service was like and it's almost always been a true one within the limitations of its dramatic form. I think, speaking as a servant, it's done something else. It has given my life's work a dignity and purpose that was not recognised before, and has shown myself and my friends and colleagues as human, real and useful members of society, a society that people today look back on partly with nostalgia and partly because they can find little to look forward to.

# A FRIEND IN SERVICE

### Gordon Grimmett

The first of my friends to tell his story is Gordon Grimmett. I've chosen him to open partly because he was the one I visited first on my journey of rediscovery, and partly because he's such a good raconteur and able to describe not only his own duties but those of his fellow servants with accuracy, and finally because he began work at Longleat, the seat of the Marquess of Bath, from where he was able to glean so much about the history and conditions of service during the nineteenth century.

Gordon, despite his poor early education, which he made the poorer by his behaviour and high spirits, has a sharp and inquiring mind, an excellent memory and an eye for detail. He didn't stay long in full-time service and after a few minor jobs made a career as a salesman of agricultural products, ending up as area manager in some of the most prosperous farming land in the country. His was a successful business life, the more so because of his humble upbringing; yet whatever company he is in he inevitably brings the conversation round to the days when he was a servant and from his expression and the way that he speaks of them it's apparent that this is the time he enjoyed most and they are the memories he treasures.

I didn't meet him when he was employed full time, though I heard plenty about him when I joined the Astors, and it was not long after this that our paths crossed. It was when he came as part-time footman to dinners and receptions at St James's Square. He was tall, good looking and with a permanent twinkle in his eyes, and today at the age of seventy-four he is very much the same. He could never be serious for long and because of his attitude I was astonished that he and Mr Lee got on as well as they did. I soon discovered that, frivolous though he might be, Gordon was an excellent footman. He was like an actor; he'd be playing the fool in the wings but from the moment he went on the stage he was straight into his part. It was the theatre of service that appealed to him, the dressing up in livery with almost period movement and big gestures that fitted the Louis Quinze dining-room at Cliveden, the throwing of the voice when announcing the guests, their beautiful clothes and jewels, the style, the grace. He loved this flitting in and out of the grand scene. He was stage struck, which is why he took every opportunity to return to what was his theatre.

# II

# THE LAMP BOY'S STORY

## Gordon Grimmett

Many of my friends thought that, because my father was a postman, as a family we were a cut above them. Perhaps it had something to do with that picture of a lurching coach and rearing horses battling against the elements, with the caption 'The Royal Mail must get through'; that was the sort of pop art of the time and could be seen on many cottage walls, alongside Landseer's 'Stag at bay'. Or perhaps it was the uniform that in their minds placed the postman on a par with the policeman, a figure of authority, if not of power. If Dad was aware of this image of his he didn't try to live or play up to it; neither did I. It wasn't easy for him to think big when he was only earning eighteen shillings a week, and keeping a family of eight on it. Nor for me at school where I cut a pretty poor figure, at any rate in the eyes of my teachers. Indeed I might easily have felt inferior had it not been for my ability to organise the 'in-fighting' both in the classroom and the playground. I suppose I should be ashamed of my tearaway childhood, but I'm not. Because I found learning hard to come by it meant that I had to find compensations, and I got them in the streets of Ascot and roaming the Berkshire countryside with a gang of boys. We didn't do much harm, a few practical jokes on the shopkeepers and raids on orchards, more for the excitement than for the fruit we stole. In those days getting caught meant a first-class thrashing from the man on the spot, and another at home if Dad got to know about it. The purpose and the thrill were trying not to get found out.

Ascot at the turn of the century was a quiet marketing town which came alive a few times each year when the fashionable race meetings were on, when we kids could earn a copper or two holding the carriage horses of the nobility. It was toppers in the daytime for men and tiaras at night for the ladies in the many large country houses that surrounded the town. Little did I think at the time that it wouldn't be long before I'd be living in one of them, and spending my time dressing and looking after these Lords of the Land.

Although my parents disapproved of my behaviour from time to time, and made their opinions felt, I had a very happy home life. Mother was a good manager; she had to be on so very little money. Fortunately she had spaced her family so that when I was eight one brother and two sisters were away working – my brother as a gardener, one sister as a stillroom maid to the Duke of Northumberland at Alnwick Castle, and the other a parlour maid in a London house. All three sent money home, it was the expected thing for children to do in those days and this helped to provide for me, my younger brother and sister. Clothes of course were passed down, patched but still wearable. Dad earned extra money working as a bearer to the local undertaker and I eventually brought in a bit by caddying at golf courses and selling the golf balls that I found on my way round. So we never went short of food, but it was plain fare, never a lot of meat, and indeed I never tasted chicken until I went into service. We might I suppose have been better off but for Dad's nightly visits to 'Sally's'. It wasn't that he kept another woman; Sally was the landlady of the Nursery Inn, our local pub, where he would sit every night drinking beer and playing dominoes. Sometimes he'd visit there at lunch-time as well, particularly if he had a funeral in the afternoon. I know because there was speculation among his friends as to how long it would be before he fell into a grave while he was lowering a coffin. Still, none of us ever resented Dad's drinking, least of all Mum. It kept him happy and contented, and in most families it was the accepted thing; it was only the do-gooders who tut-tutted their way around the town causing nothing but trouble among working class people.

Thinking back to my early days I'm sure I must have been a disappointment to Mum. She'd set her heart on having a son who'd win a scholarship to nearby Windsor Grammar School. All good parents, and there were many, wanted their sons to do better than they had and to get out of the working class rut; but education was not for me at that time. It began when I went into service and it developed through my watching, listening and imitating. Poor Mum, I couldn't even compensate her by being good at sport, for there were no organised games at school.

I did excel at one thing, however, stone throwing, at which I was a crack shot, but unfortunately it brought me nothing but trouble. I've mentioned the top hats worn by the gentry at race meetings, and these were far too tempting a target. They also supplied the element of excitement and the risk of being found out and caught. At first I was careful to take good cover, and delighted my friends with my marksmanship, but success brought over-confidence; I was caught three times in a week and having been ruffed up a bit by my victims was reported to the headmaster. Although I was accustomed to the cane by now, three beatings in seven days took it out of me, and when bath night came and Mum saw the marks on my backside, the cat was out of the bag. I anticipated further punishment, either from her or Dad, but although Mum's lips narrowed and I was sent to bed without supper, I heard nothing more from either of them. A few days later my headmaster sent for me, 'Ah boy,' he said, and he was beaming all over his face, 'your mother and I have had a little chat. We've come to the conclusion that you need a change of environment. Next week you will join another school at Cranbourne (a village near Windsor), it will give you the opportunity of making a new start. Let's hope you'll make the best of it – eh.'

He said it in a tone that only expressed doubt that I would. As I left his study he called after me, 'I understand that the stones are not so thick on the ground in Cranbourne as they are in Ascot,' and he burst out into a guffaw.

It was the first time I had heard him laugh. It was not a pleasant sound.

I'd like to be able to say that I seized my new opportunity and made the headmaster a false prophet. I didn't; it wasn't so much changing schools as changing canes. I was allowed to leave at the age of thirteen. My new headmaster then said he'd taught me all he could, but I didn't care for the way he said it.

The First World War had now been on for a year, so, as my contribution to the war effort, I went into munitions. It sounds quite impressive, but it wasn't. The factory was a converted garage, and I was put on the night shift, dull, repetitive and unfriendly work.

Physically I'd developed fast for my age and although I still went around with a gang of boys I found I was becoming increasingly aware of the charms of the other sex. In order to earn a bit more money, I worked as an errand boy delivering vegetables for a local greengrocer, and in the course of my duties I used to visit a small house in Ascot called 'White Cottage'. Two young Kentish girls, the Waterhouse sisters, worked there as cook and housemaid. I took a shine to them both and must have amused them, as they constantly invited me round for a cup of tea, a chat and a smoke. I felt no end of a dog puffing away at their scented cigarettes – 'Sweet as a rose' it said on the box. I remember also stealing the odd kiss, more like a peck I suppose, and I was absolutely unconcerned which sister I took it from.

But it was not my introduction to the joys of the other sex, however innocent, which was important in my life. It was my friendship with these girls that led me into domestic service. They talked of the grand houses, mostly it must have been from hearsay, and it seemed to me the nearest I was likely to get to a glamorous life. So when one day they told me they were leaving Ascot to go and work at a country house at Bath, I went back home determined to follow them. I first informed Mum of my new-found ambition. She jumped at the idea, but, I thought, for the wrong reasons. 'Now that the younger children are growing up we need your room,' was the first thing that came into her mind. 'I'll write to Mrs Hunts straight away.'

Mrs Hunts was the famous London servants' agency, or registry office as such places were called then. 'Make sure you tell them the area around Bath,' I said.

She promised she would, although she couldn't understand my reason for wanting to go there in particular, and said so. I didn't enlighten her. If I had it would have provoked nothing but merriment at my expense. Youthful romance was considered as something peculiarly comic in those days, particularly among the younger members of the family, and I knew I should be teased unmercifully.

To my surprise Mum had a reply almost by return. I hadn't really thought that anyone would want to employ a young inexperienced boy like me. I'd forgotten that there was a war on and that by 1915 there was already a shortage of men servants. I was offered the position of lamp boy to the Marquess of Bath at Longleat House in Wiltshire. I'd no idea what a lamp boy was or what his duties were, so I inquired around. Nobody else seemed to know, though they made one or two peculiar suggestions. 'You'll find out soon enough when you get there,' was Mum's unhelpful remark.

She bought me a second-hand brown tin trunk, more like a large tin box, packed my few things into it, tied it up with a bit of rope and only about a fortnight after I'd first spoken of going into service I found myself sitting alone in a train on my way to Warminster, the nearest station to Longleat. I felt miserable and lost at first, Mum had shed a few tears when we parted, and it was almost as if I was going away to the war; I'd managed to control myself but the lump in my throat felt as big as a cricket ball. I soon discovered my spirits though, after all it was an adventure for me and I'd always have a home to go back to; Dad had made a point of telling me that. Only one thing worried me, I'd bought no uniform; Mum had told me this would be provided when I got there but I wasn't sure how she knew. Still, I thought, as no one in Ascot knew what a lamp boy was they weren't likely to know at our local tailors how one should be dressed.

I was met at Warminster at half past two by the Longleat carrier in a covered cart drawn by a shaggy horse. Thinking about him now he was like Barkis, the Dickens carrier in. *David Copperfield*. He handed me a packet of sandwiches, 'Yer lunch,' he said, 'and you'll need it 'cos I've got things to deliver around the estate and you'll not get to the big house until around five o'clock.'

I munched away at my sandwiches as we trotted along. After a time he started chuckling to himself, quietly at first, then more lively. I began to doubt his sanity. He broke into a guffaw, then suddenly stopped. 'You'll be wondering why I'm laughin',' he said. I agreed politely. 'It's that tin box of yourn. It reminds me of a time when I came to the station to collect a young housemaid, strapping girl she was. I met her at Bath and I'd gone on to the platform so that she wouldn't leave the wrong way. "Your carriage is over the bridge, miss," I says. "But I've got a tin trunk," she says. "Tin trunk, I don't care if you've got a tin arse, the carriage is still over the bridge," I says, quick as a flash.' Then he burst into thunderous laughter.

I didn't get the point of the story but I made what I thought were appropriate noises. He wasn't satisfied, 'Don't you see, tin trunk – tin arse.'

I was still baffled but tried to roar as loudly as he did. He seemed satisfied at this, but at intervals during the rest of the journey he kept bursting forth with his 'Tin trunk – tin arse.'

After what seemed an interminable journey we began the drive up to Longleat. With every step the horse took it loomed larger and I felt smaller, more insignificant and not a little frightened. He drove round to the side of the house, and with his 'whoa there' the horse came to a halt. I jumped down, and with a final 'Tin trunk – tin arse' he handed me my trunk. 'So long me lad, I'll be seeing you,' and he drove off chuckling as he went.

I walked to a door and rang the bell. It was answered by a boy a little older than myself. 'Hello,' he said, 'you must be the new lamp boy. My name's 'Uthwaite, Bob 'Uthwaite, with a aitch. I'm a Londoner. I've instructions to take you to the steward, Mr Brazier, and if you'll take a bit of advice from me see that you call him "sir" when he speaks to you, it will get you off on the right foot.'

Even if Bob Huthwaite hadn't warned me I would have still called Mr Brazier 'sir'. He was an imposing figure, tall and austere of around fifty, with a fresh ruddy complexion and a head of beautiful silver hair. He addressed me in a gentle kind of way; it could be very deceptive, as I discovered later. 'You are Grimmett, Gordon Grimmett?'

'Yes, sir,' I replied. It had the required effect.

'Very good, Gordon, I trust we shall get on well together. You've eaten your sandwiches, now Robert will see that you get some tea, after which he'll show you where you're to sleep and explain your duties to you. That will be all for the moment.'

Bob and I went to the servants' hall, a vast room with a refectory table in the centre and benches round the sides, and two large carving chairs at either end. I was nervous of course and over-awed, but not so much so that I didn't notice the housemaids gliding about in their black dresses. My thoughts went to the Waterhouse sisters. I'd written to them in Bath telling them that I was going into service nearby, and that I hoped we could meet soon, but I had had no answer. I wasn't sure now that I was worried as I studied the girls around me. Then Bob told me that the second floor of the house had been given over to the army for their use during the war as a convalescent home for wounded soldiers. Apparently, like me, he had a taste for the girls for he lingered in his descriptions of the charms of the nurses.

Tea over he took me upstairs to show me my sleeping quarters. These were in a kind of small dormitory with six beds in it; mine was in the corner. There was linoleum on the floor, a dressing-table and about four rickety chairs; that was the sum total of the furniture. I was sharing, I was told, with two under footmen, one of the odd men, the pantry boy and Bob the steward's room boy. I didn't know whether to be pleased or disappointed with the conditions; having nothing to compare them with I just accepted them. We went down to the servants' hall again and stayed there for the rest of the evening.

I met one or two of the other servants, and Bob did his best to explain my duties, to give me some idea of the layout and the history of the house, and to describe the make-up of the inside staff at Longleat, together with their likes, dislikes and eccentricities. Although there wasn't quite a full complement with war having claimed one or two of the men, women had taken over their jobs so the inside staff was almost complete, and this is how I remember it:

There was a steward (butler), an under butler, groom of the chambers, valet, three footmen, two odd men, a pantry boy, a steward's room boy, a hall boy and me, the lamp boy. Of the women staff there was a housekeeper, two ladies' maids, eight housemaids, two sewing maids, two stillroom maids, six laundry maids; in the kitchen a cook, two kitchen maids, a vegetable maid, scullery maid and a daily woman. The outside staff I was never fully able to account for; chauffeurs, grooms, a steel boy (his job was to burnish the metal on the horses' harness) and a young lad called a 'tiger'.

Tigers were preferably small and sweet-faced, they sat on the box of the carriage. Today I suppose they would be considered figures of fun, sitting there in their livery with their arms folded over their chests and concentrated stern expressions on their faces, but we didn't think of ours like that and he took himself very seriously indeed. Part of a tiger's job was to lead the young children's ponies when they went riding, but of course this didn't happen at Longleat as the children were past that. The chauffeurs and the grooms were at that time, and in any house, sworn enemies; the ringing-out of the old and the ringing-in of the new caused almost continuous conflict. During the war, of course, the pageantry was suspended from all state occasions, nor was there a London season in the true sense, but I was told of those grand days and indeed saw the yellow coach that drove the Marquess and Marchioness to events like a coronation, a ball at Buckingham Palace, a levée, a presentation for the opening of parliament, and splendid though the coach was I think the coachman must have rivalled it in his six-tiered cape fastened from neck to hem, with silver crested buttons, wearing a three-cornered hat trimmed with silver braid.

There were also the gardeners, some forty or so men and women, the latter having been recruited as a result of the war, and the home farm staff of twenty-odd as well as a maintenance outside force of carpenters, bricklayers, painters and the like, so it could be seen why it was that our weekly dances and concerts were crowded, especially with the addition of nurses, ward maids and other medical staff. We were particularly lucky at this time because there was an Australian camp nearby and regularly they would send a concert party over to entertain the patients, and we servants were allowed to occupy the back of the hall.

Bob found it easier to describe the staff than the house, and his efforts at its history were abysmal. Mind you at the time I wasn't one for the old things; the present was exciting enough for me, but by the time I left service I'd managed, through my surroundings and the people I worked for – and with – to find a thirst for education, and it's one of many things for which I shall always be grateful to my early livelihood. Today I could give you a conducted tour round Longleat and explain its furnishings and its history accurately and impeccably.

It was built by Sir John Thynne, the foundations being laid

in 1567 and it was finished thirteen years later. Sir John, who was born in 1515 and died in 1580, was a favourite of the Duke of Somerset, the Protector, by whom he was knighted in the battlefield at Pinkie. The Protector had wide powers of patronage and so helped enrich Sir John. Sir John also helped himself by marrying an heiress, Christine Gresham, daughter of a Lord Mayor of London.

Queen Elizabeth of course slept at Longleat, nosing around as she did among her wealthier subjects and seeing exactly how much they'd got and what they were doing with it. Charles II also slept there and he it was who created Sir Thomas Thynne Viscount Weymouth.

The second Viscount started a legend which was a familiar bit of history with all the servants. He fought a duel with his wife's, Lady Louisa's, lover, killed him and entombed him in the cellars. The bones were found centuries later and years after I'd left, when the fifth Marquess was having central heating installed. His jackboots appeared to be in perfect condition, but they crumbled away as soon as they were exposed to the air. He caused me enough trouble during my stay at Longleat, appearing in places that were my province. As if his presence wasn't enough Lady Louisa's ghost haunted the passage where the duel was fought. It was known as 'the Green Lady's walk'. It's also my opinion that she and her fancy boy used to get together from time to time because I saw both of them in the cellars.

George III was another sleeper at Longleat, in the third Lord Weymouth's time, and caused another change of name in the family, for he created Lord Weymouth Marquess of Bath during his stay.

This is an example of how you get that quaint mix-up in British noble families. The younger sons and daughters are called Thynne, with of course an Honourable or a Lady in front of their names, the eldest son is Lord Weymouth, and the father is Marquess of Bath. It causes quite a lot of confusion, even among the initiated.

History doesn't report any more English kings and queens who visited Longleat. Queen Victoria certainly didn't, though Lord Beaconsfield did during the time of the fourth Marquess; perhaps this accounts for her absence, because although a special temporary lavatory was constructed for him in his bedroom, he hated the place. He wrote from there complaining about the cold and apparently had difficulty getting any ink!

I was to serve the fifth Marquess, who was in his fifties when I joined. I found him a great gentleman, kind and considerate, handsome but without conceit, an example to all with his perfect and natural good manners. The Marchioness I was in awe of. She was about the same age as her husband but somehow seemed much older to me. She was highly religious, which because of my chapel duties (which I shall describe later) brought us together. She was always most kind in a distant sort of way, seeming so far off I sometimes wondered if she really saw me at all.

There were four children – three daughters, Lady Kathleen Thynne, Lady Emma, who was to marry the Marquess of Northampton, and Lady Mary, later Lady Numburnholme, and one son Lord Weymouth, aged about twelve, Lord Henry as we knew him. He'd succeeded to the title when his elder brother Lord Alexander was killed in action in 1916.

The girls, like their mother, remained very distant. It seemed to me that they led dull lives, buried in the country with very little opportunity of mixing with young men; in any case most of the eligible ones were away serving their country. They occasionally visited London where they stayed at their town house at 29 Grosvenor Square but were always closely guarded and chaperoned. Perhaps they did find opportunities for some fun and games on the side, but I never saw any signs of it. Lord Weymouth I was to get to know well as time went on.

But I'm in danger of getting ahead of myself. When it came to my duties Bob got a bit vague, 'It's no good my describing them,' he said, 'I'll take you around tomorrow and explain them to you.'

He was a wily one was young Bob, a proper cockney. I later discovered that the reason why he didn't want to commit himself was that he was going to try to palm a number of his own jobs on to me. He succeeded for a time but the other servants soon put me wise to him. I didn't bear him any malice over it for as I came to climb the ladder I tried the same thing on myself.

It was time now for bed, something I was not looking forward to as Bob had told me that the others I was sharing with would probably rag me for the first night or two. He wasn't wrong. I was a bit shy about getting undressed, so they helped me, making coarse remarks and certain comparisons as they did so. Eventually they quietened down a bit but when I opened my trunk and took out a new pair of bedroom slippers, which had been a parting present from my mum, they broke out into screams of merriment. Come to think of it I must have cut a comic figure standing in my shirt, for in those days pyjamas or nightshirts were not worn by the working class, with a pair of bright red cloth slippers on my feet. Despite their taunts I continued to wear them. It was better than padding about on the cold lino in bare feet. There was no central heating in any part of the house and many's the morning I was in agreement with old Lord Beaconsfield, for often he had had to break the ice in the water jug before he could wash.

I was up next morning at six and Bob and I went round the

house collecting the shoes. Eventually we had about sixty pairs (family and nurses) down in the cellar waiting to be cleaned. From time to time one of us would break off and go to a landing, fill a number of white enamel jugs with hot water and take them around the bedrooms. Six at a time I could manage, three in each hand, though I clanked about a bit as I carried them. At eight o'clock we had breakfast in the servants' hall. It was a picnic kind of meal with people coming and leaving as their duties required. There was little variety, it seemed it was always kedgeree on weekdays and bacon on Sundays. As it was war time we were each given a quarter of a pound of butter a week, which we kept in a small tin; once that was gone it was dry bread.

After breakfast there was knife cleaning, steel knives with bone handles. This was done with the help of a large round knife machine. It had holes in it into which was shaken Oakley powder, then the knives were inserted and the handle turned. After the knives, the forks, not the silver ones of course, but those that were used in the servants' hall; all others had to be cleaned by hand.

By now it was a quarter to nine, time for me to rush over to the chapel for one of my daily duties, as candle boy. The chapel was lit by one hundred and forty candles, and a very beautiful sight it was. It was my job before the service to light them. I did this with a taper on the end of a stick, on the other side of which was a snuffer which was used to put them out. It was supposed to stop them smelling. It didn't. The smoke and stench pervaded the place and it became like a gas chamber.

I also had to put the vicar's cassock and surplice ready, and to help him into them. He needed help too for he'd had to walk a mile and a half from Horningsham village come rain come shine. I've seen him staggering in exhausted in winter after trudging through a foot of snow. My final job was to sharpen his quill pen.

There was a service every day lasting about twenty minutes, and of course two longer ones on Sunday. All the servants who could be spared had to leave their duties and it was generally only the kitchen staff who were excused. Either their souls were considered beyond redemption, or our masters put their stomachs before their God. Judging from the language and general behaviour in the kitchens wherever I've worked I think it must have been the former.

The Marchioness, as I've said, was particularly religious. She always carried a little notebook and I used to see her in the gallery where the family sat, peering down at the commoners below. In between prayers she'd sit up and make a note; either she had noticed an absentee or she'd seen someone chattering or fooling about. Never did she have the opportunity of booking me, for on top of my other duties I was organ blower. Some might have found this boring, but I didn't, out of sight being out of mind, and I could read a book or a comic during the prayers or the sermon. There was also an additional attraction to the job which I suppose I ought to be ashamed to mention.

Every other Sunday evening an attractive young girl would come up and sing a hymn or an anthem as a solo. She stood on a platform just above where I was blowing. She'd got lovely legs and there were very few who knew them as well as I did, because my eyes would get caught by them and I had a sort of competition with myself seeing how far up I could peer. Once or twice I got so entranced that I'd forgotten what I was supposed to be doing, and the organ would run out of air. This got a laugh from some of the congregation for I'd confided in my colleagues about my salacious Sunday evenings. When the organist reprimanded me I told him I had been carried away by the beautiful singing!

After I'd snuffed the candles when the service was over, I had to attend to them, breaking the wax from the sides and repointing them so that they looked like new. When they had burnt down to within two inches I replaced them. Candle ends were my 'perks', I sold them to the local grocer at so much a dozen, and this way I made an extra pound or two each year. In those days every penny counted.

After I left the chapel I began work on the things which gave me my name – the lamps.

Now it occurs to me that people may wonder at my title of lamp boy. After all by 1915 electricity was no new invention, and some big houses by that time were either on the mains or, if they were too remote, had their own generators. Others had compromised by using gas. Not so the Marquess of Bath, who felt that to install either would disfigure the house. The rooms had been designed for oil lamps or candle light, and if he were to change to electricity not only might it mutilate the ceilings and the walls but the character of the rooms would change. He had the same feelings about central heating.

Many of the gentry agreed over this, mainly I think because it was considered unhealthy, if not downright effete. The British public school system had instilled in them the virtues of a Spartan life, and early principles, it seemed, died hard. It was all right for the foreign aristocracy, they were a soft lot which was why the British Empire was there and would always remain there. It was also why every day I had to collect, clean, trim and fill four hundred lamps.

Actually here I'm not telling the truth because it would have been humanly impossible to have done so many, and of course the quantity was increased because of the hospital. From time to time the odd men, steward's room boy or hall boy would be sent down to help, and if I got very behind the butler would send a footman down to give me a hand. But officially the lamps were my responsibility. In other words if things went wrong with them I was called to account.

Collecting and replacing them itself meant a few miles' walk every day, though again the bulk were delivered to me by the housemaids and the footmen. They came in all shapes and sizes, bracket lamps, standards lamps, table lamps, hanging lamps. Many of them were of great beauty and value, gathered from all parts of the world.

First I would examine the wicks and trim them if necessary with special scissors, rather like an ordinary large pair but with a circular tray piece attached to the blades which caught any wick trimmings and prevented them falling back into the lamps; I wish I had kept a pair, they've become collectors' pieces now.

Then I would fill the lamps from the large oil tanks, paraffin for the corridor and staff lamps, and colsa oil for the house. It was considered that colsa oil gave a kinder more mellow light, and also that it didn't smell so much. I didn't care for colsa as it was thicker than paraffin and, if by chance I left the tap on in the tank the oil fell silently to the floor. So many times my cellar was flooded before I became aware of what had happened. Then there was the polishing of the funnels or the chimneys as they were called, the glass globes, and finally the cleaning of the stands. Fortunately these couldn't be polished, but they had to be free from any traces of oil.

As each batch of twenty or so were finished there would be the journey round replacing them and collecting others. The sheer monotony of the job took some beating. Of course it must be remembered that the lamps provided only the general lighting. Candelabra and candlesticks were used in the dining-rooms and the drawing-rooms, but fortunately these were the responsibility of the footmen. Some of the lamps were counter-weighted from the ceiling, and were in groups of three, each hanging on chains in the galleries. These I had to clean and fill on the spot, as they were too heavy to carry.

I remember one day I was showing off to a housemaid, 'They go up like this,' I said, and woosh – up this one went to the ceiling, and crash – down came the shattered reflector.

The noise startled the Marquess and he came running up the stairs. Fortunately I had the presence of mind to stoop down quickly, pick up a handful of glass, stick it on to my head and stand there shaking.

'My poor boy, are you all right?' he said, putting his arm round my shoulder.

I felt my head, put on a brave smile, 'Yes, my Lord, just a little stunned, please don't worry yourself on my account.' I was beginning to enjoy my performance.

'You must go to your room and lie down,' he said, as I staggered away. 'You're a very brave lad.'

I thought I was too until I stumbled into the arms of Mrs Parker the housekeeper, who was standing on the stairs. 'You lying little devil,' she hissed, 'I saw everything that went on. Playing up to his lordship like that. You wait till I tell Mr Brazier. Now get that glass out of your hair, and back you go to work.'

She was true to her word. I was summoned to the steward's room and given a dressing down by Mr Brazier, who also docked the price of a new reflector from my wages. He didn't tell the Marquess though, who from then on was very solicitous about my health. I reckoned it was worth it. At least now he recognised me when he saw me. I felt I had become part of the place.

I broke away from my lamps for lunch at midday. This was the ceremonial meal when the staff all came together, except for those in the kitchens who were a law unto themselves, or rather unto the chef or cook. It was a strange ritual. First the under servants would assemble standing at their places round the long table. A hand bell was rung by the odd man and then the upper servants filed in arm in arm in order of precedence, the butler and the housekeeper leading, followed by the ladies' maids, valets and the groom of the chambers, and of course any visiting senior servants. They had previously met upstairs in the steward's room, the 'pug's parlour' as it was called.

At a signal from the butler, all sat. The meat course was brought in by the odd man and the hall boy, which Mr Brazier either carved or portioned and which was then handed round again by the odd man and hall boy. Vegetables were placed round the table.

When the meat course had been eaten the remains were cere- moniously removed by the steward's room boy, followed by the upper servants in the order in which they had come in. Then they retired to the steward's room where they ate the remain- der of their meal. After this they would move to Mrs Parker's room for a cup of tea or coffee. Longleat was no exception in the performance of this custom, it was the recognised practice in most of the large country houses of the time.

We fed very well at Longleat; indeed as visiting servants reminded us, 'You wouldn't know there was war on.'

Each week three sheep of different breeds were butchered for the household, a Southdown, Westmoreland and a Brittany. We also had pheasant, partridge, goose, venison, hare and rabbit. Rarely was beef served. The meat course was followed by a variety of puddings and cheese. Since there was no gas or electricity all food was cooked on charcoal. Again Longleat was the only place I served in where there was a fish still. In it swimming about were pike or trout in their season. They were caught in the lakes on the estate and put in the still to cleanse them of the taste of mud.

I once caught a twenty-pound pike, and after giving it a spell in the still, killed it, parcelled it with great care and sent it home. Something went wrong with the post, it took a fortnight to reach there, and instead of a thank you letter, I got a dressing down from Mum.

Beer was allowed regularly. Indeed until just before the war we had brewed our own. It was served in copper jacks, sort of large jugs, and was even drunk at breakfast time.

Perhaps the fondness of beer dated back from the time of the third Marchioness of Bath who in 1829 wrote a book on how to be a good cottager. It begins with instructions on the art of good brewing and follows with a dissertation on tea drinking. 'Tea,' she says, 'besides being good for nothing has badness in it because it is well known to produce want of sleep in many cases, and in all cases to shake and weaken the nerves.' She does some arithmetic to show that tea drinking would cost a family ten pounds a year doing nothing but harm, whereas home-brewed beer would cost seven pounds, five shillings, and benefit them in every way. About bread making she says, 'Every woman high or low ought to know how to make bread. If she does not she is unworthy of trust and confidence.'

Back now to the servants' hall. We ate our main course in absolute silence, indeed the only conversation I can remember was when game or venison were being served. The cook was inconsistent over the length of time necessary for hanging, so Mr Brazier would serve Mr Pigrim the valet first, and would inquire, 'High or low?' Mr Pigrim would then sample it, patter with his lips and tongue, blink through his glasses and eventually give his opinion. If the verdict was 'High', Mr Brazier would sigh, continue serving but when he came to himself would leave his plate empty and be content with a large plate of vegetables.

With the departure of the senior servants, leaving the under butler and the head laundry maid in charge of the servants' hall, discipline relaxed and we were able to talk, though never lively in case one of them returned to give instructions to some member of the staff. I sat near the steward's room boy and it wasn't long before I noticed how, towards the end of the meal, he began to get edgy and impatient.

It appeared that he was a greedy fellow, and the reason he was anxious to get away and clear the dishes from the 'pug's parlour' was that the upper servants had better puddings than we did, and these were not always eaten. It was a race between him and two sewing maids who lived in the village and brought their own sandwiches, as to who could get there first when the exodus to the housekeeper's room had taken place. The venom on that boy's face if he was beaten to it I shall always remember as being something particularly vicious.

The meal over it was back to the lamps again for me.

I've omitted one daily duty that I had to perform just before lunch; to put a day bed out on the terrace near the front door at Longleat. Rain or shine it didn't matter.

This was for Lord Weymouth, the son and heir. His health was not of the best, and at that time he was unable to go away to school and was educated by tutors. Later as his health improved he went to Harrow.

Generally I finished the lamps by the early afternoon and the habit developed that, when I went to collect his day bed, Lord Weymouth would suggest that we took a walk together with the dogs, a greyhound and a terrier, Drake and Ben, a wonderful pair for rabbiting. Ours was a strange relationship. I was some two or three years older than he was so in a way I took the lead, yet by position and birth and by the social customs of the time he was very much my superior. I learnt a lot from him and I think perhaps he did from me. I didn't envy him, nor have I ever been jealous of any of my employers. I think Lord Weymouth helped me to come to terms with myself and my life as it was to be at an early age. He also helped me to learn to read, by which I mean to enjoy books. He had a wonderful collection of Cowboy and Indian stories which he lent me and which formed the basis of many of our games together.

At four o'clock we had tea, which was an informal meal again, bread and butter and sometimes jam, with a cup of tea. After this in the winter came lamp lighting and shutter time for the duty footman, the hall boy and me. The footmen did the lamps in the drawing-room and the other ground and first floor main rooms, while Bob and I did the corridors, the basement and cellars. We all helped with the shutters, which was in itself a tedious job. They were big wooden things which folded back into the wall and when drawn they were fastened with an iron bar which locked into a recess. On this we would then clip in a hand bell, the burglar alarm, the theory being that if a thief tried to break through the shutters the bell would ring. In practice of course no one was likely to hear it, though it was never put to the test in my time I'm glad to say. I was a very imaginative youngster and there were a sufficient number of ghost stories about Longleat to fire my imagination without the possibility of burglars as well.

I've already told you the one about the 'Green Lady'. Of me it can be said, tell him a ghost story and he'll give it form and shape, and that goes for today as well, though of course the lamp or candle light was of great help to the imagination.

When the house was shuttered and lit it was time for supper, consisting of a meat dish and pudding, although the meal was not so formal or so plentiful as the midday one. I was then free until about nine and filled in the time generally by playing cards.

As nine o'clock grew nearer my concentration lessened as I thought of another journey round the house refilling the smaller lamps in the corridors. Sometimes on one or two occasions these might have gone out and the later the hour the more scaryfying it was. Looking back I'm amazed that I stayed in the job. I suppose it was that I had no option. As if the Green Lady wasn't enough for me I was soon fed with another legend, that of Charlotte Wicks.

'Have you met Charlotte yet?' I was asked by one of the housemaids when I had been there a few weeks.

'No,' I said. 'What does she do?'

'Oh, our last lamp boy got to know her very well,' was the reply. 'In fact it was because of her that he left.'

I sensed a sexy story and was all ears, so I demanded to know all about her. It was not the kind of story that I had expected and hoped for. Charlotte Wicks had been head kitchen maid to the fourth Marquess of Bath and was responsible for all the roasts. It was her job to hook the huge haunches of venison or saddles of lamb on to the spits, and with a long-handled metal ladle baste them with hot fat from a trough underneath. When the roasts were cooked, she would remove them and place them in a heated oven until they were wanted for serving.

One day as Charlotte was removing the joint she slipped, her hair became entangled in the revolving spit and she was drawn into the fire. Her hair caught alight and so did her dress. Dragging herself free she rushed down the corridor like a flaming torch, beating against the wall with her ladle to attract attention. No help came, and eventually she collapsed and died on the floor of my lamp room. According to my information she had taken a liking to the place ever since, constantly appearing there to the consternation of my predecessors. When I told Bob Huthwaite the story he described it as 'stuff and nonsense', only in more forthright language, and so did some of the other servants but despite their denials it stuck with me.

A few days after I'd heard it I was late refuelling the corridor lamps. I'd collected four and, carrying two in each hand, made my way to the lamp room. Along the cellar corridor two went out, then as I started filling them another went, and in my nervousness I turned the wick of the last one the wrong way and found myself in the inky darkness of my dungeon, with neither lamp light nor matches. I was no longer nervous, I was petrified!

I knew the corridors well and decided to feel my way back to the servants' hall which was about a hundred yards away. I'd only gone a few steps when I thought I heard a tapping sound. I stopped. Yes, it was a regular beat, tap, tap, and it was coming in my direction. I felt my hair rise and stiffen at the back of my neck, 'Charlotte and her steel ladle', that was what it must be. That's all it could be. The tapping became nearer and louder. I plucked up courage and looked in its direction. In the distance I could see a light which seemed to be swinging from side to side, 'Charlotte and her burning hair'. Panic-stricken I rushed towards it, screaming at the top of my voice, and lashed out at what I was certain was her apparition. My fist hit something of substance, I heard it fall with a shout and the light crashed to the ground. I didn't stop to reason, I rushed on blindly to the servants' hall screaming with fear. Fellow servants comforted me and some of the braver ones made their way with lamps to investigate. They found a body lying in the corridor where I'd struck it in terror, but it wasn't Charlotte Wicks it was 'Peggy' Williams.

Let me hasten to say Peggy was not a woman, he was a one-legged fire prevention man who joined us with the hospital staff. He had smelt the smoke which had come from my two lamps, and had come along to investigate. Peggy had a wooden leg and it was the tap of that that I had mistaken for Charlotte's ladle. 'But Peggy,' I said, after I'd apologised for my unjustified assault, 'why was it that I didn't hear the noise of the boot on your sound leg?'

'Ah, lad, that you may well ask. Look,' and he raised his foot. He'd soled and heeled his boot with rubber cut from an old car tyre. 'I don't waste good money on leather when I can get this.'

At least I learnt something from my experience, for from then on neither did I. That's how I became known as 'the silent footman'.

Though my experience with Peggy should have dissolved my fears, I was glad when the summer months came. Somehow I was never quite convinced that Charlotte's presence was not still lurking in the gloom of the Longleat cellars, just as I was sure that the 'Green Lady' wafted along that top corridor.

Another thing for which I have to thank the Longleat ghosts is that they gave me the opportunity of indulging my fondness for the opposite sex. The housemaids and kitchen maids were also fanciful like me, and so when they were asked to go down the cellars to fetch something they jibbed at it. They tried to persuade me to go for them but I was too wily for that, 'No, I'm frightened too,' I'd say, 'but I don't mind coming with you to frighten the ghosts away.' So down we would go together and it proved an excellent opportunity for a little slap and tickle. It got to be so frequent that if anyone came into the servants' hall and asked where I was they'd be told, 'Oh, he's down in the cellar frightening the ghosts away.'

Heaven knows it was difficult enough to indulge in any

amorous pursuits. Mrs Parker the housekeeper kept an eagle eye on all the girls, those that showed a liking for boys being dubbed as 'frivolous', not a thing that anyone wanted written into their reference. Mr Brazier too was in that respect a spoil sport and frequently admonished me, 'You'll get into serious trouble one of these days, you must learn to curb your lusts, your baser emotions, boy.'

I must say that even in those times when we were suffering the backlash of Queen Victoria I thought he was going it a bit, he made a kiss in the dark sound like an orgy.

One night after he'd berated me I thought I'd get a bit of my own back. There was an oil lamp outside his room and the stairs up to my bedroom overlooked it. When Bob Huthwaite and I were retiring for the night I bet him he couldn't spit the wick out. Leaning over the banisters, with my first shot I hit the side of the lamp which exploded with a report like a shotgun. We dashed upstairs but Mr Brazier was quicker. He flew out of his door, realised what had happened, and who had done it, and he barked at us to report to him the following morning. When we did, he dressed us down and made our lives hell for the rest of the week.

An example of the kind of restraint we were expected to exercise had happened some time before I had joined, but was still talked about. A nursery maid and the groom of the chambers announced their intention of getting married. The house was in an uproar, both above and below stairs. How could they have met, let alone have been together for the length of time that acquaintanceship could ripen into affection?

A full-scale inquiry was launched. The children eventually gave the game away; the couple's tryst had been the nursery sink. Not, one would have thought, the ideal place for romance, but beggars couldn't be choosers. They had to leave, of course, heaven knows what the children might have seen and heard.

There's no question but that servants were owned body and soul. In service in London things were much the same. A maidservant who had 'followers' didn't stay very long. What a tawdry term 'followers' is, yet it lasted up to the beginning of the Second World War. No wonder service went out of fashion as a career.

After I'd been a year at Longleat I was promoted to third footman. I'd grown and filled out fast, and despite Mr Brazier's prognostications I'd kept my nose clean. I was now fitted out with the family livery. I learnt that it had been designed in the eighteenth century, which sounded all right but didn't mean much to me. The coat was of mustard yellow, worn with a black waistcoat trimmed with silver braid. Underneath were knee breeches and heavy silk stockings elaborately clocked.

I was also given a black hat shaped like an admiral's, braided with silver and decked with one large crested button. This I was told was for state occasions, which had been suspended for the duration of the war, and which I rightly never expected to have to wear. I was also told that for such occasions and for special dinner parties I would be expected to 'powder'. Indeed there was a special 'powder room' for footmen at Longleat. It led off the servants' hall, and down one side were long mirrors with wash basins next to them. The footmen would troop in there, hang up their jackets, and with towels round their shoulders would douse their heads with water, lather them with soap, comb it out and then take turns in sprinkling each other's hair with violet powder. At some places they used ordinary flour, more economical perhaps. Whatever was used one had to be careful that it didn't shake off, as it was a grave offence if any was seen on a livery jacket.

I myself only ever used powder in one job and that was when I'd left service as full-time employment.

I was occasionally asked to go as an auxiliary matching footman to Arlington House. A matching footman meant that we were selected because we were all of the same height and build. We powdered for state occasions, visiting royalty and such like. We were chiefly there as ornaments, for after we had dinner we lined up in the beautifully dim-lit corridor and just stood there for the rest of the evening. It wasn't easy because we weren't expected to move, and powder as it hardens on the head seems to drag the hair from the roots and this caused the scalp to itch! Nevertheless there's something artistically satisfying in wearing full livery and carrying it well. It encourages graceful movement and gesture and adds a bit of theatre and glamour to the occasion. With the shift towards the ordinary and the tawdry we could well do with a bit of it in our lives today.

Another advantage of powdering was that it paid more. We auxiliary footmen were given two pounds five shillings a night for a regular dinner and ball but we got five shillings more if we had to powder. It was a kind of danger money as it was considered we ran the risk of catching cold by wetting our hair. It was good pay in those days, though of course there was always a deduction. At the end of the evening when you went to collect and sign for your fee you threw five bob back to the butler and got a 'Look forward to seeing you again' for your pains.

But back to Longleat and my new appointment.

I learnt now how to serve at table, how to clean silver, how to welcome and valet guests, how to appear as if by magic, how to seem not to listen to conversations, how to put rugs round ladies' knees in carriages or cars with a steady hand, as well as the thousand and one things that are in a footman's inventory of duties.

I very much enjoyed the new job. It was a challenge, it brought me more into contact with the family who were easy and delightful to serve and seemed instinctively to know how to treat servants. I got past my probationary period with only one slip-up. Her ladyship suddenly decided to have tea served in the ornamental garden, so with Mr Brazier I carried the tray there. He poured the tea and I handed the cups and plates round. As we were leaving the Marchioness said, 'Brazier, tell Gordon his gloves are dirty.'

Mr Brazier stared at my hands and frowned. As we moved away I said, 'What does she mean, I haven't got any gloves on?'

'Exactly, you bloody fool, that's one of the things she's getting at and the other is that your hands are filthy.' This was a slight exaggeration but then Mr Brazier was given to overstating things.

I now began to find out more about other people's work, or perhaps it interested me more. At Longleat for example the first footman was considered to be the lady's footman. He stood behind her chair and anything the ladies' maids required to have done for their mistress was his responsibility. When she went out driving he would sit in the box with the coachman or in the front seat with the chauffeur, and would open the door for her. If she had dinner in her room he would carry the tray up. I discovered too that I'd been born a bit too late, that the third footman there was the nursery footman, at the beck and call of the nanny (I wouldn't have fancied that). But he was also the Lothario of the nursery maids (who in my later experience were attractive and skittish) and the hero of the children. When later I went to Lady Astor at Cliveden, the hall boy looked after the nursery. He, poor lad, was too young and puny to appreciate the advantages of his job.

The groom of the chamber's work interested me, but I didn't

envy him. He was responsible for the reception rooms, tidying them after the family or guests left, making sure that the writing tables were always properly equipped, seeing to the post, delivering any notes or messages, looking after the fires – never refuelling them, that was the job of the odd man – attending to the comforts and needs of the guests, and one other rather strange morning task, toasting and ironing the newspapers.

The housemaid's work I noticed more, since if I was valeting I would be with them in the corridors. It was the rule of the house of course that we should never be in a bedroom together. For a man and a woman to see a bed in company would, in the eyes of our employers, only excite evil thoughts. The maids were up at six cleaning, scrubbing, laying and lighting coal fires in the bedrooms, dashing up with hot-water jugs, opening the shutters, taking up trays of morning tea, then after breakfast making beds, changing linen, brushing rugs and carpets – there were no Hoovers then – they wouldn't have worked by paraffin anyway! They constantly had the head housemaid or housekeeper snapping at their heels, so by comparison my job was easy and peaceful. I enjoyed the housemaids more in the evening when they had changed from their print dresses and long aprons into the daintier black ones with frilly aprons and caps. Uniforms on girls do something for me, even today, and I put this all down to my early environment. There were some establishments that, as the sons reached adolescence, made a sort of tally of their maids' attractions. Those girls that came high on the list were gradually phased out and replaced by plain ones. I'm glad to say that in my experience this didn't happen, and as far as I know none of the girls, or the sons, were any the worse for it. The early evening meant some tough work for the housemaids with which they were often grateful for my assistance. Hip baths had to be carried into bedrooms, then placed in front of the fires and filled, and this meant countless jugs of hot water, the towels warmed and hung around the bath. Now this may sound archaic but when recently I've spoken to some of my earlier employers they look back on the hip bath with wistful nostalgic memories.

It was towards the end of the war that my heart strings were plucked by one of the stillroom maids. It was the first time that I had been serious with a girl, and a lot of trouble it caused me, though I must say now that when I look back to those days it's not my heart but my nose that stirs. The smell of that stillroom was something out of this world, a delicate mixture of hot bread, biscuits, coffee, lavender, potpourri and herbs. Perhaps it was the scent which pervaded dear Alice that I loved, and not her pretty face and sturdy body.

The only trouble with the stillroom was that it could be approached from the housekeeper's room by a spiral staircase, and although Mrs Parker was busy part of the day – checking the laundry, giving out the stores, finding work for the sewing maids to do and generally supervising the cleaning and running of the house – she enjoyed spending much of her time in the stillroom; preserving fruit; making jam and marmalade; candying peel; bottling morello cherries and arranging them in squat, round jars so that they resembled a parade of guardsmen; distilling rose water – as well as making the most delicious scones, cakes and pastries. So when I yearned for a glimpse of dear Alice I had first to be sure of the whereabouts of Mrs Parker, and I could never be certain that she wouldn't have returned to her room to descend from above and catch us together. Fortunately like all housekeepers she carried her keys in bunches round her waist, so the jingling of these heralded her approach.

She did of course surprise us once or twice. I was reprimanded and sent packing, while Alice had the sharp edge of her tongue for the rest of the day. Then came jam making time and whether Alice believed the way to a man's heart was through his stomach or not she now made a habit of presenting me with a slice of bread and butter with the warm jam skimmings on it whenever I visited her. Caution was thrown to the winds and again we were caught together. 'Gordon,' Mrs Parker said through her thin lips, 'get back to work, I shall report your conduct to Mr Brazier.'

As I left I heard her lashing into Alice. Mr Brazier began playing the heavy father, 'Gordon, I've now spoken to you several times about controlling your lower instincts. In future you will keep your hands off the maids, if you don't you will have to go.'

'But, sir,' I said, 'I couldn't have used my hands, I had a piece of bread and jam in them at the time.'

He shook his head sadly as if that made my behaviour more serious, 'That will be all Gordon. You may go.'

I don't want to give the impression that Mr Brazier and I were constantly at loggerheads. In fact generally speaking we got on rather well. I was anxious to learn and there was a lot he, as butler, could and did teach me. He was a good man to work under, reliable, predictable, he didn't drink to excess – a fault in some butlers that made them hard to tolerate – and he was fair. The fact that he was of the old Victorian school was an advantage to me in almost every way, except to my roving eyes. He succeeded, where my schoolmasters had failed, in making the beginnings of a responsible citizen of me.

I can remember him one day showing me a wages book. 'You seem interested in the history of the place, Gordon, look at this,' and he pointed at certain pages. One entry read, 'to Mary

Morgan, for sweeping chimneys'. The book covered the period from 1853 to 1861. 'I've heard of sending boys up the chimneys to clean them but never a respectable married woman. I suppose if you'd been around you'd have been peeping up after her,' he added with a chuckle. I realised then that although he'd admonished me over my behaviour with the maids he wasn't the cold fish he'd seemed at the time.

I had three Christmases at Longleat, all in the truly traditional style for that part of the country. There would be a huge decorated tree in the hall with the house a mass of holly, ivy and mistletoe. On Christmas morning after chapel, all the servants would line up to receive their gifts from the Marchioness. This was not the exciting moment it should have been, as we knew exactly what we would be getting. It was what had been given over the last fifty years at least, and was the same in almost every house in the land; a dress length for the women, and half a dozen starched collars for the men. 'Useful' presents were for servants, nothing that might excite them to ideas above their station. What opportunities employers missed in getting feelings of gratitude and loyalty from their staffs.

The day passed much as any other, then in the evening the junior servants, whatever the weather, would dance set dances in the courtyard, watched and applauded by members of the household and the senior staff from the cosiness of the upstairs windows. Then followed the carol singers from the village accompanied by the hand-bell ringers, and a troupe of mummers clowned their way through one of the Elizabethan Christmas plays. When these ceremonies were over we were all ready to make our way to the warmth of the servants' hall, where piled on the refectory tables were boars' heads, roast turkeys, game pies and dishes of roast pheasant and partridge, which we swilled down with beer from large copper jacks.

Then the fiddlers would arrive from Warminster, a nearby town, french chalk was sprinkled around the floor and the servants' ball began. It was the custom for the Marquess to open it in the arms of the housekeeper, and the Marchioness followed partnered by the butler. Nothing loath I remember my first Christmas asking one of the young ladies of the house to take the floor with me. It was a fiasco. I had no idea of the steps and judging from the pained expression on her face my feet spent more time on hers than on the floor. I must say the family was extremely tactful, they sensed that their presence gave the proceedings an unnatural tension and withdrew after what they considered was a nice time. It was then that the fun started thick and fast, and it was the one night of the year when Mrs Parker's, 'tut-tuts' and Mr Brazier's 'steady theres' fell on deaf ears.

On Boxing Day it was back to work with a vengeance. There was always a shoot which meant a big house party. Lunch was served in a large marquee that was put up in the woods. It was a proper three-course affair taken out in hay boxes and served by us to those who were taking part, piping hot. Many of the hardier and more adventurous ladies joined them; I myself couldn't see the point for these picnics on cold, freezing days. The upper crust were good trenchermen because, having made an excellent lunch, they returned for a dinner in the evening, of which this menu is typical:

Consommé à l'Imperiale
Filats de Sole à la Norvégienne
Crème de Volaille aux Champignons
Noisettes d'Agneau à la Riche
Canetons rôtis aux Petits Pois
Bombe à la Sicilienne

When the war came to an end I was informed by Mr Brazier that I was to go to London to open the Baths' place in Grosvenor Square, a large fashionable town house. Reg Fisher, his lordship's ex-valet, went with me as butler and engaged a full staff. After five years everyone I think was looking forward to a London season again, and I must say that I enjoyed the glamour and busy-ness of the big city.

Although my home was at Ascot, which was thirty miles from London, I'd only paid a couple of visits there as a boy on church outings, and on such outings you see only what they want you to see. I now enjoyed walking in the nearby Hyde Park. I'd parade there in my waistcoat, with my starched shirt, white bow and livery trousers and the girls would all turn their heads and say, 'There's a footman', and I'd feel no end of a dog. I was a gayer bird than the soldiers in their khaki, and a rarer one. Everything looked set for an interesting and amusing life.

Unfortunately there was 'a fly in the ointment' – Reg Fisher – he and I didn't get on. His new-found authority seemed to go to his head and he made things as difficult as he could for me. With the family and only occasional visitors, the senior servants treated the place as their own for much of the time and I was expected to wait on them and the many friends they invited round in the evening.

I was also detailed to do jobs that were not in my province, such as lighting the stove to heat the hot water first thing in the morning. I didn't like this so if I was late getting up I'd pretend it was the boiler that wasn't working properly and slip a lighted candle inside the draught doors so that it looked as if the fire was alight. Unfortunately one morning Fisher opened the top and the game was up. I knew I was for the high jump but I didn't care. There was now a demand for trained footmen, and anyway I thought it was time I had a change.

A few days later I got what we called then in service the 'Dear John' letter, giving me a month's notice. It was pleasantly enough written. It said there was to be a reorganisation and they felt I needed a change, and I was promised a good reference.

In North Audley Street, Mayfair, a short distance from Grosvenor Square, was a well-known registry office for butlers, valets and footmen called The Mayfair Servants' Agency. In the front window were cards showing many different jobs. They made interesting reading even if you weren't wanting a change as it kept you in touch with the market price for men servants. When you were in work employers kept very much to the status quo and to ask for more money was like Oliver Twist with his soup bowl – very unpopular. I now kept a sharper eye on the window. One day a card aroused my curiosity. It stated that a Mrs Charles Sandford required a young man of good character as second footman. It also inferred that he would stand a better chance for the job if he were a total abstainer, a non-smoker and a lover of animals.

All three things were easy to be the day you applied for the position, any habits you acquired after that I reckoned couldn't count. The address was 102 Eaton Square, Belgravia – a solid one. The 'fondness of animals' bit which had worried me slightly at first sight, couldn't mean that they kept a zoo there, the house was on the Duke of Westminster's estate and I knew he wouldn't have allowed it.

I checked in at the agency, who gave me a card of appointment, and walked round to Eaton Square allowing myself sufficient time to make a reconnaissance of the place. I walked slowly backwards and forwards by it hoping to catch a glimpse of my potential employer. I was lucky, a figure came to the window – came to it, she overflowed from it! As she opened it her two massive breasts surged out. Her fingers, I noticed, were covered with rings, and ropes of pearls spilled on to her bosom. She also appeared to be wearing a small fur round her neck, 'Mmm, throat trouble', I thought.

I reasoned that size was no criterion of behaviour, that fat people were often bright and happy, anyway I hadn't got to accept the job so I went to the front door and rang the bell. A man whom I rightly assumed was Mrs Sandford's butler answered it, looked me up and down, and frigidly asked me my business. 'I have come,' I said, 'in answer to the advertisement in The Mayfair Servants' Agency; I understand they have telephoned and made an appointment. You require, I believe, a second footman.'

'I'm not sure we shall require you as second footman,' he said after a further head to foot survey. 'For if you had known your place you would have gone down the area steps and to the back door. I do not accept applications for employment here at the front.' With that he closed the door in my face. 'Bugger you, and your job,' I thought, and began to walk away.

I walked as far as Hyde Park and sat down on a seat there to collect my thoughts. It dawned on me that the butler was quite right; if the same thing had happened at Longleat Mr Brazier would have behaved as he did; anyway, why 'cut off my nose to spite my face', so back I trudged to Eaton Square, down the area steps and gave a tug at the old-fashioned bell handle.

After a considerable time I heard footsteps, the door opened and there again was the butler. He scowled at me, 'This is the second time this afternoon you've woken me. Let's hope it's worth my while. You'd better come inside. Mrs Sandford does the hiring, I'll let her know you're here.'

Eventually I found myself in a small drawing-room in the presence of Mrs Sandford. 'What's your name,' she inquired.

'Gordon, madam.'

'If you come to me you'll be James, all my second footmen are called James, just as all my first footmen are called William.'

It didn't call for any reply, though I was a bit apprehensive about the 'alls', it sounded as if she changed servants as often as she changed her clothes. I found myself looking at the fur round her neck and wondering why. 'Tell me, James. Do you drink?'

'No, madam,' I replied.

'Do you smoke?'

'No, madam.'

'Are you fond of animals?'

'Yes, madam, you can take it that I'm very fond of animals.'

'Very well, James, say peanuts.'

I hesitated, I was not sure that I had heard her correctly. 'Say what, madam?'

'Peanuts, James, I don't want to shout it, P-E-A-N-U-T-S.' I swallowed. 'Peanuts,' I croaked.

'Louder, James, louder.'

'Peanuts,' I shouted despairingly.

With that the fur uncurled itself from round her neck and flew across the room landing on my shoulder. I was about to blaspheme but her 'James, don't be frightened' stifled my epithet. 'That, James, is Peanuts my marmoset, you needn't worry he doesn't bite.' We then resumed the interview with the marmoset sitting on my shoulder and Mrs Sandford tossing it peanuts which it caught, held, ate and then deposited the shells in my breast coat pocket. 'Can you make tea?' she asked.

'Yes, madam, I think I can.'

'Aren't you sure, James? Come I'll take you to the kitchen and we'll soon find out.' We went downstairs and the cook was asked to produce a teapot, tea and boiling water. As the cook showed no surprise I took it that this was a common occurrence. When the kettle had boiled I was told to commence.

'For how many people do you require me to make tea, madam?' I asked. She clapped her hands.

'Well done, James,' she cried, 'you're the only applicant to ask that very important question. We will engage you and I hope you will stay with us for many years.'

It was with mixed feelings that I returned to Grosvenor Square. What on earth, I wondered, had I let myself in for. It was surely the most bizarre interview any servant could ever have had. It was I suppose that very thing that determined me to go there, anyway I'd nothing to lose so 'What the hell,' I thought, 'I'll chance it.' I saw my notice out with the Baths in an atmosphere of acrimony. Even if you continue to pull your full weight you're accused of idling by the butler, so I decided I might as well be hung for a sheep as for a lamb and coasted along keeping out of the way as much as I possibly could. I suppose I should have been sorry to leave the house that had given me my first start in life but the job had gone sour on me.

The Sandfords kept a fair house of servants, Jim Billet was butler/valet; the first footman, Bill Ruth, was an ex-navy man who didn't let you forget it; there was a cook and a kitchen maid, a housekeeper and two housemaids, a chauffeur/coachman, and a lady's maid. I found I had to do many things that were not normally expected of a footman but this was easier to accept in a place of this kind than in the Marquess's establishment. One thing did annoy me; every night Jim Billet would hand me a quart beer bottle and tell me to go to the Star pub in Belgrave Mews and get it filled up. It wasn't my place to do it but I couldn't argue with him so early on in my new job. After a week or two I was really browned off so I put a spoonful of icing sugar in the bottom of the bottle and swilled it round until it had melted. After I had returned and Mr Billet tasted it, he said, 'Christ, this beer's sweet, where did you get it?' I was able quite honestly to assure him that it came from the usual place. 'Here, taste it,' he said.

'It seems all right to me,' I said. After I'd worked the same trick for three days I believe he thought something had happened to his taste buds. 'I'm giving up bloody beer,' he grunted, and from then on he contented himself with Mr Sandford's whisky.

The Sandfords were an ill-assorted couple and yet they seemed to get on well together. It was his second marriage, whether she'd been married before I never did find out; they'd been together for ten years.

Charles Sandford was a Southern American. It was rumoured among the servants that he was a millionaire; how they knew was a mystery to me. But still he never seemed short of money. He usually went to the City each day. He was coming up to eighty, though spry with it.

Mrs Sandford, Hettie, or Hett as her husband called her, or 'That tart from Streatham' as she was known in the servants' hall, was of an indefinable age. She might have been anything from forty to fifty. She had, as the saying was, 'let herself go'. She'd have gone still further if it hadn't been for her corsetier. The lady's maid used to come sweating down to the servants' hall. 'Give me a cup of tea, love, I need it, I've just got a quart into a pint pot!' According to her Hett was over fourteen stone. 'It's a lot of ground for me to cover,' she'd complain.

Hett's best feature was her long, blonde hair. 'That's because we wash it with egg yolks,' the maid explained to me when I commented on it. To sum them up Charles and Hett were like Mr and Mrs Jack Spratt. This was confirmed at meal times: she ate like a horse, while he played with his food. This annoyed her. 'Now, Charles,' she'd say, 'let's see a clean plate this evening.'

'Hett,' he'd reply, 'I eat to live, I don't live to eat.'

As I've already hinted, I was more a Jack-of-all-trades than a footman, but I enjoyed the situation. There was little entertaining; the Sandfords were not society, and I got plenty of time off.

I must say Hett did her best to nibble in to the upper crust. Many's the afternoon she would summon Dick Williams the coachman to take her 'card calling'. It was the job of the footman on duty to drive with her, riding on the box of the carriage, dressed like the coachman in top boots, long carriage cloak and a silk hat with a cockade 'up' at the side.

Although, as I've said, the Sandfords had a car, a large American one, Hett preferred the carriage. It was slower, more dignified and people noticed her more. She was hard to miss in her flashy clothes, dripping with mink, flashing with diamonds, and over it all a large bird cage of a hat. Thank God she left the marmoset behind otherwise she'd have looked for all the world like an organ grinder.

She'd set off about three; in one hand she held a speaking tube through which she'd give a string of instructions to the coachman, and in the other a list of acquaintances she hoped to find at home. We'd be going at a trot, say round Belgrave Square, when she'd yell, 'Stop at number six.' I would dismount. She'd pass me a visiting card for me to present at 6 Belgrave Square. 'Card calling' was quite an operation. I'd ring the doorbell which would be opened by the butler or the head parlour maid, hand them the card saying, 'With the compliments of Mrs Charles Sandford. Is your lady in today?' The door would be closed while inquiries were made as to whether their mistress was at home to Mrs Sandford.

If she was I would, after much effort on her part, get Hett out of the carriage, help her up the steps to the house, and remain standing outside until the visit was over. This could go on at one or two addresses during an afternoon, then we would take a final jog trot round Hyde Park, and return home.

If a person was not at home, and sometimes the alacrity with which the butler or footman returned showed that he had standing instructions if Hett called, the card was left with the corner turned up, which indicated that Mrs Sandford had called personally. Often footmen had the job of going round on their own delivering cards. The purpose of this was to show that their mistress was in London, and was receiving. In this case the card was not turned up and this indicated that a messenger had presented it.

It was now that I became acquainted with the outside at any rate, of the London theatres and Covent Garden Opera House. Hett was a great theatre goer, sometimes seeing the same show three or four times. Again it was rumoured in the servants' hall that she'd been on the stage, 'back row of the chorus' I'm afraid was the general agreement.

The dress for me for evening occasions was a long brown coat, peaked cap, with the cockade on the cap. As we set Mr and Mrs Sandford down I would jump off and open the coach or car door. If Mr Sandford didn't feel strong enough he would beckon to me to escort his wife up the steps. There'd be a gesture of dismissal, I'd salute, then Hett would say, 'Home, James, carriages at eleven,' or whatever time the show was over. 'Silly old cow,' the coachman would say as I got up beside him, 'she knows we're not going home.' Then he'd whip up his horses, 'To the pub, my darlings.' And off we'd trot for an evening's tank-up. Before we went into the pub we'd remove our long livery coats and caps, changing into a jacket, mackintosh and cloth cap, so losing all the marks of our offices. You couldn't be too careful, and livery was a great give-away.

It's interesting how small things give indications of people's characters. Although Hett seemed to be able to get anything out of Charles Sandford, it was to him that Jim Billet and the housekeeper had to present their account books, and according to them he'd bicker over halfpennies. 'Bloody old skinflint,' Jim would grumble in the evening as he sipped the Sandford's whisky.

I was given a first-hand example of what Jim meant. Charles always left for the City by car at ten to nine. One morning he was late and as I was standing by the front door ready to open it for him Hett said, 'James, go to the master's room and inform him that the car is waiting.' Up I went. At first sight he didn't seem to be there, then I saw a pair of heels moving under the bed. I coughed delicately and, flushed and disturbed, he withdrew himself. I gave him the message and was about to leave when he said, 'Oh, James, tell Mr Billet I've dropped a sixpence under the bed, ask him to find it and leave it on the dressing-table.' This, I thought, is one for the book. When I delivered the message I thought Jim would burst.

'The mean old bugger. Thought the housemaid would pinch it. Here,' he said, and pulled a sixpence from his pocket, 'take this up and put it on the bloody table. If that's how the likes of him gets rich and stays rich I'd rather keep my pride.'

Loss of pride was something we saw a lot of at that time. Soldiers were coming back from the front and finding the country was no place for heroes to live in. We had constant callers at the back door, not for money but for a bite to eat. It got so bad that Mr Billet called a halt. 'No more beggars,' he said, 'we're getting a name for being an easy touch. It won't do.' I found it a hard instruction to carry out.

One day when I was alone in the servants' hall there was a ring at the back door and I answered it to a middle-aged chap with his medals in his hand. He spun me the yarn only rather more explicitly than usual. I gave him some food and we continued talking. 'What work are you looking for?' I inquired, thinking he might do well in service.

'I'm an actor, music halls, Bill Newman. On the top of the bill I was at one time, but nobody wants me now. My only chance is pantomime and Christmas is a long way off.' Then he began a string of reminiscences about his life in the theatre.

'Where do you live?' I foolishly asked.

'Oh, I doss down where I can, any chance of using that shed of yours out there?'

I fell for it and of course one night led to another – and then another. Then he got careless, frightened one of the housemaids and Mr Billet was on to him like a flash. He split on me. I suppose he had no option as Jim had threatened to call the police. He was sent packing and I thought I would be too but I got away with just a hell of a dressing down. 'Well,' I thought, 'that's the end of that, I'll never see Bill again.'

About a week later I was strolling up Piccadilly when I noticed a man selling matches and underneath his tray a notice said – 'Blinded in action'. I looked at his face and he winked at me. It was Bill Newman. He'd found himself a part. I walked up and greeted him. 'No hard feelings?' he queried.

'None, but what are you doing this for, you're not blind.'

'Ssh,' he whispered. 'Matches! Matches!' he called as two ladies passed. 'Bitches, bitches,' he mumbled, as they moved on. 'It's the only thing that works now, there's too many of us, it pays to be blind.' I left him a shilling, feeling sick as I moved away, not sick with Bill for cheating, but sick with the world that only paid you if you were blind.

When I'd been with the Sandfords for six months they announced their intention of going to the States for a while.

It appeared that they were in future going to spend half the year in Britain and half there. I was excited about the prospect of seeing the new world. I didn't doubt that I would be asked because of Hett's remark when she engaged me, that she hoped I'd be with them for many years. It was bitter gall to me when I learned that except for her lady's maid and Mr Billet, all the servants were to be laid off. I complained to Jim. 'That's the way of the world, me lad,' he said philosophically, 'and it's as well you learnt it while you're young.'

It was back to the footmen's agency in North Audley Street for me. I decided that I would return to the gentry. It seemed that they were more predictable and reliable. I saw a card in the window which read:

'The Honourable Mrs Claude Portman of Goldicote House, near Stratford-upon-Avon, and Lower Grosvenor Street, London, urgently requires a second footman of two. Wages £28 a year, plus 2/6 a week beer and washing money, one morning suit and one suit of livery supplied, must be Church of England.'

I went into the agency expecting to get a card to go for an interview since Mrs Portman, I was told, was in London. 'You'll have to write.'

This I did and was astonished when a few days later I was summoned upstairs. Mrs Portman had called, I suppose to get the low-down on me from Hett. She must have liked what she heard about me since after she had interviewed me I was engaged. For the time being I was told I would be working at Stratford-upon-Avon. This suited me as a romance I was having was getting a little out of hand and the shift of ground I felt would be beneficial to all concerned. Then again to speak of

Stratford was to think of Shakespeare, and I felt that sniffing the air that he had might do something for my education.

I had a fortnight of my month's notice to see out and I could find no reason for over-exerting myself, either on Charles or Hett – they hadn't exactly considered me. I think I was most sorry to say goodbye to Peanuts with whom over the months I'd established an excellent relationship. I spent a few days with my parents at Ascot, and eventually caught the train to Stratford-upon-Avon, where I was astonished to find the butler, Mr Tubb, to meet me, at the station, in the governess's pony and cart. It was putting his dignity at stake early I thought.

During the four-mile journey he gave me a general picture of the family and the house. The Honourable Claude was about fifty years old, and his wife a few years younger. They had three children – two girls, Sylvia and Jocelyn both teenagers, and a son Edward who was in the army – the Blues. They did a fair amount of entertaining, but mostly small parties of local friends. 'There's to be one tonight, for eight,' Mr Tubb informed me, 'and you will be required in the dining-room.' I hastened to say that I had yet to be measured and fitted for my livery clothes so that this would be difficult. 'Oh, we've one or two spare sets, one of which I'm sure will fit you,' he replied smoothly.

'I must inform you, sir, that it has never been my custom to wear another man's trousers,' I said shortly. It looked to me as if we were getting off on the wrong foot.

'Let us compromise then. You wear your morning trousers, and I'll provide the jacket and waistcoat.' I wasn't happy but I accepted.

I was less happy still when he said, as we neared the house, 'By the way, David Jones the first footman is Welsh, and like many of his compatriots in my experience has a very vivid imagination. Don't therefore take much notice of what he says.'

'That's rummy,' I thought, 'very rummy indeed.'

On our arrival I was introduced to those of the staff who were on duty. 'Now David will show you to your quarters,' said Mr Tubb. 'You'll be sharing with him.'

In silence David and I climbed the stairs; when we reached the bedroom he shut the door quickly and turning to me said, 'Have you got your return railway ticket?'

'No,' I replied, 'why should I?'

'It would have saved you money. You're the fifth second footman we've had in eight months.'

Things suddenly fell into place, that was why Mr Tubb had come to meet me personally. He was afraid to send any other member of the staff in case they'd told me and I'd taken the next train back to town. It also accounted for the certainty Mr Tubb had about being able to fix me up with a set of livery; he'd got at least five for me to choose from.

When I inquired why the footmen had left David replied darkly,

'That you must find out for yourself.'

As it happened I never did, but I had a strong suspicion. It was nothing to do with the Portmans, it concerned David. He had a peculiar stomach, it rumbled a lot during the daytime but at night it, as it were, let off steam! The noises were disconcerting, the other effects were vile. My bed was near the door and many's the time I had to get up and wander up and down the corridor. As if this wasn't enough he also had asthma and his coughing and wheezing were not conducive to sleep. Some nights, too, he would wail like a banshee. 'It's the spirits, man,' he would explain when I complained. 'We Welsh are visited a lot by the spirits.' I felt like telling him that I knew it was the beer that affected his mind, and his body.

But back to the moment. As David was playing Job's comforter, Mr Tubb appeared in the room with a suit of livery over his arm, a Cambridge blue jacket and a gold-coloured waistcoat. 'Please present yourself in the dining-room at eight o'clock. Before that David will have shown you around.'

Whether it was apprehension after what I'd been told or whether one of David's spirits had entered me I don't know, but that first evening at dinner was a fiasco, a footman's nightmare.

The soup and fish courses passed easily enough. Roast saddle of lamb was the main course and Mr Tubb indicated to us that he would carve and serve. David was to serve the vegetables and I was to follow with the awkward ones, two salvers of gravy and mint sauce on a silver tray in my left hand, and a large bowl of salad in my right. I'd gone about half way round the table and was making to hand the tray to one of the lady guests when the gentleman on her left turned sharply round to her, jogged my hand and sent the salvers of mint sauce and gravy into her lap. In my attempt to save the situation I lost control of my right hand, and the bowl of salad went down her back. She screamed, uttered some most unladylike words and rushed into the small drawing-room followed by the Honourable Claude, her husband and Mr Tubb.

I hurried to get some towels which I handed to her husband, so that he could mop up the mess; it was not in a place where a well disciplined servant could do it. 'Get some brandy,' barked my master. Mr Tubb complied. 'And soda,' cried her husband. I fetched the syphon from the dining-room. When I returned I found Tubb had handed her a generous measure. 'Just a little,' she gasped, holding out her glass to me.

Now normally I give the syphon a trial squirt before serving because some can be a little fierce. This one was a tiger, for as I squeezed, the soda cascaded out taking the brandy and itself over the wretched woman's face and neck. As a circus act it would have brought the house down. David was the only one present to see the funny side; he started to cackle like a demon. This didn't help and everyone began yelling at once. I did the only thing I thought possible, left and went to my room. I began to wish now that I had taken a return ticket as David had suggested; it looked as if I had raised Claude Portman's tally to six footmen in eight months.

It wasn't long before David joined me. 'The party's over,' he said, 'and it's you and me for the high jump tomorrow. I know I shouldn't have laughed,' he went on, 'but it's the funniest thing I've seen in all my years in service. You did the lot in one go didn't you, boyo.' Then we both began to chuckle, and to relive the scene over again.

Strangely enough when he and I were called before the Honourable Claude the following morning we got off lightly. Fortunately he'd seen that my arm was jogged, and it seemed that he and Mrs Portman had also been able to look at the funnier side of it all because there was a definite twinkle in his eye as he admonished us. Mr Tubb was more severe, but the rest of the staff enjoyed the joke. I was quickly accepted as one of them, and settled in to the job.

Although the family's main interests seemed to be in hunting and outdoor activities, Mrs Portman was also keen on the arts and in a small way something of a patron.

A frequent visitor to the house, almost at times a lodger, was Miss Marie Correlli, the writer whose romantic novels had an international reputation at that time. In the summer she would arrive at the house early and make her way to the garden where she'd spend the day writing. It was my job to make her refreshments at regular intervals. I remember meeting her for the first time in the rose garden. She seemed to fit her surroundings perfectly; she looked like a country woman, apple-cheeked, short and dumpy, not a pretty woman but alive and vital; later on when I met him I was able to compare her with Sir James Barrie, another country-looking character, though more wiry. I can see her now in her long silk beige dress with a red sash round her waist. On her head a large wide-brimmed straw hat, with another red silk bandana wound round it.

'Your refreshment tray, madam,' I said as I approached her. She didn't look up but continued to write in what seemed like a child's exercise book. After a decent pause and in a louder voice I said, 'Madam, I've brought your lemonade and biscuits. Shall I place the tray on the grass beside you or would you like it on the table?'

With that she placed the cap on her fountain pen, snapped the book shut, looked at me piercingly and said, 'Now who have we here?' I told her I was Gordon the second footman, only recently arrived to join the household. 'I see,' she remarked. 'Now Gordon, first things first. I'm not a madam, I'm a miss, and for your information, Miss Marie Correlli.' This was said as a fact and not out of conceit. 'I am a novelist, constantly searching for characters, plots and situations. I believe on that score I am already in your debt. Wasn't it you who bombarded poor Katie Brook's back and front with salad, gravy and mint sauce?' I admitted my guilt. 'A delicious situation, Gordon, I shall use it.'

'It would appear, madam – er miss, from what you have said that you did not hear the conclusion.' I then told her about the brandy and soda. She dissolved into laughter. Then her eyes lighted on the tray with the lemonade and biscuits. She got up from her chair, removed the notebook from the table and stood well to one side. 'While I look forward to hearing many of your other stories Gordon, you must excuse me if I take precautions to see that there's not a repetition of the last.'

As I'd found when I was at Longleat the trouble with work-ing in old houses is that there always seemed to be ghost stories attached to them. Goldicote House was no exception. David's Welsh ancestry no doubt contributed to his ability to spin a mys-tical story. One afternoon when the family were out, he took me by the arm and led me to an oak door studded with iron bolts, and producing a key opened it. Then taking a candle end from his pocket, he lit it and shone it into the darkness. By its light I could see stone steps descending into what looked like a cellar. 'It's a secret passage, man,' said David, leading the way down.

The steps took us to a brickwork tunnel, but we were only able to go a few yards before a fall of rubble stopped further progress. Back up we went, with David making kind of shiv-ering noises.

'Gives you the horrors, darkness, don't it? Not surprising,' he said, when we reached the door again.

'Why?' I queried.

'I'll tell you tonight, when we get to bed, I've got a job to do now,' and he was off.

That night he didn't need any reminding of his promise, and when the light was out he began. 'About that tunnel. You probably didn't know that at one time this house was part of a monastery.' I assured him I didn't. 'Yes,' he said, 'and some of these monks, although they'd taken vows of chastity, were a randy lot. Some four miles from here there's a convent, or nunnery.'

'Where?' I queried.

'You must sort that out for yourself, lad,' he said. 'But these monks burrowed this tunnel to get to the nuns, and at night they would go down and have their way with them.'

'Long journey to have to make for a bit of the other,' I volunteered.

'Didn't I tell you they were a randy lot?'

'It's not only the journey there I'm thinking of,' I said, 'it's the miserable bloody way back.' He thought about this for a moment.

'Sometimes they met in the middle,' he explained. 'Rumour has it that many of the nuns were murdered to preserve the secret, which accounts for the screams I and other footmen have heard lying here at night.' I tried to laugh it off. 'All right, don't take my word for it, boyo, you just wait and see, but don't say I didn't warn you.' With that he made a rude noise, and went to sleep.

Well of course when he told it the story was palpably absurd, but half an hour later with me lying in the dark alone with my thoughts, it seemed more plausible. I must eventually have fallen into a shallow sleep, when I was woken by a screeching and a whirring sound, like the flapping of wings. 'It's the souls of those poor nuns trying to escape,' I thought as I did what anyone else in my position would have done and dived under the bedclothes. David was made of sterner stuff; anyway he knew his story wasn't true; he jumped out of bed and across the room. 'I've got it,' he said. I emerged to see him holding an owl which was screaming and pecking at him. He rushed to the window and hurled it out. We cleared the room of the feathers the bird had lost in its struggles, and returned to bed. David's last words before he went to sleep were, 'That, Gordon, is a bad omen if ever there was one. An evil portent that augurs ill for this house.' As if I hadn't enough to think about that night!

The Portmans had a summer residence, Uckfield House, about nine miles from Lewes. We went there in 1919 taking in what was fashionably known as 'The Sussex Fortnight', with racing every day at Goodwood, Brighton, Lewes and Folkestone. The family went to Uckfield by car. We servants preceded them by a couple of days, taking what seemed to me to be mountains of luggage; though by comparison with what I was to see and cope with later we travelled light. In the carriage with me were Mr Tubb, David, Lady Portman's maid (an elderly German spinster whom we called Fräulein) and Brigit the cook. As we were nearing Uckfield, the Fräulein said, 'Ah, vee shan't be long now. Dat vas tree britches.' (Meaning of course Three Bridges station.) Then she turned to me and said, 'Gordon, do you believe in goats?'

'Of course I believe in goats,' I said. 'I've seen some though I've never had many dealings with them.'

'Vat vill you do if you see a goat trying to break down zee door of Uckvield House?' I was getting a bit lost.

'Shoo it away of course.'

Mr Tubb came to the Fräulein's rescue. 'She's trying to tell you the legend of the ghost of Uckfield House, Gordon, some cock and bull story about a gamekeeper whose love affair with a maid there was discouraged by the lady of the house, and who one night went there, tried to break in and as he hammered on the door his gun went off in his face and killed him. He's buried in the churchyard at the back of the house.'

'Ja, but ee doesn't stay still vere,' interrupted the Fräulein. 'Ee rises up and goes bang, bang on zee door.'

'Nonsense, don't take any notice of her Gordon, that stuff's only for fanciful and impressionable people.'

I'm one of them, I thought.

The first two weeks passed pleasantly and uneventfully. We had little to do as the family were out most of the time. Mr Tubb seemed pleased with the way things were going. 'You can have the day off tomorrow, Gordon,' he said. 'I should take the opportunity of a visit to Brighton.' I was of the same mind. I borrowed Jim Turner's, the groom's bicycle, and off I rode.

Brighton was about twenty miles from Uckfield; I had a good day there and set off for home about half past six so that I could get back before dark. I was a bit weary and saddle sore so my calculations were wrong and it was pitch black by the time I was nearing Uckfield.

I dismounted as I got to the village, I didn't want to get caught by the local bobby for riding without lights. I knew there was a short-cut to the house through the churchyard and decided to take it. I was about half way across when I saw something that caused my eyes to stare, my hair to stand on end, and my body to freeze. There just in front of me was a light swinging from side to side and rising up from an open grave. As I stood watching in horror a head appeared gnarled and horrible.

'It's the Fräulein's bloody gamekeeper,' I thought, and I leapt forward and hurled my bike into the grave. It did the trick, the light went out and the figure disappeared with a curse I shall remember to this day.

I dashed to the house and panted out my story to a disbelieving Mr Tubb and a fascinated David. They decided to investigate. Despite his 'pooh-poohs' I noticed that Mr Tubb carried a knobkerrie. They weren't gone long.

'You're in trouble, my lad,' were Mr Tubb's first words when he came back. 'Your ghost turned out to be the local grave digger doing a night shift. He couldn't finish in daylight and was down a ladder completing the job. You caught him as he was coming up to go home, so did your bike. He's got a nasty cut over his right eye. He's also swearing vengeance on who did it, so if you take my advice you'll stay indoors for a day or two because if he sees you he'll eat you.' I was pleased to take his advice. Indeed I wasn't particularly sorry when the holiday over, we returned to Goldicote House.

We hadn't been back a fortnight when David and I were called into the sitting-room by Mrs Portman. She greeted us with the news that the family were in serious money difficulties, 'It either means Mr Edward resigning his commission in the Blues, or dispensing with footmen, so I shall give you both a month's wages in lieu of notice and you will leave at your convenience.'

At the age of eighteen I could afford to be philosophical. I'd had a few summer months in the country, socially the coast was clear now of my amorous involvements and I fancied a return to the lights of London. There was however one small matter to be settled before I left. It had been part of the agreement when I had been engaged by the Portmans that they would provide me with a morning suit. This had been 'forgotten' and I had had to use my own clothes, so I reminded Mr Tubb of their obligation, and he passed on the information. It was as if I had asked for the crown jewels, I couldn't have met with a stronger reaction. I was sent for once again. 'Do I understand it right that you wish to have a suit of clothes after the short time you have been with us, Gordon?' And so it went on with her trying to convince me that I was doing my utmost to ruin the family. I stood my ground though and eventually settled for eight pounds. The gentry were often strange in their attitudes towards servants and money. They could constantly destroy their relationships with them by their seeming meanness.

Once again there I was outside Campbell and Hearn's agency studying the cards. There were two positions as second footman that attracted me, one for Viscount Astor, and the other for the Duke of Buccleuch. While I was too young to promote myself in rank it was, I thought, time to promote my employers. I couldn't make up my mind which to choose so I decided to toss a coin. Heads the Astors, tails the Buccleuchs; and it came down heads. I was given a card and instructed to go and be interviewed by Mr Lee, butler to the Astors, at 4 St James's Square.

I went down the area steps of this imposing building and was greeted by a young lad.

'What's your business?' he inquired. I handed him the card. 'I'm Eric, the schoolroom boy, follow me and I'll take you to see the skipper.'

I met Mr Lee in his sitting-room. 'What's your Christian name?' he said.

'Gordon, sir,' I answered.

'Very well, Gordon, where have you worked over the past years?'

'With the Marquess of Bath, the Honourable Claude Portman and Mr C. H. Sandford.' I thought this an imposing list, but by Mr Lee's expression I could see he was not impressed.

'Done any valeting?' I said I had. After a few more brusque questions he arose and said, 'Right, Gordon, we'll go and see her ladyship.' By the way he said it I was convinced I was not going to get the job. He took me to what I was to learn later was Lady Astor's boudoir, told me to wait outside while he informed her ladyship of my presence and left me for what seemed a long time, with my heart now nearly in my boots. Finally the door opened. He beckoned me in and said, 'This is Gordon, my lady, applying for the post of second footman.' I looked at Lady Astor, a beautiful trim figure of a lady, with a smile like a spring day. (I was to learn later how quickly it could turn to winter.)

'A very good afternoon to you, Gordon,' she said. 'He looks a big strong boy, Lee. Where is your home, Gordon? And have you a mother and father?'

'I have a mother and father and my home is in Ascot in Berkshire, your ladyship,' I replied.

'Well now, isn't that nice. We have a country house at Cliveden, near Taplow in Buckinghamshire. You'll be able to go home to your parents regularly.' Then she sped towards the door. 'How soon can you join us? We want you in one week's time. Goodbye, I must fly to the House of Commons.' And out she went.

'You can consider yourself engaged,' said Mr Lee, I thought a trifle unnecessarily.

My wage was to be thirty-two pounds a year, with two shillings and sixpence a week beer and washing money, and I discovered that any beer I wanted would have to be bought outside, but that this was not encouraged as Lady Astor was very strong against liquor. It had to be mentioned in the terms though because it was in the tradition of the time. I was then instructed to visit Robert Lillico, their tailor in Maddox Street, to be measured for suits and livery. 'Are we allowed to choose our own pattern, sir, for the morning suit, or do you insist on pepper and salt?' This was the footman's term for a grey and white pinhead suiting which many families instructed their tailors to supply their men servants with, which looked as was intended – a servants' suit.

'Within reason you may select any pattern you wish,' was Mr Lee's non-committal reply.

I went to Maddox Street and was duly measured by Mr Lillico. When he had finished he drew me aside by the arm and whispered, 'Dear boy, you're entitled to a long pair of woollen underpants to go under your livery trousers, we give them with each suit. If, however, like many other footmen you don't choose to wear them go downstairs and my brother will give you something in their place.'

'Downstairs' I found was the cutting-room. Seated at the table was brother Bob surrounded by three other men who like myself were being fitted for livery. All had glasses in their hands.

'Ah,' he greeted me, 'another no-nonsense pants man, I presume. Come and sit down and join us.'

He then took a glass and filled it with whisky from a cask at the end of the table. 'Here you are, Astor, this is your reward.'

He replenished his glass, and wished me luck in my new job. I eventually staggered out into the air a little worse for drink, but not so far gone as to wonder what my clothes would be like when I got them, for brother Bob was the cutter and how he could work after paying the footmen for their pants and drinking the health of each one was beyond my comprehension. In the event my clothes fitted perfectly, and I was later to join Bob in many similar celebrations; but I never ceased to wonder at his capacity.

Although I didn't realise it at the time, looking back now at my life in service it was at the Astors that it really began. All right, I'd learnt the rudiments at my three other places, but I lacked the skills, the polish, that make a real servant. Professionalism I believe is the art of making the difficult job simple. Edwin Lee, Lady Astor's butler, was not only the highest skilled professional butler I've ever met, but he also had the ability and the patience to impart those skills. Moreover he did it in a way that made you want to learn, want to please him. He was perhaps a hard taskmaster, sometimes to be feared but always respected, and a word of praise from him would keep a man happy for a week. There was no job in the book that he couldn't do, and do superbly, and no job however menial that he wasn't prepared to do himself to demonstrate how it should be done. Lord Lee of Cliveden he was known as in servants' halls all over the country, a title he richly deserved. I met many great men during my time as a servant but no one impressed me as much as the 'skipper', as we called him behind his back. When you were with him you felt you were in the presence of greatness. Everyone who knew him was the better for it. I understand he is to relate his story later in the book. It will I know be told modestly, though I ask you to remember my tribute to him as you read it.

A good captain means a happy ship, and being with the Astors was happy. We had our moans and groans of course, but life was fun. Lady Astor contributed to this with her personal gaiety. She brought to Cliveden very much the way of life of the Southern States of America. She came from Richmond, Virginia, and her art of mimicry and impersonation of the deep south was remarkable. She was constantly digging at the too pompous British, and her *pièce de résistance* was her impersonation of Margot Asquith. She even carried a set of false teeth in her bag to make her performance the more real. Sometimes at the luncheon or dinner table she would begin her antics; these were the moments when it was difficult to play the imperturbable servant who must never be supposed to be listening.

I remember once when Charles Dana Gibson, her brother-in-law, was visiting she told the story of an unfortunate man who was in the local jail awaiting trial. The window of his cell looked on to the street and he was peering through the bars asking passers-by the time. He was ignored until an old grey-haired man came up. 'What yo sayin'?' he asked.

'Ah jus want to know de time of day.'

'What yo want to know de time of day fo' you ain't got no 'pointment has yo?' replied the old man.

It doesn't read as the funny story of the year, yet the way her ladyship told it, it was. As she came to the end I was standing behind Mr Gibson ready to serve him with potatoes, he threw his arms into the air and caught my dish, upsetting the potatoes over the lady next to him. She was leaning forward laughing and one potato lodged in her cleavage. She screamed and foolishly clutched her hands to her bosom. Now everyone knows that a potato that's hot on the outside is scalding inside, and a squashed scalding potato between the breasts is no laughing matter to the person concerned. It is, however, to the onlookers and coming quickly on to Lady Astor's story it was impossible to tell exactly at what the company were laughing. I knew of course, so did Mr Lee. I was able to dive to the floor ostensibly retrieving the potatoes, and Mr Lee turned to the sideboard. It was left to her ladyship to try to restore some sort of order. She led the injured party from the room, and then the laughter knew no bounds. I had to retire to the serving-room, so did the skipper. How eventually we finished that lunch I don't know.

Another episode which required, but didn't get, the fullest restraint occurred during a weekend house party. It had been a gruelling day for both Mr Lee and me and we were glad when the final duty came round at ten o'clock. It was a nightly ritual, the taking up of the 'Grog' tray, so called I suppose because there was no grog served, just slices of lemon in tumblers contained in silver holders set on a salver and carried by me with Mr Lee following with a silver jug of hot water. It was considered by Lady Astor to be a good digestive drink on which to retire to bed.

We entered the drawing-room with due ceremony. As we did so one of the young guests, Miss Joan Poynder, began to walk out of the room. As she drew near us she suddenly stopped, clutched at her waist but was too late, her knickers fell to the floor. We both stopped in our tracks,

'Christ,' I thought, 'what action is a well-trained servant

supposed to take now. Nothing I can do with my hands full, I'll leave it to Lee, he's got one free hand.' Lee stood to attention looking to his front like a well-trained soldier. Miss Poynder with modest composure stepped out of her knickers, picked them up and as she passed said, 'Oh Lee, I'm so sorry.'

I couldn't resist it, as she left I whispered, 'It's a sure sign she fancies you, sir.'

Mr Lee gave me a withering glance and started forward. As we got to the table I noticed his face begin to go. He turned round, beckoned to me and together we left the room still laden with tray and jug. When we got outside he began laughing then suddenly stopped and turning on me said, 'You insolent bugger, don't you ever do that to me again.'

We then returned to the drawing-room. Half way across I noticed his shoulders shaking, he did an about turn and we left the room again. 'You bloody young fool, look what you've done to me.'

He pulled out his handkerchief, mopped his eyes and went back for yet another go. He was determined to try and make it this time. Then Mrs Phipps, Lady Astor's sister, said, 'Are you feeling all right, Lee, has something happened to upset you?'

This was too much for the skipper, I could see the scene passing again before his eyes. He put his jug down on the table, and left the room. I stayed behind and finished serving.

'What's the matter with Lee, Gordon?' her ladyship asked. 'He looks as though he's had a nasty shock.'

'I believe he has, my lady,' I replied.

'Oh,' she said, 'I must remember to ask him about it tomorrow. Good-night, Gordon.'

'Good-night, my lady,' I said just making the door before I collapsed helpless with laughter. It was one of the few occasions that I ever saw the skipper completely scuttled.

Not all the fun at Cliveden was unconscious or accidental. Bobbie Shaw, Lady Astor's son by her first marriage, would often visit there for a weekend and bring down a party of the younger set who would lighten proceedings in their own way with dancing, moonlight bathing, playing tricks on unwary servants and generally putting a certain amount of devilment into the house.

I remember one particularly cunning plot they hatched for J. L. Garvin, a journalist and later Editor of the *Observer*, a paper Lord Astor owned. He was a serious-minded chap who expounded a lot at the dinner table on the state of the world. Always, according to him, we were on the brink of disaster. One particular night, although he didn't know it, he was.

In the corridors of the east wing there stood 'The Venetian Lady', a life-sized figure of a woman in the national costume of Venice. Reginald Winn, Alice Perkins and Joan Poynder, led by Mr Bobbie Shaw, carried this dummy up a side staircase, placed it in Mr Garvin's bed, and then removing the bulb from the main light in the room and putting a chair where he was likely to stumble over it they retired to his dressing-room and lay there in wait until he came to retire for the night. Mr Garvin behaved as they expected; he tried the light and finding it didn't work groped his way to the bedside trying to find the light on his bedside table, knocking the chair over and crying out as he did so. One of the conspirators then burst from the dressing-room with a torch. 'What the devil do you think you're playing at, sir, making your way into a lady's bedroom like this. It's not the kind of behaviour that's expected of a gentleman in this house.'

Mr Garvin mumbled something about thinking it was his room.

'A likely tale, sir, but if it is the case I suggest you look for the nightwatchman, he has a list of the guests, and will take you to your room.' With that he shut the dressing-room door.

Poor Mr Garvin stumbled out of the room and went looking for the watchman. Meantime the others replaced the light, removed the Venetian lady, straightened the bed, returned to the dressing-room and waited for his return.

'But this is the room I came in to, I swear it,' declared Mr Garvin to the nightwatchman.

'Was it indeed,' he replied in a patronising voice of disbelief. 'Well there ain't no lady in 'ere now.' Then he sniffed a bit and chuckled. 'A lot of gentlemen get a bit muddled around this time of night, especially after a drink or two, eh?' Mr Garvin was not amused.

'But I haven't been drinking,' he explained.

'Of course not, sir, how could I have thought such a thing. Well we'll say no more about it, eh?'

Garvin by now was speechless. There was a rustle as he removed a note from his wallet. 'Here you are, my man, and good-night.'

'Thank you and good-night to you, sir.' And the nightwatchman went away, ten shillings or a pound richer. The next day Mr Garvin appeared sheepishly at breakfast time, and was uneasy for the rest of the day. It's my opinion he was glad to get back to London after that weekend.

But life wasn't all fun and games. Every morning would see us up at seven, running down to the stillroom, eventually emerging with six small morning tea trays arranged on one large butler's tray, distributing them round the guests' rooms, opening curtains and gently but firmly waking them. We didn't want them slipping back to sleep again and blaming us for their having missed breakfast. Then collecting their clothes from the night before, whipping them into the brushing-room, sponging, brushing, folding and hanging them. Then laying up the breakfast table, and bringing in the various dishes, kidneys, bacon, eggs, fish on one side of the dining-room – hams, brawns and galantines and game pies on the other. And the constant running to and fro with fresh toast and hot rolls.

After breakfast came the cleaning of silver, then hall duties; at St James's Square the duty footman would be stationed all day in the front hall sitting in a large hooded leather chair. There were constant callers of all nationalities to see either Lord or Lady Astor. Unless they had appointments the reply was always the same, 'They are not at home.' Then there was the running and taking of messages. We were permanently busy.

And then lunch, and what a pandemonium this meal could be. Each day Lady Astor's secretary would advise Mr Lee of those that had been invited, he in his turn would tell Monsieur Gilbert the chef, of the number the kitchen should prepare for. Experience had taught him some strange arithmetic; if he had been told six by the secretary he would tell the chef ten, if ten, sixteen and so on. Even with this kind of exaggeration he could be wrong, last-minute guests would be invited, then some would arrive who were not on the list and whose names had not been mentioned. Phone calls to the kitchen could go like this, 'Monsieur, there are now sixteen for lunch.' Five minutes later, 'Monsieur, the number is now twenty-four.'

'What can I do!' would cry the chef. 'First you say ten, then sixteen, then twenty-four.'

'Give them anything, monsieur, scrambled eggs, bacon – anything,' pleaded Mr Lee. In the meantime we footmen would be pulling the dining-room table to pieces and putting in extra leaves. Then Lady Astor would rush in the front door, see the hats and coats and shout, 'Lee, what are all these people doing here. I never invited them?' The skipper learned to take no notice, it was always happening.

Dinners in London were generally formal affairs, at Cliveden more family and friends, jollier occasions. Some of the dinners were on the grand scale, something never seen in the London society of today. Forty or fifty places at table, with a dance or reception afterwards in the ballroom with anything up to two thousand people, with extra waiters employed. These were grand if exhausting occasions for us as well as the guests.

I particularly remember my first dinner, given for the royals, King George V and Queen Mary. It was my afternoon and evening off duty the day before but when I was just about to go out I was summoned in to the steward's room by Mr Lee.

'Gordon,' he said, 'I want to remind you about the party tomorrow evening. It will be a long and exhausting day, so make sure that you're in tip-top condition for it. By that I mean no gallivanting tonight, do you understand?'

I said I did, and at the time I meant it. Unfortunately just around opening time I met Lloyd George's detective in Oxford Street. Since the Prime Minister was a frequent visitor to St James's Square I'd got to know this detective and he'd been well looked after in the servants' hall.

'Hello, Gordon,' he said, 'come and have a drink. I'll take you to our club at the police station in Hyde Park.'

I suppose I saw the red light but I ignored it. They prided themselves on their Younger's beer there, and I found their pride well justified. After an hour or two it was suggested that we went on to the Gate Swings High near St George's Hospital, where the Bass was considered to rival the Younger's. It must have. I remember going in but that's about all. Apparently I was eventually driven back to St James's Square, propped up against the wall by the back door, then the bell was rung and the detective rushed up the steps and away. Jack Gammon the odd man opened the door, got me upstairs without anyone seeing, and put me to bed.

Well of course I felt like death the next morning, and looked like it. Mr Lee gave me some old-fashioned glances as we got everything ready. It was of course the full treatment, the gold plate with the racing trophies decorating the table, a hell of a lot of cleaning and polishing. There were twenty of us waiting that night and everything went without a hitch. The King's equerry, I remember, brought two decanters with him, one of sherry and one of port, thinking that as the Astors were teetotallers he might not get his accustomed drinks. Mr Lee politely but firmly rejected them saying he was sure that His Majesty would be satisfied with the wines the Astors kept for their guests.

After the party was over and everything cleared away and cleaned Mr Lee invited us all into his sitting-room and gave us a glass of champagne. As he handed me mine he said,

'Gordon, I want to see you first thing in the morning.'

My heart missed a beat, I knew what it meant. If I hadn't been so exhausted I wouldn't have slept that night. It wasn't as bad as I expected.

'Look, my lad,' he said when I reported to him, 'don't think I don't know what you were up to on your night off. I'm not used to having my instructions ignored and if you hadn't carried out your duties to the letter yesterday we should have parted company; as it is don't you ever disobey me again. That's all.'

He was right of course, I learned my lesson, I controlled my future drinking and I suppose most important of all I made sure to cover my tracks on any future escapades.

Although invitations to the Astor parties were widely sought after in society it was generally accepted that they would be dry since her ladyship's opinion on strong drink was continuously and forcibly voiced both in and out of parliament. The Duke of Windsor, then the young Prince of Wales, made the same mistake as his father. So later did George VI when he was Duke of York.

Sometimes of course the parties were teetotal. Certain people would ring up beforehand to find out and bring their hip flasks if there was any doubt, and the lavatories were often used more for the consumption of drink than for their real purpose.

I remember a large reception being held for the Rhodes scholars. Dignitaries of every kind were invited to St James's Square to meet them. Arthur Bushall, his lordship's valet, and I were in the hall to attend to the guests on their arrival, taking their hats and coats and directing them upstairs to where Mr Lee would announce them to Lord and Lady Astor. A rather brash and flashy American came in a little late, with a peer of the realm at his heels. He handed his coat and hat and a gold-knobbed cane to me saying, 'Look after that stick of mine, it's kinda fragile.'

'It looks robust enough to me,' said the peer.

'Take a look at that,' said the American unscrewing the knob and withdrawing a long glass tube containing an amber-coloured liquid. 'There's a pint of rye in there, comes in real useful in these prohibition days in the States. It should come in useful here tonight too.'

'Goodness gracious me,' murmured the disapproving peer, and moved hastily away. 'Whatever will people think of next.'

The American winked to me, I responded with a stony sort of stare, a stock-in-trade of a good footman. But as he went I turned and grinned at Arthur; it was a very cold November night and the continual opening and closing of doors didn't help matters. Both Arthur and I started stamping around, blowing into our hands to keep warm. Suddenly Arthur turned to me and said, 'Are you thinking what I'm thinking?'

'I believe so,' I said, and without another word I walked over and got the gold-topped cane, while Arthur fetched a glass from the lavatory. We both of us thought that the American gent had been exaggerating when he said the tube contained a pint. We finished the lot in under five minutes.

Some time later the owner of the cane appeared waving his cloakroom ticket.

'Your hat and coat, sir?' I inquired.

'No, just hand me that cane,' he said.

I did so and with it he disappeared into the lavatory. After a second or two he was back. 'What the hell's going on around here, who's drunk my rye?' He looked at us accusingly.

'What rye, sir?' said Arthur innocently.

The American partly withdrew the container from the cane. 'The rye whisky that was in there, you saw me show it to that old buffer when I arrived.'

'That might account for it,' I replied. 'Yes I remember now, a gentleman did come down and ask to see the cane. I thought he was a friend of yours so I gave it him, thinking he was going to show it to some other friends. He handed it back to me a minute or two later.' I thought the American would explode.

'Give me my hat and coat, I'm off. If this is British hospitality I've had it!'

'No,' said Arthur when he was out of earshot, 'it was American hospitality, and we've had it.'

An interesting character who was employed for all dinner parties and receptions at St James's Square was James Hopkins 'Oppy, the linkman. He was a gnome of a man, not five feet tall, with a wrinkled face, long arms and a big head. Nevertheless he was a spry, bird-like creature. He had a voracious appetite and could put down a pint of beer without swallowing. A linkman's job was to stand outside the front door with a lantern and control the flow of traffic as guests arrived, and to call up the carriages or cars as they left.

'Oppy had his own uniform, he wasn't provided with the liveries of the houses he served. He wore a scarlet frock-coat, black dress trousers and a silk top hat. Round his neck, attached to a piece of string, was a whistle. As the guests arrived he would swoop on their vehicle, quickly rid it of its occupants, then would wave the coachman or driver away to park in or around St James's Square. While the party was on he'd first go round the Square checking and memorising where the various vehicles were parked, years of experience having taught him to recognise to whom they belonged. He would then retire to a local public house to refresh himself. He seemed to sense when the guests would depart, I never knew him to be late. The routine would be for the footman to announce the departing guests and shout, 'Lord so and so's carriage.'

'Oppy would bound round the Square, whistling as he went, and when he was in hailing distance of the vehicle would shout, 'Get a move on, your master wants 'ome.' Then he would rush back to be at the door, put his head into the hall and say, 'Lord so and so's car stops the way.' If Lady so and so was with her husband he would take her elbow and lead her down the steps, assist her into the carriage, remove his topper flourishing it in front of the occupants and refuse to move it until he heard the thud of a florin or a half-crown as it fell inside.

'Oppy was of course as well known to society as they were to him. His ingratiating manner must often have made them squirm; it did me. I could never stomach the way he would lean into a vehicle after a debutante and her mother and say, 'I 'ope the young lady 'as a successful season – in every possible way.' Meaning of course that he hoped she would land a husband.

One night Bert Jefferies, Lady Astor's second chauffeur, and

I got together about 'Oppy. We thought he was getting a bit big for his boots; the last time he'd been with us he was boasting about how well he did with his tips. Then he said that the Astors' friends were an exception. 'Probably it's because they're mostly teetotal,' he said.

Bert and I didn't care for this comment, we were nothing if not loyal. So when he arrived to have his supper and to dress before going on duty we waited for him. His routine was always the same. He went straight to the servants' hall, unpacked his scarlet coat and topper from an old kit bag, took out a couple of bottles of stout and a velvet pad, and while drinking he would polish his silk hat. This he then placed on a side table and would begin his supper, which he ate fast, noisily and with great relish.

This particular evening, while Bert engaged him in earnest conversation throughout his meal, I removed his hat and generously plastered the inside with black boot polish. When he went on duty opening car doors and lifting his hat with a flourish he got some very peculiar glances from the occupants. Eventually one looked at him, burst into a loud guffaw of laughter.

'Oppy rushed inside, took a look at himself in a mirror, went down to the servants' hall, changed and disappeared for the night. In a way the joke back-fired on me since I had to take over his job. From then on whenever 'Oppy came he ate his supper with his topper in front of him on the table, and he refused to speak to Bert or me. He took himself very seriously.

I hadn't been with the Astors long before I found that her ladyship's forecast that I would be able to visit my parents at Ascot frequently was a pipe dream. If life at St James's Square was busy, life at Cliveden was busier. There were continual weekend parties, and these meant late nights. Indeed the nearest I got to Ascot for months was by standing on a roof at Cliveden and gazing towards it with a pair of binoculars; then I could only manage the race-course grandstand, and that only on a fine day. During the season the name of Ascot was almost a dirty word among the servants. Ascot week was the jewel in Lady Astor's social crown and while it lasted it meant continuous feverish activity from the servants. Far from being a week, it was well over a fortnight for us. The early days of preparation and anticipation were almost the worst; then it began with a weekend party, and ended with one. No time off was granted, nor was it expected, and we were on duty from seven-thirty in the morning to well after midnight every night.

It was then that the job of valeting assumed enormous proportions. I would be looking after about six gentlemen throughout the period, with often a change of clientele at week-ends. It was a job I enjoyed. It was the most personal side of service. I got to know many gentlemen and, though a few were uncommunicative, many of them seemed anxious to talk and indeed at times to share intimate secrets and gossip with me, much of which must remain locked in my memory box.

Not only for Ascot week but before every weekend a list would be put up in the brushing-room of gentlemen that the footmen would have to look after. I'm a little ashamed to say we studied it with some interest and for the wrong motives. We made our selections with no regard for rank or importance; it was related only to their reputation as tippers. This repu-tation was based not only on our own experience but that of the underground telegraph of the below stairs world. When I first joined, Mr Reginald Winn, although a young man, was considered high on the list of people who were a good touch. He was then courting Alice Perkins, her ladyship's niece, and was anxious I think to make a good impression all round and wisely considered that to be on amicable terms with the staff could increase his standing in everyone's eyes.

Americans varied, some could be almost absurdly generous, particularly on their first visit, others tight-fisted. I think it was either through inexperience or because they thought that we would put it down to that. Our expectation was a currency note of either ten shillings or a pound. Paul Phipps, known in the servants' hall as 'Poor Phipps', would only give half a crown, even though he was Lady Astor's brother-in-law. His apparent meanness was excused because of his great courtesy and charm; as Mr Lee said, 'You must remember he's only an architect.' And he spoke of him as though he was in trade.

An American who was one of my early charges was Admiral Simms, the Supremo of the U.S. Navy. He was given the Tapestry bedroom and dressing-room at Cliveden which over-looked the River Thames. As I was unpacking his bag he said to me, 'What's that little creek down there?'

Now the Cliveden reach of the Thames was then and is now considered particularly beautiful, so with some pride I answered, 'That sir, is the River Thames,' and demonstrating my inadequate schooling added, 'it's the largest river in the world, you know.'

'You don't say,' said the admiral. 'Where did you go to school, boy?'

'Ascot, sir,' I said brightly.

'Well either you had a bad teacher, or you were a bad listener. Let me tell you we've got a little old stream where I come from called "Big Muddy", the Mississippi River, and if that ain't ten miles larger than that stream out there my name ain't Simms.'

He then removed his naval tunic and asked for a towel and his beard trimmers (he sported a magnificent white goaty beard), sat down and while I held a small oval hand mirror in front of his face he said, 'In America we remember the Alamo, you remember the Amazon, boy, that's the biggest river in the world.'

The next day I called him, laid out his day uniform, gave him his morning tea and ran his bath. I returned after the gong had sounded and thinking he'd gone down to breakfast picked up his beard trimmers and ran them up the back of my neck. At this moment the admiral walked in from the dressing-room. 'Here, son, let me do that for you.'

He bounded over to me, grabbed me by the scruff of the neck and ran the clippers up and down pulling out more hairs than he cut saying while he was doing it, 'The largest river in the world is the Amazon, it's in South America and it's four thousand miles long. The largest ocean is the Pacific, there's nearly sixty-four million square miles of it, and I've sailed the lot.' Then he put me down and went to breakfast. A grand old man and an excellent teacher!

Another American I served, though somewhat against my wishes, was Senator 'Pussyfoot' Johnson the famous prohibitionist. I was wrong in my prejudgement. He was a charming old man, and very interested in the make-up of the staff. He couldn't believe that the Astors had some one hundred and fifty servants to keep their houses and gardens running. 'How much do you earn, son?' he asked.

'Thirty-two pounds a year plus two and six a week beer and laundry money, sir,' I replied unthinkingly.

'Beer money! Lady Astor pays you beer money?' I thought he'd explode. I tried to explain that it was a traditional term, and that we didn't have to spend it on beer. I'm not sure that I convinced him. I heard him grumbling to himself in his dressing-room. 'Beer money, indeed.'

I got a nasty shock the first morning I went to wake him. I opened his curtains and was about to put his tea tray on the bedside table when I saw he had a set of false teeth, a wig and a glass eye looking up at me accusingly. 'Beer money,' it seemed to be saying. My final memory of him was as a kindly and generous tipper.

I eventually learned the hard way what Mr Lee had tried to impress on we footmen, not to give service in the expectation of a reward, but for its own sake.

Lady Astor had had one of her memory lapses and an American Episcopalian parson arrived at the front door one weekend with his suitcases. Mr Lee summoned me, and after a quick phone call to the housekeeper, a room was found for him. I made a mental cash assessment of him as I took him to his room, and gave him a zero rating. This was confirmed next morning, because it was the custom for men to empty their pockets on to the dressing-table before hanging their clothes. I glanced there and saw neither small change or a wallet. 'My reverend travels very light,' I remarked to the other footmen as I gave his clothes only the most casual sort of brushing, and ran a cloth over his shoes. He got scant treatment from me during the next day and night.

On the Monday morning Mr Lee called me and said, 'Your reverend is leaving and wants packing up.' I slung his things in in any old way and was just closing his case when he came into the room. 'Oh, Gordon,' he said, 'will you allow me to do something?'

'What is it, sir,' I queried.

'Will you permit me to give you this?' and he handed me three pounds. Three pounds! I could have wept.

'No, sir, it's too much,' I heard a voice saying which sounded like mine.

'Please, Gordon, you looked after me so very well.'

So very well! If only I'd known what was coming, he'd have had the royal treatment from me. As I said, it taught me a life-long lesson. That evening I sought out the skipper and told him the story. 'I now see, sir, what you meant about service,' I said. He didn't respond, just gave me a pat on the back as he moved past me to the cupboard, poured me a glass of port and sat down and began talking of other things.

Although Lady Astor was a Conservative member of parliament she didn't restrict her friendship to people of her own political leaning, as indeed her great and lasting friendship with Mr Bernard Shaw witnesses. Her Liberal opponent when she stood for election for the Sutton division of Plymouth was Isaac Foot, father of our present minister. He was a regular visitor to St James's Square. It was there that I was called upon to valet for him. He travelled up from Cornwall to attend a dinner party and reception, arriving at about six in the evening. As I was unpacking his case he asked me what dress would be worn. 'Full evening dress and decorations,' I said off the top of my head and began laying the things out. 'And what time is dinner?'

'At eight fifteen, sir.'

'Good, I will have a little rest till then. I imagine Lord and Lady Astor will be too occupied to see me now. Call me at seven forty-five.' This I did, helped him with his clothes, and he went down resplendent to the drawing-room, where the guests were received. To his dismay and chagrin he was the only one wearing evening dress. Even his hosts were informally clothed. I'm glad I was not there at the time, it was bad enough the next morning when I woke him. He glanced over the bedclothes at me and said, 'And what am I expected to wear at breakfast – pyjamas!'

A Labour minister whom Lady Astor befriended was J. H. Thomas, the Railwaymen's Union Leader, who became prominent at the time of the general strike in 1926. Befriended is probably an under-statement, it was more in the nature of a take-over. She gave him and his family the boat house, where the Astors had picnic teas when there were river parties, to live in rent free. Later they moved into 'Rose Cottage', another small house on the estate, and his family of two boys and two girls were brought up there. My wife 'Pop', then the head gardener's daughter, knew and liked them. It was Lady Astor who first invited him to a real dinner party and Pop's sister Rose who helped to dress Mrs Thomas, because she was uncertain of her clothes sense. Later on as J. H. Thomas became more powerful politically she didn't have to worry much as she'd accompany him to some of his meetings round the country and come back loaded with rolls of material and a variety of other presents, 'political perks' I believe they were called. He got to enjoy the high life though he could never get away from his working class origins.

There's a story that at one of the Astor's dinner parties when he was sitting next to F. E. Smith, later Lord Birkenhead, and asked by him how he was feeling, he said, 'I've got one 'ell of an 'eadache.'

To which F. E. replied, 'Why don't you try a couple of aspirates for it, Jimmy.'

A rum lot I found these Labour M.P.s. They may have resented the crumbs from the rich men's tables for their constituents but they weren't ashamed to share the cake with them.

While I have a great respect for the British public school system and the kind of person it turns out, my only experience of one of them at close quarters was disastrous. It was during Mr Billie Astor's first half at Eton. After he'd been there for about eight weeks Mr Lee sent for me and said that according to Nanny Gibbons, the Astor children's nurse, someone, and that on this occasion it was to be me, had to go to the college to examine his suits and shoes to see if any repairs were needed.

Any shoes which wanted heeling – and I was informed that there was some sort of competition as to who could first wear them down to the soles – were to be taken without argument to Ganes, the old established cobbler in the High Street, and any clothes that required mending were to be returned to Nanny Gibbons.

I was driven by Bert Jeffries, then his lordship's second chauffeur, in the Daimler to Mr Conybeare's house. It was a rambling old place. Outside there was a group of boys, top-hatted and all carrying badly rolled umbrellas. 'Could you,' I asked them, 'inform me which room the Honourable William Astor occupies?'

'Try the top floor and knock on every door until you come to his,' was suggested.

This I did. Grinning faces appeared and I received comments like, 'Go away, you annoy me', 'Your looks revolt me', and, 'Never heard of him my good man'.

Finally by threats and perseverance I found the room and achieved the purpose of my visit, leaving with a pair of trousers and two pairs of shoes. On my return, half way down the passage, doors suddenly opened and I was ambushed by a dozen boys who chased me downstairs with a rain of blows from hockey sticks, cricket bats and umbrellas. When at last I reached the car I explained to Bert Jeffries what had happened. It wasn't really necessary. Unsympathetically he roared with laughter. 'You were lucky,' he said, 'they usually de-bag outsiders like you who come on a clothes and boot check.'

When I returned I reported the incident to Mr Lee and told him that never again would I visit the place. He, too, was unfeeling. 'You'll be all right next time, you won't have to make enquiries, thereby finding it unnecessary to open the boys' doors and advertising your presence.' I stuck to my guns though and when the next visit came round another footman took my place. Like Bert Jeffries I saw no reason to inform him what to expect. He gave a better account of himself than I did, however, and returned as good if not better than he got, coming back to Cliveden with nothing more than a badly battered top hat.

My only other experience with Mr Billie's clothes came later when he was more grown up. I was looking after him in the holidays and finding that he only wore shirts, vests and pants for one day and knowing that he took a bath twice a day I decided that this was an extravagance, so I wore them for another couple of days before putting them into the laundry basket. Although I wasn't found out I was shown the red light by Nanny Gibbons who one day went to the basket, held up some of Mr Billie's things and said, 'Look at these, Gordon, fancy you letting Mr Billie wear his clothes until they get as dirty as this.' I stopped wearing them after that. I was lucky because a week or two later one of the footmen was caught wearing Mr Bobbie Shaw's socks and was sacked on the spot.

It was however possible to accumulate a small wardrobe from some of the visitors. It was Mr Dana Gibson, Lady Astor's brother-in-law, who put me wise to this. I'd been valeting him during a long stay he had with us and as he was leaving he gave me his customary generous tip, then slung some ties at me. 'You can throw these away, Gordon, I've no use for them any more.'

I looked through them and could find nothing wrong, many of them seeming brand new to me, so I took them down and showed them to Mr Lee. 'This is the way gentlemen of breeding offer you their old clothes as a present. You may keep them.'

It was a different story some months later. Flushed with the success that Mr Dana Gibson's ties had in my social skirmishes with the ladies and finding my other charges showed no anxiety to throw anything my way I began 'accidentally' to leave the odd things out when I was packing a case at the end of a stay until I had a tidy collection of shirts, vests, underpants and socks. I even 'won' a pair of shoes from Mr Reggie Winn, though this was a genuine mistake.

He was the only commoner, apart from Dana Gibson, whose clothes I wore, which accounted for Mr Lee's reaction when he came to my room after I'd been doing my personal laundry. He glanced at the articles hanging on an improvised clothes line and said,

'You know, Gordon, if you were to be knocked down in the street and taken to hospital the authorities there would have to send for a copy of *Debrett* to determine from these coronets and coats of arms your real identity. It could indeed cause a major incident. I'm sure that even if the noble gentlemen gave you these clothes they did not intend you to assume the crests embroidered on them.'

The skipper had a way of getting his message home. I pondered over it for many days but I'm ashamed to say I didn't act on it. I was just a little more careful when crossing the road.

To me the most comical occasion that concerned borrowed plumes came much later in life. I was living in Luton and, though working as a salesman of cattle food, I still enjoyed the odd evening as a footman in the stately homes round about. Cliveden was quite near and one day George Washington, then butler to Lord Billie Astor (it was after Mr Lee had retired), asked me to help him with a dinner party there. It was a hectic evening and after the meal, as we were washing and cleaning the silver, George said to me, 'Your shirt's wringing wet and filthy, Gordon, I reckon you'd better let me lend you one for the morning.'

I agreed and as I was going to my bedroom in the servants' quarters he handed me what looked like a silk shirt. 'It's an old one of Lord Waldorf's, you needn't bother to return it,' he said.

Next morning I had to be up at dawn to go to the Hitchin corn market and while dressing I saw that, instead of a shirt, George had given me one of his lordship's old nightshirts. Well, it had a collar so I found a couple of safety pins, shortened it about a couple of feet and put it on.

I was a bit conscious of it as I went round the stands of the corn market passing the time of day with the millers and farmers, so when I bumped into a friend of mine, Lob Illott, I told him what I was wearing. His eyes twinkled, he grabbed me by the arm, pulling me round behind his stand. 'By gum,' he whispered, 'this is where we have some fun and make a bit of money into the bargain.' I looked bewildered. 'It's Jack Garratt,' he said, sticking a thumb towards the next stand.

Now Jack, like Lob, was a Pickwickian character, owner of a roller flour mill and a bit of a dandy. 'He's always going on about his tailor,' said Lob, 'and about how all his clothes are custom made and in particular about how he has his shirts specially made to come down below his knees so as to keep his arse and his other precious parts warm in winter. He once offered to bet me a sovereign that he has the longest shirts in the country. I'll take him up on it and we'll prove him wrong.' He managed to get Jack to join us for drinks around lunch time, then brought the conversation to shirts and their length.

I played my part by saying, 'I bet I've got the longest shirt in the company.' Jack took the bait and the wagering started.

'How are we going to prove it,' one of the punters asked.

'Jack and I will go into the lavatory and compare lengths,' I suggested.

But that didn't suit at all. 'No, we've all got to see,' was the universal decision.

So back we trooped to the market and the interested parties

made a circle round Jack and me. 'Who's going to drop first,' I said. We tossed for it, Jack lost and down his trousers went. I must say it was an impressive sight, his shirt stretched half way down the calves of his legs. He stood there, proud, impassive but looking bloody stupid. 'Let's see you beat that,' he said.

I had, of course, previously removed the safety pins and as I lowered my trousers it was like a curtain falling at the theatre as my nightshirt enveloped my ankles. I got a round of applause, such as an actor would have welcomed, except of course from Jack.

'You bleeding cheat,' he screamed, 'that's not a shirt it's a bloody shroud!' We dragged him back to the pub still protesting. He refused to pay his debts but he settled in kind. If mine was typical there must have been many sore heads the next day.

Although work dominated our lives with the Astors their sort of dual nationality and her ladyship's lust for travel gave us leisure opportunities not granted to servants in other similar positions. They made frequent visits to the United States, which in those days meant sea voyages and usually lengthy stays. Because it was not considered necessary to cater only for the servants left behind we were all put on 'board wages', that is we were given money, generally around a pound a week, out of which we bought our own food.

Freddie Alexander, the under butler, and I used to work in together over this. We'd scrounge whatever we could from the kitchens, and steal a bit here and there. I remember one time when we lived for nearly three weeks on bread and dripping, bacon and sausages and Freddie said, 'I reckon my pores are so clogged with grease if I don't get a change of diet I'll turn into a slithering eel.'

That sparked an idea off in my mind. 'What about some fish, Freddie,' I suggested.

'Now you're talking.'

'Right, we'll borrow a couple of rods and try our luck in the river.'

He didn't seem too pleased about this.

'Seems a waste of good drinking time,' he grunted, so I had to go on my own and as luck would have it I caught a sizeable pike. There wasn't a fish still at Cliveden but beggars couldn't be choosers so we straight away opened it up to clean it. We had the shock of our lives, there in its stomach was a half-digested rat. That finished Freddie. 'I'm off to Maidenhead, we'll open an account at Budgens (the Astor's grocer), and worry about paying when the bill comes in.'

It did of course several times but we ignored it, happy in the belief that Budgens wouldn't make a fuss as the Astors were very good customers. We were right, but it's the sort of thing you can only do once. I suppose I should feel ashamed of our behaviour, I can only excuse it by saying that with the family abroad there was no entertaining, and therefore no tips, and this deficiency had to be made up somehow.

The first week that the family were away was usually one of feverish activity in all departments. It was a chance to give everything the cleaning and refurbishing that constant usage didn't offer. However, after all was done things slowed down, we were able to look around, to consider our social lives and enjoy some entertainment. For me this meant the opportunity to concentrate my attentions on the opposite sex, interspersed of course with pub outings with the boys when I could boast of my prowess. Freddie Alexander, although many years my senior, shared my tastes. He had a steady lady friend, Flo Hillier, a cook who had a cottage in the nearby village of Cookham. According to Fred it wasn't just food she was interested in. He showed me a letter from her in which she told him she'd got hold of a book by some Indian fellow, which described various sexual antics, and she ended by saying, 'Won't we have fun, Freddie, trying them all out.'

My first bit of dalliance at Cliveden was with Elise, a red-headed Swiss girl who came to us as nursery maid. Nursery maids were looked on as footmen's perks. This Elise, although as pretty as paint and flirtatious, was also very strong willed. She told me she'd come over to England to learn our language and that there were other things that she could just as easily learn at home. So I had to content myself with the occasional kiss and cuddle, and with the envious glances there were thrown my way by other young men as we walked the streets together.

I was more fortunate one night when Freddie asked me to join him for a drink at the Feathers. I was held up and got there about an hour late to find him plying a rather charming young lady with port. He'd had a few drinks himself and his intentions were written all over his face, and didn't make a very pretty sight. When he left to answer the call of nature his girlfriend grabbed me by the hand and said, 'Come on, we're getting out of this place,' and together we fled into the woods.

If Freddie's face had been an ugly sight that night it was nothing to what it was the next morning when he saw me. 'You're a nasty, thieving swine,' he said, then meanly added, 'you owe me the price of three large ports.'

Paying homage to the ladies also made us liars; we had to be if we were to expect any serious attention from them at all. I think as a result of the First World War domestic service was considered inferior employment for both men and women. I couldn't understand why, and even if I had there's nothing I could have done about it. I and others like me had to condition ourselves to accepting the general verdict. This meant that whenever we went dancing and started chatting to the girls we always had to be ready to speak of some other job if we were asked about our work.

I became friendly with a dance band set in Maidenhead and it was agreed amongst us that I'd be introduced as a saxophonist from London; thank God nobody ever asked me to play. Members of these dance bands were a lusty lot and, like pop groups today, had the pick of the girls. One particular night stands out in my memory. Stan Bennett, a conductor, took me round to a flat in Maidenhead where a composer called Arthur Bliss kept two girls.

'Never heard of him,' I said, as his name came up on our way round there, 'what's he written?'

'Nothing you'd know, he's sort of classical.'

'Sort of classical' was an under statement. *Sir* Arthur Bliss, when he died, was Master of the Queen's Music. Anyway when we got round to the flat and met the girls it was apparent that at that time he was behaving like a young Chopin.

Stan didn't waste a lot of time talking, he whipped one of the ladies into a bedroom. I liked chatting a bit first, so my one and I made ourselves comfy on the sofa. Sure enough she got round to what I did for a living, and I spun her my usual tale. 'What rough hands you've got for a saxophonist,' she said, just like Red Riding Hood. 'Oh I spend a lot of time gardening, you know,' I explained. This may have got her thinking about the birds, bees and the flowers. Whatever it was she came out with the fact that she was pregnant and did I know where she could get something done about it. Pregnant! With that my sexual fantasies flew out of the window. I daren't even kiss her in case she might use this in evidence against me. I took my first opportunity of a get-away, and walked back home in a cold sweat. Apparently there must have been some sort of inquest about my behaviour because Stan tore into me about it the next time I saw him, ending up with, 'You needn't have worried about it, it was her appendix and she had it out the following week.'

It was probably lucky for me that shortly after that incident I got pierced by cupid's arrow and fell in love with someone whom I'd observed and admired from a distance all the time I'd been at Cliveden; Poppy, the third daughter of the Astor's head gardener. She it was, as I've previously mentioned, that became my wife, but before that we had a deal of fun and got ourselves in and out of no end of scrapes.

Pop had a job in the house as floral decorator and this meant that she was responsible for all the plants and flowers in the rooms at Clivedon. It was considered a superior position as it brought her into contact with the family, and close to Lady Astor who took a personal interest in the flower decoration. Although Pop was close to her ladyship they never really hit it off; as Frank Copcutt – one-time decorator and later head gardener – said, 'It was hard enough for me to come to terms with her ladyship, I'm certain no woman ever could have in that job.' But as I've said, it was a position of some authority and therefore it wasn't surprising that at first Pop took scant notice of the glances and occasional wise-cracks of a second footman.

We first met properly at a dance at a nearby village. I may have been no Fred Astaire but comparison with some of the other men there made me a near relation, so I might say without conceit that I swept Pop off her feet. She loved dancing as I did and it gave expression to the gaiety, fun and mischievousness that were so much a part of her. From that night on we sought each other's company. Young people today complain that in the country there's nothing to do, yet they have clubs, television, radios and money to burn. We had none of these things yet our lives were exciting and at times idyllic. In a way we were 'star crossed' lovers. We knew that no one would approve of our relationship – not Pop's family, because of her father's position, not Mr Lee, because 'that sort of nonsense' was bound to interfere with the smooth running of the house, and certainly not Lady Astor. So our meetings were conducted with stealth and were in a way all the more valued because of that. Just a touch of hands as we passed each other in a corridor was a thrill and sensation to be remembered, and if our work brought us together for just a few moments it was as if the world stood still. We plotted and planned our surreptitious meetings in whispers or with the passing of silly little notes, and when those times came we would wander hand in hand, speechless and bewildered by the wonder of it all. We danced, of course, always choosing places where we hoped we would be unobserved. We walked the fields and parklands around Cliveden and saw the countryside in a new light together. We rowed and swam in the Thames.

In a way the river shared our secret since by crossing it we could make short-cuts to the town of Maidenhead and many of the villages we visited. Also by making our way down there individually there was less chance of our being seen by anyone. We would meet at the boathouse. Old Joe Brooks, the ferry-man and boatman, was a simple soul given more to grumbling to himself than talking and unlikely, even if he suspected our secret meetings, of telling anyone about them. He was, however, very fond of his bed so that the chances of getting him up from it to ferry us back on our return journeys were light. We didn't find this out until I'd had to swim the river a couple of times to get the ferry and to retrieve Pop, which not only cooled my ardour but offended my dignity, for no man cuts much of a figure in dripping wet underpants, shivering cold and covered in goose pimples.

We eventually decided to borrow a boat each time and leave it out of sight downstream. This worked well in good weather, but there came one terrible night when a storm had blown up. When we got to the river the current was in full spate. We were already late so there was nothing for it but to take a chance. It nearly cost us our lives, for despite my pulling on the oars like a long-shoreman we were carried downstream and began shipping water as the boat turned sideways into the current. When I thought we were finished a wave flung us towards the quieter waters near the bank and although we were a mile downstream of the boathouse we were safe. Our night wasn't over, we had the job of dragging the boat against the stream back to its moorings, stumbling along the bank and often having to wade into the water, with the screeching of disturbed birds and the red eyes of the water rats adding to the discomfort of soaking clothes and mud-coated legs.

Having survived that ordeal and many other near discoveries we grew bolder and took more chances so that eventually, although we didn't know it, our romance became an open secret. I think in the end Lady Astor was the only one who didn't know about it. I suppose in a way both of us wanted to be found out otherwise we wouldn't have acted so foolishly, for one day after lunch, while I was clearing the table and Pop was preparing the flowers for a dinner party, I said, 'Come on, there's a good film on in Maidenhead, let's leave this till the evening.'

It was madness of course and I think we both realised it because we stayed in the town far too long. Mr Lee, finding the table undecorated, rang Pop's father who came storming up to the house to finish her work. My absence was then discovered, two and two put together, her ladyship informed and the trouble began. Love thrives on opposition so the more they stormed the more firmly we held our ground. I, of course, was sacked, but Pop came away with me, the Gods smiled on us, we married and almost immediately I found employment as a floor manager in one of the Lyons Corner Houses, and despite some occasional hard struggles I think I can say we have both enjoyed our lives together, and have made a success of our marriage.

It now looked as if my life in service was over and that I would have to make a new set of friends. It wasn't and for this I have to thank first Edwin Lee the butler. Before I left Cliveden he spoke to me in his room. 'Don't imagine that this is the end of the line, Gordon,' he said, 'it's just a storm in a teacup. I'll do anything I can to help you both. I've had a word with her ladyship and told her that you are too good a footman to lose entirely and that after a decent period I shall ask you to come and assist at any dinner or reception that we hold. She has seen fit to agree with me so we hope we shall see plenty of you in the future, that is of course if you are willing to come.'

Today it may not seem much for him to have said but in the context of the times it was a magnificent gesture. There were others in plenty he could have employed without risking her ladyship's displeasure. I think though that she was pleased with his attitude because she was always one to forgive and forget, and the way she greeted me whenever I visited the house was a sign of this.

Charles Dean was another great friend and ally who, when he became butler to Alice Astor, employed me regularly. He seemed to sense when Pop and I were finding the going a bit hard and would give food parcels and the like to me whenever I visited him.

I remember him one evening ringing the Corner House and asking me over to Hanover Lodge, Alice Astor's London home, for a drink and a chat. At that time she was married to Prince Obolensky, the Russian émigré. 'The prince and princess will be going out for dinner tonight,' he said, 'so we can enjoy ourselves over a few glasses of port.'

When I arrived at about eight o'clock Ernest the footman told me that the princess had changed the plans and that they had in fact a small dinner party of ten. 'Help yourself to some supper, though, Charles will be down in about half an hour.'

I sampled the various dishes as they were brought down to the pantry. Then I saw three quails resting in a silver plate. I'd had my fill but I thought to myself that Pop would like to sample them, so I wrapped them in paper, threw the garnishing into the pig bucket and stuffed them into my overcoat pocket. It was now getting quite late and I decided that I had better be getting back home. I left a message for Charles and was making my way down the drive when I heard my name being called and running feet making towards me. I looked round and there was Ernest the footman, 'Come back, Gordon, the princess is asking for the quails.'

We both ran back to the house together, I unwrapped the unfortunate birds that had suffered a few bruises and broken bones in the packing, arranged them into some sort of shape, while Ernest picked the garnishing out of the pig bucket, put it under the tap and sprinkled it hastily around the silver dish. By now I had missed my train so I waited for Charles to come down so that I could apologise to him. 'All's well that ends well,' he said, 'the princess thought them the tastiest birds she'd ever eaten.'

Poor Pop was disappointed when I told her the story. It must have stuck in her memory for when many years later she was asked if she had ever tasted quail she replied, 'Only once, very nearly.'

Although my hands were empty that night there were others when they were too full. The Obolenskys entertained many visiting Americans and one night the guest of honour was the composer and pianist Cole Porter. After dinner it was decided that the family and their guests would have a quiet musical evening, followed by cards and backgammon. Down came Charles and handed me his keys, 'Get the champagne up, Gordon, they've decided to stay in.'

'How many bottles?' I inquired.

'Oh about three dozen.'

Ernest filled the bath with ice and we began taking the wire off about half of them. Then the bell went, up and back went Charles. 'Bloody women,' he said, then he began mimicking the princess. 'Oh Dean, we think we're going clubbing so we shan't need the champagne.'

The footman and I continued the theatricals. 'Oh Dean, what a pity because we've taken the wires off some of them, do you think we might have a little drinkie ourselves?'

'I can't put them back in the cellar like that, they'd probably blow the bloody roof off – help yourselves.'

We did. A number of bottles later I was poured into a taxi, to catch my last train. By this time everyone was in a happy, generous mood, Dean shoved two bottles of champagne into my coat pockets, someone else handed me a couple of food parcels and finally some joker threw in a seven-pound tin of soft soap, saying I might need it when I got home and Pop saw the state I was in. As I drew up at Paddington station the taxi driver said to me, 'You'll need a porter, mate, I shouldn't try carrying all that stuff in your condition.'

'I'm not going to,' I replied.

I put the soap on the pavement, seized the two parcels in my arms and dribbling the tin along with my feet ran through the ticket barrier. Everyone stood looking at me in amazement. Panting up to a carriage I threw the tin and the parcels in and sat down. There was a report like a gun going off, my fellow passengers ducked straight into a shower of champagne that spurted from one of my coat pockets. I tried to stop it by putting my thumb over the bottle. This was an error of judgement, it squirted in a venomous jet into the face of a man sitting opposite me. I had a lonely journey home for, despite my apologies, the carriage emptied fast.

Charles wasn't the only one to show generosity. May, Lady Astor's kitchen maid, had a big heart and was open-handed with her food. One night as I was leaving for home she gave me an extra large parcel and a basket of fruit for Pop, who was very pregnant at the time carrying our son Bill. I was so anxious to get home to see how she was, I ran most of the way from the station, into the house and threw myself on to the end of the bed. Its legs buckled under my weight and threw Pop forward into my arms. From the expression on her face I thought she was going to hit me, then I saw it change to one of deep concern. 'Oh heavens, it's started,' she cried.

I don't remember much about the rest of that night, except that it was one of the most exciting and frightening of my life. I do remember thinking the following evening, as I set about repairing the bed in the knowledge that I had a seven and a half-pound son, that it was a fortuitous thing to have happened. The basket of fruit was timely too.

One of the criticisms levelled at servants is that we were servile. I'm not quite sure what that means. We were certainly not slaves in any sense but like other men or women in employment we had to obey those in authority over us. We had our own established code of behaviour to which we conformed, so did those in society at that time, and if either side broke the rules and was found out they were punished for it.

I was fascinated by the way certain people reacted towards royalty. High society, I found, behaved impeccably, but the faster-monied set that often surrounded the Prince of Wales seemed a fawning lot and the behaviour of many of them was enough to make the most hardened footman flinch.

I remember one particular party; it was before the story broke in this country of Edward's relationship with Mrs Simpson, though at the time she was constantly in his company, and it was a time of great mental and political insecurity for the prince. He hated the injustice of mass unemployment and was rowing with his ministers in order to get something done about it. Then he also knew that eventually the problems of his emotional life would have to be made public, and that decisions would have to be made on the future of the monarchy.

On this particular night he was expected as a guest with his brother George and, as usual when royals were invited, the other guests assembled a quarter of an hour before the expected time of arrival. Among them was Mrs Simpson, surrounded by a sycophantic lot, who a few months later were to behave like Judas Iscariots towards her. I was serving cocktails and was accompanied round by a footman. We made our way towards Mrs Simpson. 'Would you care to have a cocktail, madam?' I asked.

'What kind have you?' she queried.

'There are Paradise, White Lady and Champagne, madam,' I answered. 'Huh,' she said, 'whoever heard of a white lady being in paradise.' It was not, as I think you'll agree, the funniest remark of the year, yet the circle around her screamed with laughter and clapped their hands as if she was the greatest wit since Oscar Wilde.

When eventually the princes arrived it was obvious that Edward was thoroughly exhausted. As was customary I placed a glass and a small decanter of brandy at his side. As I made to pour one he said, 'No thank you.'

I stood near by in case he should require anything else and within the course of three minutes half a dozen people came forward and tried to persuade him to drink. Eventually he lost his patience. 'I want to eat,' he cried.

Dinner did little to improve his temper and there was an air of tension all round. Rawitz and Landaur, the famous piano duetists, were doing their best to lighten the proceedings by playing Strauss's waltzes, but this didn't suit the prince, 'Why don't they play some bloody jazz?' he said to his brother.

An equerry, 'Chips' Channon, was called over; he went and whispered to the pianists, who easily switched to razmataz. Things got a bit more cheerful after that and so did the host and most of his guests.

One of nature's gentlemen that I had the privilege of serving was Charles Chaplin, at a dinner given by Count Lemur, a secretary at the French Embassy at 86 Eaton Square, with the Prince of Wales at the party too. It was one of those nights when drink got in the way, although this time it happened below stairs. Jimmy Gordon, the count's steward, had over the years developed what is known in service as 'the butler's complaint'. It comes from taking a drink every now and then to get through a heavy evening and ends up with becoming a confirmed alcoholic. Jimmy was such a one and by the time dinner was over he was paralytic. On occasions of this kind everyone does his best to cover up, so I took over from him and explained to the count that he was unwell. I'm glad to say everything passed off without a hitch, Mr Chaplin was on top of his form and kept everyone entertained. It was only when he was leaving that an incident occurred that embarrasses any butler or footman. After I had handed him his coat and hat, Mr Chaplin turned to me and held out his hand expecting me to shake it. Taken by surprise I ignored him, walked to the door and opened it. Waiting outside was the police constable on duty. 'Good-night, Mr Chaplin,' he said.

'Ah,' said Charlie, 'a London bobby. At least he won't be too proud to shake me by the hand.'

I was never on the staff of any Jewish gentlemen, but they had a good reputation among servants for their kindness, consideration and generosity, so when one evening I was waiting at a dinner party and a Mr Goldberg approached me and asked if I would organise a party for him, I jumped at it. All went well, there was excellent food, an abundance of good drink, dancing to one of Jack Payne's bands and entertainment provided by the Western Brothers. They were flying to Stockholm that evening and were rather nervous of it. 'Do you think you could get us some brandy?' one of them asked. I obliged with a bottle and was quickly slipped a pound. As the guests left they too were very generous and I was already a fiver in pocket before Mr Goldberg settled with me. 'A very good evening, Gordon,' he said as he gave me a pound on top of my agreed fee. 'Thank you very much, sir.' As he made to go he said, 'Oh by the way I hope my guests showed their appreciation to you by way of their gratuities.' His wallet was still in his hand so I thought fast.

'They were not very generous, sir, not quite what I'm used to,' I lied, 'but it doesn't matter.'

'Doesn't matter!' I thought he'd hit the roof. 'Of course it bloody well matters,' he was almost sobbing. 'My friends, my friends, they call themselves my friends; they come here, eat my food, drink my wine, smoke my cigars and aren't prepared to give you a few shillings when they leave. I must apologise to you, Gordon, on their behalf.' He fumbled in his wallet. 'Here take this,' and he pushed another two quid into my hand and walked away muttering some Jewish curse on his friends.

I must say I felt a bit upset and guilty as I made my way

home. It didn't take Pop long to bring me to my senses when I told her the story. Women have a way of seeing things differently. 'If you feel like that about it,' she said, 'give the money to me, so that I can cry all the way to the bank with it.'

It must now be apparent that although I left full-time service when I was dismissed from the Astors in 1924 and although I eventually rose to what some might consider a good position in the commercial world, my heart was always behind the green baize door, and at every opportunity I would join it there. First, of course, the additional money was important, it helped us raise and educate a family, but it wasn't only that that pulled me back. I suppose in a way it was the actor in me. As I went into one of the great houses it was as though I was going into a theatre as a member of a cast. It was a world of make-believe, people were escaping from the realities of life; but was this escapism such a bad thing? If the rich had surrendered their privileges and given everything that they had to the poor would it have been appreciated? Wouldn't they, as people do today, have just cried out for more.

Of course servants were underpaid, and perhaps overworked, but if ever there was a job where that out-worn cliché about money not meaning everything was justified it was in service. The loyalties alone justified it – not just from among one's colleagues but from those that one served. It may be said that Lady Astor showed little loyalty when she sacked me because I insisted on marrying Pop, but it would be wrong. I broke the rules, I knew what I was doing and I wasn't bitter then, nor am I now, about the way she behaved; she administered the punishment and later she showed compassion.

When I look back to the day I left school – I was a country lout, nothing more. It was from the moment that I went into service that my education began. It was founded on discipline fostered by my environment. It was impossible to live among

beauty without it getting under your skin; you learn to distinguish what is good and what is not, you learn taste and
appreciation, you look at books lining shelves and eventually
you pick one up and begin to read; overheard conversations
spark off a desire to know more. You also learn moral values,
not always by examples but by observation and comparison.
You absorb these things. This is real education. Then, if you're
like me, you let your sense of humour run riot over the lot and
that way fully enjoy life. That's the way I see it.

## Some Reflections on Gordon's Story

Gordon has now retired and lives in a bungalow near the east
coast seaside town of Mablethorpe. He has three children, two
boys and a girl, all of whom have succeeded beyond his expectations. He enjoys retirement and so does his wife 'Pop'. Both
feel they have lived full, useful and happy lives. They have many
friends and have plenty to do.

His story I think describes the man. If things go wrong for
him he makes light of them. He can always see the silver lining.
Perhaps it may seem to some people extraordinary, having read
of his early behaviour, that he is a pillar of the local church, but
being a good Christian to him, or to me, doesn't mean going
around with a long face, choosing actions and words carefully.
It's an inner happiness, the joy of life which transfers itself to
those around, seeing the best in everything and everybody and
giving help when it's needed and deserved.

After any meeting with Gordon I come away feeling a better
person.

Perhaps this tribute from the present Marquess of Bath,
paid in a letter to him dated 2nd August 1973 illustrates what
I mean.

'I can remember distinctly having to rest every morning in the open air as I had a patch on my lung and in those days it was one of the only ways you could prevent it from becoming serious, in fact it is owing to you that I am still alive and, believe it or not, I am very grateful. Although I am now sixty-eight I hope to live a considerable time longer.'

# A FRIEND IN SERVICE

## Edwin Lee

Of all my friends Mr Lee, the Astors' butler, influenced my life the most strongly. I have met and spoken with many famous, important and rich people but only with 'Father', as he allowed me to call him, have I felt in the presence of greatness. If anyone has ever thought that Sir James Barrie's play, *The Admirable Crichton* was an exaggeration they should have seen Mr Lee at the height of his career, and they would have believed that it was on him that the playwright mirrored his character.

I first met him at intervals between 1923 and 1928 when I was maid to Lady Cranborne and on my visits to Cliveden. As a visiting maid I used the pug's parlour and so was able to watch the way he ran things. It was impressive. It had to be, for although Lady Astor was considered a great hostess she was not a good planner, for she would fuss and interfere. If 'Father' hadn't been a brilliant organiser, and a diplomat into the bargain, her reputation could have vanished overnight.

It was when I joined the Astor household as lady's maid to the Honourable Phyllis Astor (Miss Wissie), her ladyship's daughter, that I really got to know him, or perhaps it would be nearer the truth that first he got to know me. He made a point of talking to all new staff, finding out about their background, experience and capabilities, and in exchange giving them a history of the family and countless bits of advice which, if taken in the right spirit, made life there so much easier. When eventually I became her ladyship's maid it was he who made it possible for me to continue in the job, for at first she so overwhelmed and knocked the stuffing out of me that I'd almost determined to give in my notice.

Because of his own stature he was able to recruit and keep a staff who were not only highly efficient at their work, but also fitted together as a team, which made them as much a family below stairs as the one above.

Perhaps some of the credit for 'Father's' character should be given to Lord Waldorf. They were men of similar kind and it was considered by many of us that he'd taken his lordship as his pattern of behaviour and had moulded himself into his image.

Despite his position Mr Lee was a shy man, particularly in his attitude towards women; at times he was almost the country boy. I remember once when he was recalling the temporary loss of Lady Astor's pearls and how Miss Samson, a predecessor of mine, was searched by a police sergeant, he said, in a horrified whisper, 'Do you know, Miss Harrison, he even put his hand inside her breeches.' He couldn't bring himself to say the word knickers. Yet women found him most attractive and he was never short of admirers.

Like so many good men his life may seem to some dull in comparison to other naughtier men. Not to me. It reflects so much that is good in the British character and which is able to shine out at a time when supposedly the working class had little chance to develop their qualities. Some may even say that given today's opportunities he might have done so much better; that he might even have become a member of parliament. I suggest they don't say it in Mr Lee's hearing.

# III

# THE PAGE BOY'S STORY

### *Edwin Lee*

I must beg your indulgence if occasionally events and dates get slightly muddled. It's the fault of being born in 1886, making me ninety years old, and although some things are as crystal clear to me now as if they'd happened yesterday others, strangely the more recent ones, I find difficult to recall as fully as I would like. Still I think that I can say that the more important events and the memory of the eminent people I've had the privilege of serving have stayed with me; probably because during, and indeed after, my life in service I have told and retold the stories of my experiences to those who wanted to listen, and sometimes to those of my colleagues whom I felt needed to hear them.

I was born at the Lane Farm, Dudlestone, the last of five children, and my parents, particularly my father, were getting on in age when I arrived. Dudlestone was then, and maybe still is, a little village near the town of Ellesmere, in the county of Shropshire on the Welsh border. My father owned and farmed one hundred and fifty acres, which today would make him a man of some substance. It didn't then. Farming was a hard, unpredictable business, there were none of the aids that there are today and two or three bad seasons could mean ruination. It took a very good milking cow indeed to fetch ten pounds, and I remember a cousin of my mother's telling us how he took some young pigs to Oswestry market and having no offer for them had brought them back home again. He was mulling over his ill luck in the village pub when a collier came in and said, 'I see you've got some pigs outside, Mr Philips. I could do with some, how much do you want for a couple?' After some hard bargaining two pigs changed hands for a glass of whisky.

My mother was a farmer's daughter, one of fifteen children. Like all girls, except those born into the gentry or the professional classes, she went into service when she was very young. There was no compulsory schooling, and very few schools in country areas. In those days no farmer would consider marrying a girl who hadn't been in service, since it was there that they learned to bake, clean, launder, mend, cook and make butter – all the things necessary in the taking care of a man and his farm. Looks in a woman were less important than good hips that made for easy child-bearing. Strong healthy children were necessary as a source of cheap labour, and to look after their parents and keep them in their old age. Many men were not prepared to chance taking a barren wife, and in any country parish register births will be seen to follow marriage too quickly for the kind of morality that was impressed on girls thirty years later. There's a tale that shows the truth in what I've said. In a village shop two women were gossiping. 'I hear Hilda Brown is getting married.'

'Is she? I didn't know she was pregnant.'

'She isn't, bloody snob.'

I don't think I need press the point that life was hard in those days for both men and women. There was always work to be done, even on Sundays, though we were expected to go to church and it took a brave independent man to break this rule, since many employers would sack anyone who wasn't a regular attender. I myself looked forward to Sundays; it was the day the whole village was gathered together and it gave me a feeling of belonging to a community. It probably seems strange today to say that we got such a deal of pleasure just out of singing hymns.

There were no such things as youth clubs – Sunday school was the nearest we got to that – and no organised games. I remember my father coming back home in a rage from Ellesmere because he'd seen men playing football. 'It's a disgrace to allow it, twenty-two men kicking a bit of leather about instead of working, it's a waste of God's good time.'

I must have been only about four years old when Dad had his accident. It was at threshing time; he was making a wheat stack when a sheaf of corn slipped taking him with it so that he fell and crushed both his heels. He could only walk on crutches after that, and since we were a young family it was only a matter of time before the farm must go bust. I think it was the anxiety of knowing this that killed him. After he died Mum tried to keep things going with the help of her brother, but the inevitable happened and we were eventually sold up – lock, stock and barrel. We then rented a small-holding which gave us sufficient food for our needs and what we sold provided the necessary extras. I continued to go to school at Dudlestone, under a Mr Taylor, a good teacher from whom I learned what were considered the educational necessities, Reading, Writing and Arithmetic. These provided me with a good grounding for the life I was to lead and I was able to pick up a deal more on my way through.

I stayed at school until I was thirteen, left on the Friday, was confirmed on the Sunday and on the Monday thought I was a man, for I'd got a job to go to. It was as page boy and pony boy to a doctor at St Anne's-on-Sea in Lancashire. My wages were twelve pounds a year. Mum bought me a small tin box, in which she packed my underwear and a few odds and ends, and gave me my railway ticket with instructions to change trains at Whitchurch, Crewe and Preston. To me that journey was as exciting and terrifying as flying round the world would be to a boy today. I'd only been a six-mile trip by rail before, and I'd never seen the sea. The last leg of the journey was one of complete misery, for I'd lost my tin trunk at Crewe. To my relief and amazement it was in the guard's van when I reached St Anne's and I've admired railway staff ever since for the way they answered my prayers that day.

My first impressions of my job were exciting. I was fitted for a page boy's uniform in which I answered the door and announced the patients or visitors. When the doctor went on his rounds, with me driving a pony and trap, I wore a livery jacket and silk hat, looking for all the world like a little coachman; I thought I was no end of a dog. Of course custom stales and life became very much a routine; I was at the beck and call of the other servants; a cook, parlour maid and nursemaid. Naturally the jobs I had to do were the unpleasant ones that they didn't fancy.

After I'd been there almost a year I began to consider my future. Where was this leading me? The answer was nowhere. As luck would have it I didn't have to make any plans for my future. One day as I was standing holding my pony while the doctor was visiting a patient a baker's cart drew up beside me, the driver dismounted and coming towards me said, 'What's a smart lad like you doing dressed up like a doll? Why aren't you doing a real job of work?' His attitude nettled me a bit but I thought there might be something behind it. 'Any suggestions?' I queried.

'Now it's funny you should ask that,' he said, 'because I have. I'm looking for a lad to deliver bread and groceries, come round and see me in the morning if you're interested – the name's on the van.'

It seemed to be the opportunity I was looking for, so I took him at his word, called the following morning and the next month saw me working for him. By gum I did work; I started at seven-thirty in the morning and it was often midnight before I got to bed – six days a week. Shops in those days were open right through and so were the services they offered. Many a night at around eleven a customer would call and want things delivered straight away – they were too lazy or too proud to carry them themselves. But it was interesting work. The things I particularly remember about it were the glorious smells of the goods I handled; freshly baked bread and rolls, roasted coffee beans, tea in those mysterious boxes that had travelled all the way from India, the scent of fresh farm butter and the various sugars, not refined and sterilised as they are today, and all the sweeter for it. Then there were the spices and dried fruits. Yes, we breathed God's good air on the streets in those days, and I reckon a blind man could tell where he was by the smell that came from the shops.

There was, of course, bound to be a snag about the job – my master drank – and by the time I joined him it had got a strangle-hold on him. This meant that more and more work fell on my shoulders and they weren't yet strong enough to carry it. Things went from bad to worse, people began to take advantage of his condition, the business lost money and he ended up in Carey Street broke to the wide and owing me a month's wages.

I now had to think fast. I could see I wasn't going to get anywhere as a delivery boy – what I needed was a trade – so I went calling on those tradesmen I'd made friends with on my rounds. I particularly fancied being a wheelwright, and was offered an apprenticeship, but the man wanted thirty pounds down in cash for teaching me his skills. Eventually I was taken on by a French polisher, at a wage of eleven shillings a week. This meant I was only left with twelve pence after I'd paid for my board and lodging. I managed to scrape along for about six months but by then my shoes were worn out and my clothes threadbare. There was nothing for it but to go back home.

There seemed to be two choices open to me, farm labouring or mining. In those days and in our own way we considered 'breeding', we thought we were bred for a job. It was felt that if your father and his father before him had done the same work then in some way the qualities required for it were passed on to you. Today we expect it of animals but reject it for men and women. At the time being considered the man for the job was as much a reflection on your ancestry as it was on you. A miner's son was likely to make a better miner and the same applied to a farmer's son. It was in this way that the choice was made for me. I started to work for one of my mother's brothers at five shillings a week and my food. I was now sixteen, very strong and good with horses. After a twelvemonth I thought my labour was worth a bit more; my uncle didn't. He felt that since I'd had to return from St Anne's with my tail between my legs he could dictate to me. I didn't like it. An elder brother of mine who'd found himself in the same predicament had left the land, gone into service and was now second footman to the Earl of Powis on a nearby estate. He'd recently had a few days' holiday at home and from talking to him I could see that there were opportunities for advancement that I would never have as a labourer. I made the decision which was to dictate the course of my life in the middle of a field as dusk was falling. It had been a hard day's ploughing on a banky field with the ground heavy, and me working with two young horses. My uncle came along and examined the day's labour.

'You've made a bloody fine mess of that,' he scoffed. That did me.

'If you think you can do better, get on with it,' I handed him the reins. 'You can keep your five pence a day, I'm going to look for a bit more.' He didn't like this.

'Whoa, steady boy,' he said, as though he was talking to a horse. I interrupted him.

'No, I'll have no more of it. I'm off.' I'd got a few details from my brother on how to apply for a job in service, and I wrote straight away to Massey's Agency, a London firm with a branch in Derby. I was sent the address of the Honourable Henry Mostyn, who had a house near Llandudno, the Welsh seaside town, and was engaged as a young footman at a wage of eighteen pounds a year. I had to write my own character reference and it took me some time to persuade my uncle to sign it. I stayed with Mr Mostyn for eighteen months, keeping my mouth shut and my eyes open; I was determined to learn as much as I could and when the butler and other members of the staff found I was a willing horse they put plenty of their work upon me.

The next stile I had to cross was to get me into livery service. I also wanted to see London. I wrote to Massey's again. I achieved the first object, but London had to wait for me, for I was offered and accepted the job of second footman to the Honourable Frederick George Wynn, Lord Newborough's heir at Glynliven Park, Caernarvonshire. I was still to be in Wales. It was here that I had my first experience of a country house run in the grand manner.

Mr Wynn was a bachelor of some sixty years, living alone, entertaining rarely yet keeping a full establishment of staff. There was a butler, under butler, three footmen, steward's room boy and an odd man; a housekeeper, six housemaids, two stillroom maids and six laundry maids; a cook and five kitchen maids. In the stables were a first and second coachman, four or five strappers or grooms to tend the horses and drive the broughams, landaus, bogies (small open carriages), box carts and governess carts. There was also a chauffeur, a rare bird at that time, to look after and drive a white steam car which the master used to drive round the estate, frightening the animals and locals alike. He also kept a home farm and a stud farm, some sixteen gardeners, two wheelwrights and three outside carpenters. All these people to look after one gentleman. Today it seems absurd, but we accepted it as the done thing at the time. To us it seemed that he was only keeping the same establishments as his father and grandfather had, it was his birthright, and provided employment for the village people.

The house was a grand one, not as large as Cliveden, about sixteen best bedrooms; there was a large entrance hall, a saloon drawing-room, two small drawing-rooms, music-room, a morning-room, dining-room, breakfast-room and a study. The grounds were surrounded by a twelve-foot-high brick wall, nine miles of it, broken by five drives each with its own lodge.

Mr Wynn was also master of two other country houses which were only in occasional use, Belham Fort on the Menai Straits, and Bodium Hall near Nevin. The Hall was a biggish place of about ten bedrooms, with a resident cook housekeeper, housemaid and parlour maid. He only visited it twice a year, during the shooting season, then of course it would be augmented as was Belham Fort by some of the staff from Glynliven.

He went to the Fort for fishing and yachting. I was lucky that the old man took a shine at me and employed me as his valet when we visited these places. I'd learnt to shoot as a youngster, had enjoyed it and when he learnt this Mr Wynn used me as his loader. He often allowed me to take a gun out on my own.

It may seem strange when I say that with so large a staff to look after one man we were all kept extremely busy. I suppose it was because the routine was much the same whether there was one person in residence or twenty. We were able to take time and pains over our work and it was while I was at Glynliven that I learned how silver should be cleaned and kept. Life over my two years' stay was peaceful and uneventful, things moved so much slower in those days, unchanging and unchallenged.

Mr Wynn was easy to serve but he had his peculiarities. One that I found irritating and disturbing was that he always spoke to the servants with his back to them. It was almost as if we were some strange creatures that he couldn't bear to look at. It was probably because he felt no kind of affinity with the likes of us and this made him nervous and shy. He would bark when things went wrong but a barking back is not frightening, it needs an angry face to go with it. He could also be kind in an odd sort of way. The one dread in any servant's life was breaking things of value; a careless move when cleaning could destroy something that was the equivalent of a lifetime's wages, and employers were not slow in telling you this if it happened. So my heart was in my boots when one day I had to tell him that a candelabra had slipped from my grasp while I was cleaning it and had smashed on the floor. His back listened impassively to my confession, then his shoulders shrugged and with a 'Worse things happen at sea, my boy', he strode out of the room.

Strangely the food for the staff at Glynliven was not good,

consisting for the most part of a plain unappetising succession of stew-like meals. When I was first there we were only served with one pudding a week, rice on Sundays, tacky stuff. Whether our old gentleman suddenly thought that we'd moved into more enlightened times I don't know but after I'd been there a year we were allowed stewed fruit every Wednesday.

Another change that he made which was welcomed by the maids, though how he a bachelor thought of it is a mystery, was that instead of wearing black bonnets for church on a Sunday they were allowed little toques. Church-going was, of course, a ritual. We assembled in the servants' hall and at a given moment, on a signal from the butler, we all trooped down. A matter of seconds after we were seated, in came the master through a special door which only he was allowed to use.

In the servants' hall we ate at a long slate-topped table. The food was served on enamel plates which I found would skid and bounce on the slate; this was a matter of acute embarrassment for me, for as I slid and rattled my way through a meal the maids would giggle and snigger and since at that time I'd blush when I so much as spoke to a girl, my red face protruding from a hot collar couldn't have been a very pretty sight.

I was also a fanciful youth, easy prey for any ghost story, so when we visited Belham Fort and I was told that in the next room to mine a baby had been suffocated in its cot, and that its cries and shrieks could be heard around midnight, the story stayed with me. One stormy night, with the wind whistling in the fir trees and the gulls screaming in their flight against it, I couldn't sleep for thinking about this unfortunate child. I got up and looked out of the window; then I heard a screaming and a crying. I must have got some courage from somewhere because I dashed out of my room and into the one that was supposed to be haunted. There under the window I could see a wooden cot on rockers swaying from side to side – and then I heard a noise coming down the passage.

I went to the door, there was a flickering light approaching. I didn't wait to see any more but dashed back to my room, into bed pulling the bedclothes over my head, and I lay there shivering with fear until I eventually fell asleep.

The next morning at breakfast the housekeeper said to me, 'Was that you rushing about on the landing last night, Edwin?' I was a bit cagey with her.

'Yes, I thought I heard something moving about.'

'It was me,' she said, 'there was a shutter banging so I got up and fixed it.'

She looked at me a bit searchingly as if she knew I'd been frightened out of my wits. Today people don't seem to have these kind of ghostly experiences. I don't think it's because sophistication has made them less fanciful. It was the time of the flickering lamp or candle which could play tricks on even the most unimaginative pair of eyes.

People often ask me, 'What on earth could you do in your spare time?' And I sometimes find it hard to explain. Ours were simple pleasures and we got them from the land around us. On our frequent walks we'd maybe come across a badger's set, and at night we'd go out and watch over it. It was the same with foxes and their cubs. The wild flowers were a calendar for us, and though there were so many around, we knew them all by name. We watched the birds mating, nesting and hatching, and could tell where the trout would be feeding in the streams. The woods, parklands and fields were our pleasure grounds and the thrill of being the first to hear the cuckoo was something that's impossible to explain. So was the joy of seeing the first lamb.

It was at Glynliven that I first played cricket; you might say that I learnt it there, for Mr Wynn was keen on the game and we fielded a side from the men employed on the estate. He took it so seriously that he engaged a professional to coach us, who stayed at the house during the season. With this kind of encouragement it wasn't surprising that we were unbeaten by any of the local teams.

Mr Wynn was also fond of music; he had two organs, one in the saloon and another in the Tenant's Hall. The Tenant's Hall was a large barn-like place where twice a year the farmers and villagers would assemble to pay their rents and get some of it back in the shape of a good supper, with plenty to drink. Mr Wynn couldn't play the instrument himself but would regularly engage a local organist, Mr Williams, to play for him. After dinner the music would come floating down to the servants' hall, and when our duties were done we'd line up outside the green baize door the better to hear. The one in the house was an electric water organ, a predecessor to the giant Wurlitzers that were popular in cinemas between the wars.

After I'd been at Glynliven for two years, much as I enjoyed the country life I felt I needed a change. I still hadn't seen London and the myth that the streets were paved with gold still held good for a country boy, and I told the butler I was considering giving in my notice.

'I don't know what the old man will say,' was his only comment. Giving notice was taken almost as a personal insult by all employers, no matter what excuse you might have, and seeing your time out meant an interminable month of snubs. 'It isn't convenient,' was often the reply, and if you were foolish enough to ask, 'When will be convenient?' you were told not to be impertinent. I decided to write the old gentleman a note. I got a curt one back, which to this day I have been unable to understand, it said,

'Edwin, I think you are very foolhardy to wish to leave me,

as the increase in your stoutness will go very much against your getting a good job.'

I was then as thin as a lath! Deciding there was no arguing with Mr Wynn I waited till the month was up, collected my wages and slipped quietly out of the house.

Since I'd made up my mind to get a place in London I decided not to write to Massey's. It seemed they either just sent you to the first job they had at hand or found it easier to fill the town rather than the country places, so I wrote to my brother who was still with the Earl of Powis in Berkeley Square.

He met me at Paddington station and took me to some lodgings behind Victoria Street. They were over a working class restaurant, run by a friendly fellow called Anton. I was completely bowled over by London. 'This is no place for you,' I said to myself, and if it hadn't been for Anton and my brother I think I would have settled for country service for the rest of my life.

I eventually found my way to Massey's who sent me to a Mr and Mrs Taylor, at a house in Eaton Square. I was interviewed by the lady of the house; a formidable body who shot questions at me like bullets from a gun. I must have suited her because I was engaged there and then, and moved in the following morning. I learned that Mr Taylor was a wealthy mine owner, that their main residence was Chipchase Castle, and that they were definitely not gentry. This astonished me, since the house at Eaton Square showed all the signs of good breeding and good taste. Apparently, though, it belonged to Lord Farquhar, who rented it to them for two or three months a year. I discovered that this was a habit with the nobility who, while they wouldn't mix socially with people in trade, didn't mind taking a few sovereigns off them whenever they got a bit short. They later did the same with Americans, but this didn't become common practice until after the first war. I was also warned that Mrs Taylor was both a bit of a tartar and an eccentric. She was what I call 'a stick waver', she carried one both indoors and out, using it to make all her gestures, sweeping it around, pointing it at your stomach or stamping on the floor with it in anger. She had two daughters, and a son in the army in India.

At the time I joined there was no butler – he was still at Chipchase looking after Mr Taylor – and since the other footman had been engaged at the same time as me I was a bit apprehensive as to how we were going to cope. I'd hardly got my trunk into my room when the mistress sent for me.

'We have a dinner party tonight, Edwin, for fourteen, do you think you can manage it?'

It was a bit late for me to say, 'No madam, we can't!' 'We can only do our best,' I replied.

William, the other footman and I put our heads together. We engaged a couple of waiters and with the kitchen playing their part, by seven o'clock it looked as if all was going to go easily. Then Mrs Taylor came into the dining-room, accompanied by Miss Marjorie, the elder of her daughters. She took a look at the table, swept her stick over it and said,

'This won't do, this won't do at all.'

'No madam, it won't,' I thought as I prepared to stand my ground.

'To begin with these napkins are all uniform, they should be folded one high, one low, it looks like a third-rate restaurant.'

She drew breath to continue, but I got in first.

'Madam, I beg to correct you, if you insist on having one high and one low napkin it will look like a third-rate restaurant. I have it on the highest authority that the "mitre" folding that we have given you is always used at Buckingham Palace.

I would have thought that what was good enough for Their Majesties would be good enough for you.'

This threw her back on her heels, but as she started to come forward again I thought, 'This is it, my boy, you've overstepped the mark this time.' It was then that Miss Marjorie came to my rescue, perhaps it was the moment she had been waiting for.

'He's right, Mother, I noticed they were folded this way at Lady Caldwell's last week.'

Seeing herself outgunned, my mistress retreated, and she did it like a good one.

'It seems that you are right and I am wrong, thank you Edwin.'

The dinner party went smoothly, one of the guests remarked on the silver which William and I had given a good shine and I watched this remark register with Mrs Taylor. The following morning William and I were called into her sitting-room. She addressed herself to me, or so I assumed as her stick was pointing two inches from my belly.

'You did very well last night, young man, I was most pleased with you, see that you keep it up.'

Then the stick dropped, she fumbled in her purse and handed us each a gold sovereign. We got on well after that until the butler joined us; he was frightened to death of Mrs Taylor, and behaved like a cringing little monkey, so of course the more he bowed and scraped the more she took it out on him.

Just as I was beginning to get accustomed to London life it was time for us to return to the country. Chipchase Castle, I found, wasn't a bad sort of a place, presentable enough but needing a lot of money spent on it to make it tip top. It was still lit with oil lamps but there were too few of these to illuminate it properly, and the heating and sanitary arrangements left a lot to be desired. It was also overrun with rats; they were everywhere, in the corridors, under the floorboards and of course around the drains. Coming as I did from a farm, rats were no strangers to me, but to have a pair of pink eyes staring at you wherever you walked was an unpleasant sensation, even to me. I spoke to the mistress about them. 'I know Edwin,' she replied, 'I deplore the situation but Mr Taylor won't allow poison to be put down as you suggest.'

'Well,' I thought, 'I've got to do something about the beggars.' So in the afternoons I'd sit in the pantry with my .22 rifle at the ready, and wait for them as they crawled along the pipe towards the pig bucket, picking them off as their heads went down into it.

One day just after I'd got a big fellow in my sights I heard, 'Edwin, what do you think you're doing?'

I turned round and there was my mistress's stick pointing at me.

'Shooting rats, madam,' was my obvious answer.

'Have you killed any?'

'Yes, three.'

'Let me see them.' I lifted them up by their tails. 'That's very good, Edwin; so you're not prepared to take the master's "No" for an answer, you've taken the law into your own hands.'

'Something like that, madam,' I replied.

'I'm very glad that you're doing it,' she said. 'Now you and I must strike a bargain, I'll give you sixpence for every one you shoot.'

'You've no need to do that, madam, after all I'm doing it in your time.'

She wouldn't see it that way and insisted on paying. I used to take her the rat tails each week as proof of my prowess, and she'd hand me over the money; I made quite a little business out of it. I spoke to one or two of the boys around and offered them threepence a tail, thus making a tidy percentage.

I don't know whether she thought I was earning too much or whether the master got tired of her waving these tails at him, but eventually a professional rat catcher was employed. He was the biggest little man I ever saw, five feet tall with shoulders about the same width across, and tough with it. He wasn't allowed to use poison either but for a time he was trapping up to forty a day.

It was Mrs Taylor who introduced me to horse racing. One morning as I was tidying the sitting-room she said,

'Edwin, it's your day off tomorrow isn't it?' I was surprised she even knew.

'Yes, madam,' I said.

'What are you going to do with it?' I wondered what was coming next, so I said non-committally that I didn't know.

'How would you like to go to Hexham races?'

'Well, madam,' I replied, 'I've never been to a race meeting before, I wouldn't know what to do when I got there.'

'Then it's high time you found out. Take a friend, take anyone you like and I'll give you a sovereign each towards your expenses.'

'Towards our expenses!' I thought, it was too good an offer to miss. I took one of the gardeners with me, 'But don't breathe a word to a soul,' I said. It was one of those days, we had four winners out of five races, a first class outing, a good dinner with plenty to drink and we arrived home four sovereigns to the good. The mistress asked me how I'd enjoyed myself the next day and when I told her she looked as happy as if she'd backed the winners herself. It was the kind of thing that never happened in aristocratic service but I found it a generous and warming action.

The rich are very curious about money; some are free with it to a point of stupidity, some just naturally open-handed, some generous in one way and mean in another and some so mean that they're responsible for the old cliché, 'That's how they made it and that's how they keep it'. My Mrs Taylor was plain careless at times with hers. One day she and the master announced their intention of taking a holiday together. Like any other employer they said that this didn't mean that we were at liberty to idle, that the house was to be cleaned from top to bottom while they were away. Shortly after they'd set out, the head housemaid came running to me and asked me to go with her to the mistress's boudoir. She opened the drawer to the dressing-table; it was full of sovereigns and half sovereigns.

'What are we going to do about that?' she said. 'She's gone away and left the drawer unlocked.'

The key was still in the keyhole, so I closed the drawer and locked it.

'We must find a place to hide this,' I said, holding up the key, 'somewhere that only you and I know of. Then if anything goes wrong in Mrs Taylor's absence you and I will be the ones responsible. Don't mention a word to the other servants.'

It wasn't that I mistrusted them but some employers, and all police, in my experience, immediately suspected the staff if anything was missing, and never was it deserved. When they returned I went straight to the old lady and told her what we'd done. She asked me to fetch the housemaid and together we went to her boudoir, took the key from its hiding place and handed it to her. She opened the drawer, glanced in, took a handful of coins and said,

'Thank you both, not a word to the master, now go away and divide those between you,' and she thrust the coins into my hand.

It may seem strange and perhaps a little ungrateful of me that with such a considerate and generous employer I could contemplate leaving, but I hadn't yet been in a position that was attractive enough for me to think of spending more than a couple of years in it. The only way to seek promotion and experience was to keep changing jobs, so after eighteen months with the Taylors I moved to Lord Cowley at Coldoverton Hall, Rutland.

This might easily have been a mistake for 'Toby' Cowley was at that time notorious. He'd recently been sued in a divorce case by Sir Charles Hartopp, for committing adultery with his lady. Now while adultery wasn't exactly rare in society – indeed there were some hostesses at some weekend parties who arranged the position of their guests' bedrooms with as much care as they did their places at the dinner table – such affairs were conducted with great discretion. People weren't expected to cause or make a fuss or scandal. If their philanderings were found out they had to take the consequences, which could mean their exclusion from society. I suppose it was hypocritical but it seemed to work very well and suited both society and the monarchy.

Lord Cowley apparently wasn't content just to philander with Lady Hartopp, he wanted the whole cake, and Sir Charles was determined that he should pay for it. It cost him eighty thousand pounds, close on a million at today's prices. They were the highest damages ever awarded in a divorce case; not a particularly enviable record to hold.

Lord Toby and Lady Hartopp were married when I joined them, but the affair was still fresh in everyone's memory. Whenever I mentioned that I was footman to Lord Toby I got some very queer and searching looks – I think they tarred me with the same brush as my master. 'What are they like?' was the question that often followed as though anticipating the lascivious and lurid details of wild behaviour, and their disappointment when I said that they were more respectable than many I'd served was written all over their faces.

It was a comfortable job for me there as first footman, and I stayed an uneventful year, but I was still not suited. I'm not sure what I was looking for. It was like true love; I thought I would know it when I found it.

I moved to the Dowager Duchess of Roxburghe, again as first footman. I thought that with her I could have the best of both worlds, town and country, for she had a small house in South Street off Park Lane, and the Dower House at Roxburghe Park, Dunbar. It was often hard on the widows when an entailed estate passed to the next of kin, and more particularly so if it wasn't to their own flesh and blood. My duchess had on one day been mistress and hostess of Floors Castle with its sixty-thousand-acre estate and the next she had passed into comparative social oblivion, with a much reduced purse to draw on. I suppose she was the most aristocratic of my employers, and I often thought she modelled herself on Queen Victoria, she was so ladylike, sedate, autocratic. I was sorry when the time came for me to leave; it was not by choice. The old lady's funds had begun to run out and she could no longer keep a full staff. My disappointment was heightened because, while we were living in Scotland, I had begun to learn to play golf and I was beginning to get quite good at it when I was given my notice.

I made my way round to Massey's Agency once again wondering what my fate would be. I'd fancied a big place for some time but none had come my way. I wasn't in a position to pick and choose as work wasn't easy to come by, so it was risky not to accept the first thing that was offered. I'd been lucky, I hadn't been turned down for any job I'd applied for. I don't count the time when I was interviewed as a matching footman for Lord Derby. It was no fault of mine that I only stood six foot, and it was necessary for them to have someone an inch and a half taller.

When I arrived at Massey's I told the clerk there that I wanted a larger house.

'Well,' he said doubtfully, 'they're interviewing for a first footman of three at the Astors' tomorrow, but there's seven others going from here, so I don't fancy your chances.'

'Never mind,' I said, 'I'll have a shot.'

I was seen by Mr Parr, the Astors' steward, at St James's Square.

'How tall are you?' was his first question.

'Six foot, but I didn't know that this was a "matching" job.'

'No more it is, but her ladyship doesn't like pygmies,' he replied brusquely.

I couldn't help wondering what height you had to be not to qualify as a pygmy. He then waded into me with his questions. After about ten minutes he stopped.

'Well, I think you'll just about do,' he said as he stood up.

'What does that mean, sir?' I asked.

'What do you think it means – you're engaged.'

'What about the others waiting outside?' I said.

'Don't bother yourself about the others, you just start thinking about work. Here, take this down to our tailors, Lillico, in Maddox Street, and get yourself measured for suits and livery. Then back here as quick as you can, you're able to start straight away I take it?' That then is how in 1912, at the age of twenty-six, I started to work for the Astors, with whom I stayed for fifty-one years.

It was a fascinating new world that I found myself in, a mixture of high society, politics and country and family life. I didn't have much time to think for the first month or two. Except for the train journeys between St James's Square and

Cliveden I hadn't an hour off. Mrs Astor was lying up expecting her fourth child; I include here Mr Bobbie Shaw, her ladyship's son by her first marriage. The wet nurse was already in residence, a Mrs Stephal. This was my first contact with a nursery and I was surprised what a very well spoken, pleasant lady she was, for I'd always imagined wet nurses to be big, rough and peasant-like women. A son, David, was born a few days after I joined the staff.

I was looking forward with mixed feelings to meeting my new mistress. The servants' hall had been at some pains to paint her as something of a tartar.

'She's the one you'll have to worry about, not Mr Astor,' I was told when I said how impressed I was with him and his way of behaviour. Mr David wasn't three days old when I met her, and a strange introduction it was. Mr Parr called me into his room and said,

'Mrs Astor is having a dinner party tonight for six. You and I will be serving.'

'Her ladyship,' I spluttered, 'but ...'

'But she's still in bed. Precisely, and it's in her bedroom we shall be serving the meal. She can't be still for more than two days at a time.'

When I saw her that evening I thought her perhaps the loveliest creature I had ever seen. There was a bloom about her, she had beautiful hair and skin, and lovely doe-like eyes, which I later found could change to a tiger's in a second. Her brother-in-law Dana Gibson had created his famous 'Gibson Girls' from his wife, Mrs Astor's sister Irene, but she could equally have well been his model. She must have seen me studying her.

'You're new,' she said, and then gunned me down with questions. 'What's your name? Where are you from? How old are you? How long have you been here? How do you like it? Have they made you comfortable?' Ending up with, 'Have you got a mother and father?'

I blushed to the roots and began stammering answers.

'Never mind, you can tell me later. I hope you stay. Look after him Parr, he seems a nice boy.'

Then she turned her attention to her guests and ignored me for the rest of the evening. It was as if I had ceased to exist.

When she was up and about however she cross-examined me again in the same quick-silver manner. I'd always thought that Southern Americans were slower than the Yankees; I found I was wrong, very wrong indeed. Whenever she gave me messages she fired them at me in the same way, expecting me to understand and remember them immediately, for she hated repeating herself. She suffered even intelligent people badly and if you forgot anything it was no good trying to cover up, because she couldn't suffer liars at all. I found it was her general behaviour that was so difficult to reason with at the beginning. I'd been in service some years, I knew what was expected of me and what I could expect of my employers. There was an unwritten code of behaviour to which people conform. In servants' hall language, 'I knew my place, and they knew theirs.' It seemed Mrs Astor had no place, and this being the case my life was going to be unpredictable, testing and at times downright exhausting. Miss Harrison has said that shortly after she joined the staff (it was many years after I had), when I described Lady Astor I said, 'She is not a lady as you would understand a lady.' I think that sums up my impression when I joined, and it stayed with me almost to the end. She was unpredictable even when she was eighty. I don't mean to be critical, it was perhaps this trait in her character that was the reason why those who'd served with her and tried to understand her over the years were so fond of her, but at times she strained affection to its limits. It isn't any good trying to dismiss her waywardness by saying she was an American. In my experience Americans who made their home here for any length of time become more English than the English. No, she was just a wild one, and she stayed that way. She spoke without thinking, gave hurt to many and because of it gave hurt to herself. But I wish there were a few more like her today – both men and women.

After I'd been with the family a few weeks I decided that for my own peace of mind I'd got to try to come to some sort of terms with Mrs Astor. I had to do this myself, and stand on my own two feet. Mr Parr was a good butler but in no way was he a leader of men. He only thought of himself and he was not above putting the blame on others to cover his own mistakes. Mrs Astor could make mincemeat of him simply because he couldn't, or wouldn't stand up to her. It didn't take me long to discover that he was sailing on the wrong tack. I decided, as I had with Mrs Taylor, to fight my corner; to do my work to the best of my ability, and to let that speak for me but if it was challenged by Mrs Astor or anyone, to defend it. Time showed that I succeeded, but it wasn't ever really easy.

Mr Waldorf Astor was so very different from his wife. An American by birth he was an example of what I have said earlier and had become a minted English gentleman. He was a member of parliament so as a footman I didn't see much of him except at dinner parties. In politics he was a Conservative, but he was very liberal in his attitudes towards the staff. We were paid well, fed well; he'd founded a club which gave us entertainment and exercise in our spare time. He showed us every courtesy and consideration, and set a fine example. The staff held him in high regard.

This was the first time I'd been in a house with a young family, and I liked it. It gave the place a sense of life, purpose and continuity. Master Bobbie (Shaw) was eight or nine years old, Master Billie five, and Miss Phyllis (Wissie) three, the baby David born when I went there, the two other boys Michael and Jacob (Jakie) arriving when I was in the army. It was after the war that I really enjoyed the children even though, or perhaps because, they were away at school for part of the time. Even children knew their 'place' with servants. They were friendly without being familiar and though they would play tricks on us from time to time they seemed instinctively to know how far they could go. As they grew older they slipped easily into a relationship where although class divisions were not easily defined one felt they were nevertheless there. Although the Astors were rich by any standards the children were not spoiled by money; indeed they were sometimes short of cash and from time to time I or the other servants would lend them a few coppers.

As a mother Mrs Astor was splendid with the children while they were growing up. I think they were the envy of all their young friends for having a mother who was so beautiful, who treated them as equals and didn't patronise or talk down to them. There was a magic in her story-telling and in the way she sang her Southern American songs. She was an excellent mimic and the children would love to hear her imitating her friends, particularly those that were pompous. I think the highest tribute I can pay her is to say that the servants would often be found eaves-dropping when the children were in the sitting-room with their mother. Unfortunately as they grew up Mrs Astor's outward affection diminished. She became critical, sarcastic and at times downright hurtful. Nevertheless if they had to face any crisis in their lives she always stood by them and showed great loyalty, and if necessary forgiveness.

If there was one snag in having young children in the house, it was the nanny. Miss Harrison, in her first book, has said that Nanny Gibbons was an exception to this rule. I didn't find her so. Our difference of opinion is understandable; when Miss Harrison joined us the children had all passed the nursery stage so nanny's authority had diminished. She stayed on at Cliveden, as others of her kind did, as a sort of grace and favour lodger. But when I first went there and for many years afterwards, she was a power in the house second only to Mrs Astor.

The rearing of children is given first priority today almost anywhere and it takes a brave man to question this, particularly when the process is going on in his own home. It needs a slightly less brave one to question it in the abstract, and I don't mind being the one to do it. It does seem to me that we cosset children too much when they're very young. They are after all nothing but little animals, and if they are fed properly and exercised properly they should be given the freedom to grow up on their own. They should have affection and discipline but not be allowed to rule the house and everyone in it. I could go on further about this but I think the drift of my argument is clear. Instead of rushing to doctors or studying books we should look back at nature, at the farm if you like, and see how good strong, healthy, intelligent animals are reared. I'm all for the English preparatory and public school system of education, where boys have to stand on their own feet and fight their own battles, but it seems to me a bit stupid that they're not prepared for this kind of world in their homes. They are mollycoddled, fussed over, decisions are made for them up until the day they go away, so that they're unready for the Spartan life that follows. And it's the nannies that are paid to do this. To justify themselves they make demands on everyone else's time and patience, and are always allowed to get away with it. It's no good any servant trying to fight them because they have the ear of the mistress of the house. It's 'Nanny knows best', not just for the children but for the staff as well.

Nanny Gibbons was not quite so bad as the picture I've just painted but she often upset the smooth running of the house and particularly of the kitchen, which was a temperamental enough place at the best of times. Again women are strange cattle, when it comes to their attitudes towards each other. If a man takes against another they try to work things out between them, whereas women employ wiles. I remember a particularly nasty incident that happened in my early days as a butler. We'd had a succession of housekeepers, none of whom seemed to suit, and Lady Astor (as she'd then become) asked my advice.

'Why don't you promote Violet Caveny the head housemaid, my lady,' I suggested. 'She's a good worker and she knows the routine here.'

She acted on my suggestion. This didn't suit Nanny Gibbons and she made it plain. One day when the nursery had been given a particular cleaning nanny called for Violet, the new housekeeper, and complained that a few strands of hair had been left in one of the drawers, and that the job must be done all over again. Violet protested saying that they had been put in there since her inspection. Nanny went running to Lady Astor, who sent for the housekeeper. I saw her before she went in and advised her to stand up for herself. She didn't and came out with her face streaming with tears; she'd been sacked. I tried reasoning with her ladyship.

'She's a liar,' she said. When I pointed out that this was a matter of speculation she replied,

'Even if it is if she can't get on with Nanny Gibbons she must go.'

I gave up. It's impossible to argue against that kind of feminine reasoning. It may seem a piddling little episode but multiplied a few times it makes for bad feelings amongst the staff.

But back to my own career. As I settled in I found I was enjoying life. I'd begun to get part of the measure of Mrs Astor, and I'd taken to Mr Astor from the start. I'd only been there a few months when David, the groom of the chambers, left and I was appointed in his place. This meant some loss of sleep for me because my duties went on later at night as I had to look after the drawing-room after dinner and I was an early riser and couldn't change the habit of a lifetime.

David Hughes was Mr Astor's valet and whether it was drink or women, or both, I don't know, but he took to staying out late at nights and found it difficult to get up early enough to wake Mr Astor, shave him, give him his breakfast, prepare his bath and dress him before eight o'clock every morning. Two or three times I noticed that he wasn't up and went to his room to wake him. I got nothing but curses for my pains, so I decided to leave him and let him sort things out for himself. The results were inevitable. For two or three days he would pull himself together, then slipped back and eventually was sacked. It happened two days before Mr and Mrs Astor were leaving on a tour of France and Germany, so I was sent for and told that I would have to fill the gap temporarily and would travel with them.

'But I've never shaved anyone in my life,' I told Mr Parr as he gave me the instructions.

'You've got forty-eight hours to learn,' was his unhelpful reply. I looked for volunteers. 'You, you and you,' I said to a footman, the odd man and hall boy. I made what my victims called, 'A good stab at it', and by the time we left I was certain that Mr Astor would find me no Sweeney Todd. Just before we returned to England, Mrs Astor spoke to me.

'It seems you have appointed yourself the master's valet, Lee.' She used my surname for the first time, that way showing that she confirmed my position.

'No, madam,' I protested. She was beginning to get used to me by now.

'All right, have it your own way, let us say Mr Astor is well satisfied with the way you look after him and is offering you the job.'

'You'll have to get a new groom of the chambers, madam, I won't be able to do both jobs.'

A Mr Furney was appointed groom of the chambers and it was now that I was able to see the great consideration that the Astors showed to their employees. He hadn't been with us a fortnight when he was taken seriously ill. He was given a special room, the best medical attention and a day and night nurse were engaged to look after him. He recovered but was likely to be unfit for work for a long time, so he left. While he'd been ill I'd taken over his duties. Once again Mrs Astor sent for me and said,

'You seem to have combined both your duties splendidly, Lee, so I suggest you continue in them.'

As I was about to protest, she said,

'Your money will be adjusted accordingly.'

It was adjusted, but not accordingly. Mr Parr was a mean man and I had to do some hard bargaining before I ended up satisfied but not pleased.

Another advantage of being in service with young people is that you're given the opportunity of meeting their parents and through them filling in the picture of the family as a whole. Unfortunately neither of the Astors' mothers was alive. I think that the loss of his wife had particularly affected Mr Waldorf's father in his later years. He'd always been a bit of an eccentric and since the boundary between eccentricity and madness is often hard to distinguish, a good wife can prevent a man from straying over the border. I visited old Mr Waldorf a few times, first at Hever Castle his country house in Kent This in itself was an example of the old man's peculiarity. He'd bought it as a ruin, had it rebuilt paying particular attention to the gate, drawbridge and moat. Outside these he had constructed a mock Tudor village. It was here that his guests were housed. At a certain time in the evening the gate would be shut, the drawbridge pulled up and there he would be like a baron of old, secluded in his castle and protected by a moat. I also went to his town houses, one was at 18 Carlton House Terrace and the other the Astor Estate Office on the Victoria embankment. This latter was another Tudor-style place which he had built for himself at enormous cost. It again showed signs of his oddness, for there were no handles inside the room doors. When a door was shut it locked and it was not possible to get out. Some guests were shown the release mechanism, a sliding panel inside which was a press button; others were let out by a footman. I think he went in fear that someone would do him in for I know that he always slept with two loaded revolvers on his bedside table. Another thing that was a source of amazement to Mrs Astor was that he would never receive his guests personally; one of his secretaries was delegated to do it. 'I don't know why so many influential people continue to visit him,' I once heard her say. I did, they smelt his money and followed their noses.

He was a generous and good-natured old gentleman and I liked him, and his generosity extended beyond his family. He had a butler, a Mr Pooley, who after thirteen years with him took to the drink. Eventually Mr Astor could stand it no longer and decided to sack him.

'Pooley,' he said, 'because of your bad habits when you're

in the drink, I've got to ask you to leave, but because of your good habits when you're out of it and the time you've served me, here's something to take with you.'

And he handed him a bank draft. When he left the room Mr Pooley looked at it and saw it was for a thousand pounds. 'That's something worth getting drunk for,' he said to his friends in the pub that night.

Mr Chiswell Langhorne, Mrs Astor's father, was as different as chalk is from cheese from old Mr Waldorf; tough, open-hearted, a bit flashy and theatrical; like his daughter he often spoke without thinking, and didn't care for the conventions. He was readily accepted by all his daughter's friends for his own sake. He was very affable to the staff and generous with his tips. I only once heard anyone, it was Charles Hopkins the chauffeur, speak roughly of him, and when I heard why I couldn't blame him. Mr Langhorne was a tobacco chewer and spitter, and though at the time spitting was common practice among the lower classes, indeed there were spittoons in most pub bars, it was not considered a gentlemanly thing to do. Of course the old man didn't do it around the house but his habit had been reported to me by one of the gardeners. One day he was deputised by Mrs Astor to go to the station to meet the Archduke Franz Ferdinand, heir to the throne of Austria, who was coming as a guest for the weekend. Charles Hopkins was the chauffeur and he chose to drive a spanking new Lanchester which was his pride and joy. They hadn't got to the end of the drive when Mr Langhorne cleared his throat and spat straight on to one of the windows – he must have thought it was open. It wasn't. Charles stared at it first incredulously, then in rage. Then he stopped staring because he'd driven into the lodge gatepost making a nasty dent in his front wing. He returned in a towering temper. I remember thinking some months later that if his driving had been as wild as his rage he might have prevented the outbreak of the First World War by crashing and maiming his passengers.

Many people have written about Mrs Astor's conversion to Christian Science, and her religion was something that was visited on the servants as well as her friends. It's my view that it was the doctors' fault. At one time she had a succession of illnesses and while doctors, like lawyers and undertakers, seem on the outside to show deep concern, their ultimate real interest is the money. They also work in droves, so a physician calls in a specialist who seeks a second opinion, and so on and so on. I have watched this sort of thing happening all through my life in service. Then the bills come in, and no matter how rich you may be you begin to sit up and take notice. With Mrs Astor they eventually killed the goose that laid the golden egg, metaphorically speaking that is. She saw what they were up to, so she was easy to sway when other influences came along. She vainly tried to convert me to Christian Science. She succeeded in converting one of my footmen. I'm sorry to say it didn't do him much good, I still had to sack him.

I don't think any of us expected or were ready for the First World War, and when it came it took us completely by surprise. Not unnaturally Mr Astor and I discussed the situation. He was unfit for active service and he felt this very deeply.

'You must do what your conscience tells you, Lee, I won't try to influence you one way or the other.'

I enlisted in 1914 shortly after hostilities had begun. My master made it plain that my job would be open for me when I got back, and it was.

Looking back on it I enjoyed my war service. I experienced another kind of life at a time when I needed it. I got to know men from all walks of life and under all kinds of conditions.

It gave me a broader understanding. I was discharged in 1919 with the rank of Company Sergeant Major, but I'd most enjoyed my time as a platoon sergeant. Many's the time I was to regret the sergeant major bit, for whenever I had to stir things up below stairs I know the rank was referred to to my disparagement. During the time I was away I received letters from Mr and Mrs Astor, and food parcels. When the war ended, as I've said, Mr Waldorf was as good as his word and I returned to the position of valet. My wages were raised to £120 a year. It took me a little time to shake down, for there was a new staff with new ways.

At the end of 1919 Mr Astor's father died. Although I knew this was likely to cause a bit of a stir in the family I didn't realise the consequences it was to have for all of us. In 1916, while I was away at the war, old Mr Waldorf had bought himself a title. He was created Baron, and later Viscount. I learnt that at the time this had put the cat amongst the pigeons for it meant that my Mr Waldorf, whose work as a member of parliament was receiving recognition, would in the event of his father's death have to leave the House of Commons and enter the House of Lords, thus putting an end to his parliamentary career. Not unnaturally both my master and mistress were very angry; indeed from that time they became estranged from the old gentleman, but having no reason to think his death would follow as quickly as it did, they were taken quite unawares. It meant there would have to be an election at Plymouth to fill Mr Waldorf's, now Lord Waldorf's, seat.

It's a bit incongruous but typically British, that while a 'Lord' cannot sit in the House of Commons, a 'Lady' can, so suggestions were made to her ladyship that she should stand in my master's place. The to-ings and fro-ings both at 4 St James's Square and Cliveden were the stuff that nightmares are made of, for Lady Astor's moods changed hourly. Indecision didn't suit her. One day she sent for me. 'Oh, Lee,' she said, 'I've talked to so many people about Plymouth, what do you think I should do?'

'I should go for it, my lady,' I replied.

Now I'm not so big-headed as to think that my opinion swayed her in any way but a couple of days later she again sent for me. 'Lee, I've decided to take your advice. I'm going to "go for it" as you said.'

She did, and it's now history that she was the first woman to take her seat in the House of Commons.

During the election I had to go to the Astors' home in Plymouth – 3 Elliot Terrace – and run it for them. It was an exciting time, both day and night. People were in and out of the house and the phone never seemed to stop ringing. But it was all worth while and a triumph because her ladyship was elected. The day after the results she came to me and handed me a decent cheque. 'What are you going to do with it, Lee?' she asked.

'Get myself a gold watch, my lady; I've always fancied one.'

'Give me that back,' she demanded, and she tore the cheque up in front of me. 'Oh Lord,' I thought, 'Have I said the wrong thing?'

'I shall buy you a gold watch, Lee.' She did and it was a beauty, she had it inscribed and I have it to this day.

Being in parliament changed her of course. She seemed to get a renewed vigour, and heaven knows she'd been vigorous enough before. Now more than ever she became the centre of the house. Luncheons and dinner parties were almost daily events, and the staff had little warning or time to plan them. It got too much for Mr Parr the butler. He and her ladyship were constantly rowing and at the beginning of 1920 he was given the sack. She sent for me. She didn't actually offer me the job so much as tell me I was going to do it. This didn't suit me.

'No, my lady,' I said, 'I don't think I'm up to it.'

'I shouldn't ask you if I didn't know that you were, Lee.'

This I thought was getting better, but I still hummed and hawed.

'Come on, Lee, give it a go.' Her eyes twinkled and her voice softened. This was more to my liking.

'Well, my lady, I will give it a go,' I said, 'but I'm still not sure that I'm up to it.'

'I'll help you, Lee,' she replied, and skipped out of the room.

I felt very satisfied. I'd got the interview round to the way I wanted it, I'd given myself a let-out if things went wrong, and I felt very proud that I'd got the job.

It was now up to me to make it work. There's a school of thought that says a new boss should take things easily. I couldn't subscribe to it. I'd noticed since I'd returned from the war that things had got slack. 'Don't you know there's a war on,' had been an excuse for too long for not doing a job properly. Our dream in the trenches of 'A land fit for heroes' had not materialised and wasn't going to. This meant that we had to get back to the old order of things and down to some damned hard work. I therefore began by making several changes in the staff, training new men by working with them and showing them how I wanted things done. What scared me was the dinner parties and receptions which were given on such a big scale, forty for dinner and up to as many as two thousand at a reception. To give myself peace of mind I'd have rehearsals. In this way I found everyone knew what they had to do, and that I could delegate responsibilities. One major difficulty was that so much rested on precise timing, and her ladyship had no idea of time. I'd tell her lady's maid, who from 1929 onward was Miss Harrison, to make sure she was down in time to receive her guests, then I'd worry his lordship to get her and her guests into the dining-room. Sometimes he'd throw his arms up in despair. 'What can I do, Lee, it's impossible to move her.' Between us we did make some improvement but I seemed to get it both ways, the chef would scream that his dinner was ruining, and Lady Astor would say that she couldn't hurry her guests.

I learnt by experience, by successes and mistakes. One night I stopped the traffic in St James's Square and nearby Regent Street. It was before a dinner party and reception for Lord and Lady Balfour. I'd been round to the local police station and asked for three men to control the movement of horses and motor transport to the house. Unfortunately they sent three constables who wouldn't take orders from each other. Coachmen and chauffeurs were screaming, sounding their horns and cracking their whips; the guests couldn't get near us. It took me half an hour to sort out the chaos. It took me longer than that the following day to persuade the chef not to give in his notice.

I think you get the best out of a staff by example. I don't mean this pompously or conceitedly, but if you show them that you are prepared to do any job yourself they will try to do it that bit better. I particularly wanted to try my hand, or rather my voice, at announcing – that is heralding each guest for their reception by the host and hostess. I always engaged a Mr Batley; an excellent man. One evening my opportunity came; he'd had a slight cold and his voice gave way. King George V and Queen Mary had dined and there was a large reception afterwards, with full dress and decorations worn by all the guests. Among these were several senior Labour members of parliament, some of whom had principles about 'not dressing up' as they called it, in court or evening dress. Mr Will Thorne was among these. Now it's one thing having principles and another living up to them, as Mr Thorne was to find out. He came on foot to St James's Square and seeing the dazzling array of guests in full dress with their ladies in mink and tiaras, on his own admission he took fright. He decided to linger around until most of the guests had arrived. He didn't do it for long because he was apprehended by a police officer, who wanted to charge him with loitering with intent. He was able to talk his way out of this but it hadn't done his self-confidence any good, so he decided to enter. Gordon Grimmett was the footman on duty and was standing near the announcer whose role I had assumed. He had to inform me of the identity of each guest. I'd just announced a distinguished member of the peerage with a string of decorations and appointments, when up piped Gordon with, 'Mr William Thorne,' then dropping to a stage whisper he continued, 'turned-down collar, coloured shirt and tie, blue suit, cut-away short jacket.' Now I prided myself on my ability to keep my composure under the most trying circumstances, but that did me. I managed to get Mr Thorne's name out and to signal to the announcer to continue his duties before I fled downstairs howling with laughter. When I thought I'd recovered I sent for Gordon to reprimand him, but the sight of him brought it all back and both of us ended up helpless. Unfortunately the press got hold of part of the story so that it got back in a garbled way to Mr Thorne. Apparently he took it in good part and I understand that later he often told it against himself.

I've said that when I was appointed butler, Lady Astor told me she would help me. She was nearly as good as her word for two years when – as if by common consent – I was on my own. Indeed she almost seemed to take against me. She was constantly criticising and interfering. All right, by now I knew her sufficiently well not to let it upset me, it was water off a duck's back, but when it began to affect the work of my staff I knew I wouldn't be able to contain myself much longer. One evening she called me into the drawing-room and in front of the family started on at me. I found it too much. 'I'm sorry, my lady, I seem no longer to be able to please you so I must give you my notice.'

'Your notice, Lee?' Eyes began to twinkle.

'Yes, my lady, I'm off.' I turned to go and she ran towards me.

'In that case, Lee, you must tell me where you're going because I'm coming with you.'

What can you do when someone says a thing like that! We ended up laughing and she was easier in her behaviour towards me for quite a while.

Another time she drove me to distraction was just before a large dinner party; I think some of the royals were to be present. She came back late from the House of Commons, went to the dining-room, took one look at the table decoration, kicked off her shoes, climbed on to one of the tables, knocking my glass and silver all over the place and began tearing the centrepiece of flowers to bits, spilling water on the table as she did so. I stood aghast. 'This won't do, my lady,' I said, 'it won't do at all. You're ruining my work and the decorator's. If this is the way you want your dinner parties run you must look after them yourself, I want no more of it.' And I left the room. She came running out after me.

'Stop, Lee, stop.'

I turned and looked at her, she was pathetic in her stockinged feet.

'Don't worry, I'm going to change now.'

Then she dashed back into the dining-room, straightened the table out a bit, picked up her shoes and raced upstairs with them in her hand.

She also began to interfere in the appointment of my staff. It had always been her custom to see the people that I interviewed and decided to take on, but it was only her place to put, as it were, her seal of approval on my decision. By the thirties experienced footmen were hard to come by, and I'd chosen a man who I thought would make a good one. She saw him and began by saying that her footmen would always turn a hand to anything. 'Are you prepared to clean windows, bring in coals, do anything that needs doing,' she demanded.

'No, madam, I'm afraid not,' he replied. 'I am only prepared to do those duties that are normally expected of a footman, no more.'

'Well in that case you're no use to me,' she said, and she walked out.

'She doesn't want a footman, she wants an odd man,' he threw at me as he went. She told me what had happened and I gave her a piece of my mind.

'Call him back, Lee,' she cried.

'No, my lady, that I cannot do. You have created a situation from which there is no retreat.'

She couldn't learn. Another time I sent in a footman who'd been recommended to me. Apparently she'd spent ten minutes questioning him on his religion. As he came out he shook his head at me.

'She doesn't want a footman, she wants a ruddy parson.'

There was an occasion when she insisted that I did something that went completely against my principles. She made me steal a friend's housekeeper. We'd had some trouble finding the right person and she came to me one day and said,

'So and so has a woman called Mrs Moore, who I understand is excellent. Get in touch with her, offer her more money and I think she'll come.'

'But, my lady, it's like stealing,' I explained to her, 'it just isn't done.'

'You do it, Lee,' she said. Then, just like a woman, she put her conscience right by saying, 'I'm sure she needs a change.'

There are two snags about such practice apart from the offence it gives to your friend; one is that it creates in a servant a sense of power, and the other that, having done it, if she proves unsatisfactory it is hard and unfair to dismiss her. In the event neither of these things happened. Mrs Moore came to us, was superb at her job, ran the house to perfection and left to become housekeeper at Buckingham Palace, and one of the great figures in domestic service.

Mrs Moore and I once had occasion to join in battle against Lady Astor. Her ladyship had visited somewhere where real candles were used in a crystal candelabra in the hall, so she decided that we had to do the same at St James's Square. Mrs Moore and I both protested, but were over-ruled. Our worst fears were realised; the draught from the front door made the candles burn unevenly and the next morning the carpets were studded with pools of hardened wax.

'What on earth shall we do?' Lady Astor cried when we asked her to come and look at the damage.

Mrs Moore answered, 'What we shall do, my lady, is to clean the carpets as best we can. It will mean days of work and they will probably never be the same as they were.'

Her ladyship crept meekly away.

So my life with Lord and Lady Astor continued over the years. It had a sameness but it was never for a moment boring. In a way it was lonely. It may seem strange for me to say that when I was surrounded by so many people, but I was like a captain of a ship, there was no one to whom I could go with my problems. My private life had to be very private. I received little praise if things went well. I remember once saying this to her ladyship.

'What do you expect me to do, Lee, keep patting you on the back?'

Given an answer like that I never laid myself open again.

I suppose there came a time when I knew that I could never leave for another job, a time when I had become part of the place, though I find it hard to say when it was. Probably it was just before the Second World War. The war years, of course, made it impossible for me to leave.

It was the war that upset the pattern of domestic service as I had learnt and practised it. It was never to be the same again. After it was over I tried hard to return to the old order of things and I got together some semblance of a staff, but the old spirit was not there. In 1945 Lady Astor was persuaded by the family to give up her parliamentary duties. It was against her wishes, or afterwards she pretended it was, and she became even more unpredictable. Fortunately she spent much of her time travelling the world. His lordship had become a sick man as a result of his work during the war. He and I, who'd always had a mutual esteem, became closer and probably shared many more confidences than is usual between master and servant. His death in 1952 robbed me of a great friend.

I suppose I should have retired then, indeed I thought seriously about it, but Lord Billie, who succeeded to the title and the estate, persuaded me that I was needed. I'd always liked him so it wasn't difficult for me to stay. He was easy to work for, he didn't expect things to be as they were before the war, he understood the changes that had taken place. I only meant to be with him a year or so but every time I suggested leaving there seemed to be some particular reason why I shouldn't. I was lucky in a way. Lord Billie's butler/valet, George Washington, had joined the staff when his lordship took over, so I had a young but experienced man to help me.

I stayed with Lord Billie for eight years. Eventually in 1963 I insisted on leaving. It was the year before the Profumo scandal.

I don't propose to make any detailed comment on the affair, except to say that my master was tried, judged and found guilty by the public on no evidence at all. I had found him a fair, honourable and understanding man to work for. He did many fine things for people less fortunate than himself. For those who seemed to revel in his downfall I will suggest that they used him as a sacrifice for their own misdemeanours, whether these were in thought, word or deed.

I'd bought a house in the seaside town of Eastbourne, having married in September 1953. I apologise to my wife Emily for not having mentioned this before, but I've spoken about my public rather than my private life. Emily was a lady I'd had my eye on every day for many years, when she was the Astors' telephonist. I left marriage late. I can't deny that I was fond of the ladies, but fondness was all I felt I could allow myself. I couldn't see how a wife could, or indeed would, allow herself to fit in with my work.

When I left the Astor household I suppose like any other man when he retired I looked back carefully on my life. I felt I'd done my duty as best as I could and that through doing it I'd had a fuller life than almost any man of whatever class or position could hope for. If I may use Mr Rudyard Kipling's words,

'I had walked with kings, and not lost the common touch.'

## Some Reflections on Mr Lee's Story

Although at the beginning of his story Mr Lee protested that his age stood in the way of his power of recall, I don't think it shows. Partly this is because, since his retirement, he, I and others of his many friends have gone over the past whenever we have met, so that we know our lives together almost by heart. I understand that Lady Astor's name is not allowed to be mentioned at his bowling club!

I still marvel at our relationship. I've known him now over fifty years, we are very close, and yet he continues to call me Miss Harrison. I have never called him Edwin, but at least 'Father' sounds cosy. Indeed it could be said of him that his Christian name was the most unimportant thing about him; I can hardly ever remember it being used; he was known to everyone who visited us as Lee, or Mr Lee, even royalty never had to be reminded of it. To the staff he was Sir or, behind his back, Skip or Skipper.

The nickname skipper was apt; he was in every way captain of his ship. This in a way made him a lonely man, for although we could always go to him with our problems, whether they were personal or to do with our work, he had no one in whom he could confide. It was fortunate therefore that he had the kind of strength necessary to any man that commands.

In one way I was able to help him every day. When I came down after giving Lady Astor her breakfast, he would treat me as a kind of barometer.

'What's the forecast today, Miss Harrison?'

I'd then give him a report on her ladyship's 'temperature'.

I seldom heard him use bad language, and if I did it was heard only when he was reprimanding one of his men or railing about her ladyship's behaviour. We would encourage him in the pug's parlour to tell naughty stories, but he would never be able to finish one; he'd get to the bit with the sting in its tail, start blushing and flustering and we would all roar with laughter and miss the point of the story.

He was good with money. In his later years he gambled a bit on the Stock Exchange and usually seemed to come out the winner. I remember admiring his house in Eastbourne when he first went to live there. 'It's a present from Japan, Miss Harrison. Before the war I bought some Japanese shares which although they became worthless during the war, later rose to glorious heights. I sold them and converted them into bricks and mortar.'

He was helpful to others over their money. We had an odd man, 'Sailor' he was called, I don't think I ever knew his real name. He worshipped Mr Lee as a spaniel does his master. Father noticed when Sailor began drinking heavily, and also discovered that when he'd had a pint too many he'd buy drinks for all the scroungers around him. Together they made a deal so that every month Mr Lee would deduct half his wages and invest the money for him. When Sailor died he was worth a sizeable sum for an odd man, a hundred pounds of which he left to Mr Lee.

Although he never boasted about it, I know he had many offers of employment from other houses, offering far more money than he was getting from Lady Astor. Many came from America; he showed me one letter where the figure offered him was astronomical by any standards. He stayed put because he didn't like change, but also out of loyalty both to her ladyship and the staff.

And her ladyship strained his loyalty. Many employers did, to test what they thought was our devotion to them, for they wanted to be loved. I remember Lady Astor coming back one day from a visit to Hatfield House, Lord Salisbury's place. I was at the front door when she came in.

'Hello, Lee,' she said, 'I've had a lovely weekend. My word, that butler of theirs certainly knows the way to do things.'

'Yes, my lady,' Mr Lee replied, 'I also understand he has an excellent handicap at golf.'

Another brush that he told me about happened on the

Coronation day of King George VI and Queen Elizabeth. Lady Astor had instructed him that all the servants who could be spared were to be allowed to watch the procession. He gave the men servants time off and remained on duty himself. When the proceedings were over the front door bell went and continued ringing until he opened the door. There was her ladyship with her thumb on the bell push.

'Why did it take such a long time for anyone to answer the door in this house?' she demanded.

'My lady,' he replied, 'I must jog your memory. You instructed me that all the servants that could be spared were to be allowed out to watch the ceremonies. I took you at your word and gave them leave of absence. Unlike you, they had no precedence in returning home. I can assure you they will be on duty as soon as they come in.'

Smiling she dropped him a little curtsey. 'Really, Lee, you talk to me more like a husband than a butler.' Then she ran upstairs, shouting for me, while Mr Lee called after her that I too was out.

'Thank heavens there isn't a coronation every day,' she screamed back.

Another earlier tiff that he had with her was on behalf of the servants. One of the housemaids asked if she could be allowed to have her hair bobbed; it was the fashion of the time.

'When I'm next with her ladyship, and if I remember I will inquire,' promised Mr Lee. He did remember.

'Why should she want her hair bobbed,' her ladyship demanded.

'I understand it's the fashion, my lady.'

'Tell her she must keep it as it is, I don't want fashionable maids.'

'Very well,' said Mr Lee, 'but I think I should inform you that if you adopt this intransigent attitude you will shortly be lucky to get housemaids with any hair at all.' Lady Astor dissolved into laughter, and told him that the maids could do anything they wanted with their hair.

As I think I've hinted, Father was not short of money, and recently I asked him why he had never bought a car.

'If I'd wanted a car, Miss Harrison, I could have had one for the acceptance. In between the wars her ladyship was changing Daimlers, and she offered me a present of the old one.'

'And you didn't accept, why?'

'To begin with it was too grand a car for me; if I'd gone out shopping with it the prices I'd have been charged would have soared. Also I could see that I would be acting as an early morning or late night chauffeur for her ladyship, fetching and carrying guests home, or to the station. This would not have been my place, but I would have been under an obligation. In any case you know how I feel about chauffeurs.'

Nevertheless Mr Lee was gratified and flattered at Lady Astor's offer, which as he said was made in a generous and kind spirit. He then qualified it by saying, 'It's the business of looking a bit further than the end of your nose though, Miss Harrison.'

He was full of sage saws of that kind and indeed still is, for when I was last with him drawing out his stories, discussing our employers and in particular Lady Astor, he said, 'You know when all is said and done domestic service comes to this. We needed them and they needed us.'

It was a failing of Lady Astor's that she seemed unable to pay any compliments for a job well done. It must therefore have been very gratifying to Mr Lee when he read the following report in the political columns of *The Times* newspaper:

A socialist member of the House of Commons, a Mr Sorenson, was complaining of the way the evacuation of civilians from London had been handled at the beginning of the Second World War. 'One woman in my constituency who was sent to a big country house, returned home because she didn't like the way the butler looked at her. I see the Honourable Lady (Lady Astor) laughs. Perhaps she is afraid of her butler.'

'Afraid of him, never, he is a treasure,' was her ladyship's retort.

# IV

# A FRIEND IN SERVICE

## *Charles Dean*

If Mr Lee can be described as the king of butlers, Charles Dean is among the princes. He doesn't deny 'Father' his place, he bows to his ascendancy and says that he learnt almost everything he knows from him. He goes further; he feels that it is from him that he got the confidence and will to succeed. 'I was really little more than a country boy when I went to the Astors, yet when I left I was able to take my place among the big 'uns and it was all because of him.' I tried to point out that Mr Lee himself had been just a country boy when he started his life in service, but Charles shook his head, he'd have none of it, he couldn't see him as ever having been a beginner or a learner; he was like a son unable to believe that his father had ever been badly behaved at school or suffered the torments of a first love.

I first met Charles at Cliveden when I was visiting with Lady Cranborne. I didn't get to know him well immediately, our friendship has been one that has developed over the years through casual meetings, sometimes in England, sometimes in Paris, Biarritz or Switzerland; never, strangely, in the States though we were quite often there at the same time, as we found out when we shared our experiences.

My first impression of him was that he could never take anything or anybody seriously, he turned every occasion into a joke. He was always flirting with the girls, he tried it on with me but soon found out that there was one North Country maid that hadn't come up to London to stray. I shortly discovered that there was another side to him.

As under butler he was in charge of the silver and took me down to show me the silver safe; for the uninformed a silver safe is generally a fair-sized room with a heavy four-inch-thick iron door which opens on to another steel grille door through which you can see the plate, the bowls, the cups and trophies, the candelabra and other ornaments. If you are fortunate enough this steel door will be unlocked and you will be taken into the room itself and shown the contents of the cupboards and the drawers, some full of silver cutlery in a variety of styles, others containing priceless family treasures. It is a sight such as described in *The Arabian Nights*. I've seen many such safes in my time but never one as beautifully kept as was Charles's. His silver had that wonderful deep black shine that can be reached only by hours of work and continuous cleaning. Subsequent under butlers must have come to hate the name of Dean for Mr Lee would make constant comparisons of their efforts to his achievements.

Although I didn't see him in action waiting at table in the early days he was, I understand, to the manner born – discretion, confidence and speed. He moved quickly but unnoticeably. I think this was in part due to his ability as a dancer, for Charles was one of the lightest-footed partners I've ever had. As a butler, and providing he hadn't got a grin across his face, he was a most imposing figure. He was six foot tall in his stockinged feet and he stood every inch of his height. His jet black hair was the joke of the servants' hall, it shone like his boots and it was rumoured that he did indeed use boot polish instead of hair cream. He was bilingual in his use of English, the Gloucestershire accent he used below stairs quickly changed to lahdidah in the front hall. Like so many comedians he could keep a poker-face distant expression when with guests, yet the way he moved to satisfy their unspoken wishes showed that he was always conscious of everything that was going on around him. He had presence and dignity, yet could soften in an instant to put someone at their ease.

During the last few years leading to Lady Astor's death when we were together at Eaton Square no one could have been kinder or more solicitous to her ladyship, or such a friend to me and the rest of the staff. When it became difficult to get her ladyship to her room at night, Charles and Otto Dangl, the chef, would wait up and the three of us would share a nightcap until, certain she was asleep, we made for bed ourselves. But I'm in danger of telling his story for him, so let me end here as I began and introduce you to a prince of butlers.

# THE BOOT BOY'S STORY

## Charles Dean

I was born in Bisley in Gloucestershire in 1895, the fourth of eight children. Our cottage was called 'The Nest' and our street, 'The Backside', and if you don't think that's funny there was a fellow alongside me in the trenches during the First World War by the name of Caine, a school teacher's son who lived at the foot of a hill called Lashams. His house was called 'Lashams Bottom'. If you can believe that then you'll believe everything else that I'm going to say.

My father worked at the village store as butcher/baker for under a pound a week. He'd been there thirty years when I was born, which shows that wage increases are something new to the working classes. Even in those days Dad was being hard put to it to raise a family on that kind of money so, like most other men, he was prepared to turn his hand to anything that brought in a few coppers; this meant a full day's work for him since baking began at five in the morning.

Although the main purpose of the oven he used was to bake bread, buns and cakes it also served the women of the village as their means of cooking. Many cottages were without stoves and in others they were too small to take the joints, pies and cakes of the housewives. Sundays would see a procession of women walking through the village streets carrying the dinners for Dad to cook, at the cost of a penny or two. The bakehouse was a source of gossip and remarks like 'I see the Smiths are having beef today, I'd like to know where they got the money from to afford that', or 'Mrs Jones was baking a game pie, it's evident that Bill Jones has been out poaching again', were bandied around.

My school days were uneventful. I must have learnt some-thing because I could read and write, and later on in life I handled some fairly large sums of money which I had to account for. I was a member of the church choir, which didn't mean so much that I was particularly musical since every boy in the village was automatically recruited from the age of five or six; those who couldn't read or sing in tune were told to mouth the words, and it was a funny sight at the end of a hymn or song, to see them carrying on with their miming when the music was finished; they looked like fledglings in a nest waiting to be fed.

I left school when I was about ten or eleven, which I know was before I should have, but nobody seemed to notice or if they had it didn't worry them; people knew when to mind their own business in those days. I started work at the bakehouse with Dad, where my job was to deliver bread and groceries around the farms and outlying districts using a horse and cart, but as there were many places that could only be reached on foot it was tiring work for me. I continued doing this until 1910. By that year I knew every inch of the countryside around, and the business and behaviour of the men, women, animals and birds that lived in it; I could drive a horse and van and ride bareback, I could at a pinch do the baking or kill and salt a pig, and that was about the sum total of my knowledge and experience of the world. To my employers I was still worth only five shillings a week.

My mother's sister was married to a coachman in Bristol. Coachmen were considered special because they were so smartly dressed and turned out. My uncle and I had always hit it off and one day he said to me, 'How would you like to work in Bristol?' It had always been a dream of mine; I'd visited there once or twice, been round the docks, marvelled at the bigness and busy-ness of the ships and the port which seemed to me to be the gateway to the world. I told him this. He looked a bit sceptical. 'Well,' he said, 'I don't know whether being boot boy at Clifton College is going to match those dreams of yours, but the job's open if you want it.'

I took it, for at least it was a glimpse into another world, albeit a very smelly one first thing in the morning. Apparently it wasn't considered the sort of thing that I needed anyone to instruct me in. I was shown the boot room, the cleaning things and fifty pairs of boots, and told to get on with it. The trouble was that the boots were all of a regulation pattern and as many were the same size the boys later had some difficulty finding which pair was which. They began bickering, then fighting and my handiwork took a bit of a caning as the boots were used as weapons or missiles. Nobody attacked me, which was surprising since I was the cause of it all. I think once a fight got going they forgot what it was about.

Within a day or so I'd got the hang of things. Although the boys were little toffs they became quite friendly towards me, by which I mean they called me by the same foul names that they called each other, and generally abused me. My first duty of the day at half past six made me probably the most unpopular man in Bristol. I had to wake the boys by ringing a hand bell and as I went down the dormitory pulling back the curtains they used the most filthy expletives. I thought I'd heard all of those kind of expressions in the farmyards, but these were enough to have turned the cow's milk sour. At meal times I took the food from the kitchen to the dining-room, and throughout the day I was given the jobs that the other servants didn't fancy doing. I stayed at the school for two years; I suppose it was unenterprising of me as I was getting nowhere, but life in Bristol suited me and I enjoyed my new-found freedom.

In 1913 feeling like a change of scene, I went as a general servant to a tailor in Weston-super-Mare. He was what the trade and the middle classes called a houseman, keeping a cook and a housemaid, and I enjoyed a pleasant, easy life.

Then came the war.

About a week after it was declared I was walking down the promenade eyeing the young ladies when I saw a colour sergeant on a soap box shouting his head off about 'Your country needs you'. On either side of him were two of the most attractive bits of stuff I'd ever seen. Like a fool I stopped to gaze at them. Suddenly I realised that the sergeant had turned his attention on me. 'You seem a fit and strong young fellow,' he said, 'and from the way you're looking you seem to like the fairer sex. I'll make a bargain with you on behalf of these two young ladies. You take the king's shilling in exchange for a kiss from each of them. What do you say to that?'

What could I say; if I'd left then he and the crowd round him would have jeered at me, and so before I realised what I'd done I'd signed on the dotted line, had my palm crossed with silver and was walking away blushing from two smacking kisses.

A week later saw me training with the North Somerset Yeomanry, a Cavalry Regiment, on Bath racecourse, and cursing myself for having been such a mug. Actually I was luckier than most of the recruits because I could ride fairly well and knew how to groom a horse, so I escaped much of the scorn of the N.C.O.s who were training us. I remember when my squad was given the order to charge it was like the Light Brigade at Corunna; men were falling off their horses to the right of me and to the left of me, the difference being that there were no guns volleying and thundering in front of us. As one of the casualties limped back the sergeant major called out, 'Hey you! What did you do in civvy street?'

'Tram driver, sergeant major.'

'Next time you come on parade put a bloody wheel round your horse's neck, perhaps that'll help you control it!'

I was in France by February 1915, stationed at a remount depot at Rouen, where some rogue of a Canadian horse dealer had sent a batch of wild horses which we had to train. Eventually we succeeded, and by contrast actual battle was considerably less terrifying than we might otherwise have found it.

We went up the Somme, and I remember going through Ypres on the night of 12th April 1915 with the town ablaze from end to end. We went into action on the 13th May and within six hours half the regiment was lost.

When eventually we moved back to re-form, my troop was commanded by an Irish officer by the name of Annan. He sent for me and said, 'I understand, Dean, you've been in service. I'd like you to be my batman.' I knew this would mean I would eat and sleep better, so I jumped at it.

We were billeted with the village curé and, with my officer being a Catholic, this meant an easy relationship. I made myself generally useful, learnt a bit of French and with the curé's influence we were soon eating like fighting cocks. Unfortunately, as it turned out, Mr Annan invited the squadron commander and some fellow officers to dinner one evening. We did them well but envious eyes were cast and the major decided he wanted to take over the billet, and me with it. He reckoned without my gentleman, and I learned that army rank doesn't pull the weight against social standing. Mr Annan arranged for us both to be transferred to the First Royal Dragoon Guards. The major didn't get the billet either because the curé refused to take him or any other officers. With our new regiment Mr Annan was appointed billeting officer. This meant of course that he didn't do himself too badly, so apart from occasional trench duty I had it cushy.

After the armistice we moved into Germany, staying in a farm cottage where I slept in a bed for the first time in five years. Mr Annan was anxious to get back to civvy street and, knowing that I felt the same as he did, he arranged our demob together in February 1919. So in terms of my future the war hadn't been a waste of time; I'd mixed with and looked after gentry, learnt some continental cooking and a smattering of French and German.

When I returned home to Bisley it didn't take me long to decide to return to service. I took a job as footman to Judge and Mrs Woodcock of Lypiatt Park, an estate near to my home. It was a small house with only two in each department, distinguished in the neighbourhood because it was there that the Gunpowder Plot was hatched. I think it was the one bit of history that everyone around knew; indeed, whenever I mentioned where I worked people would say, 'That's where the Guy Fawkes business started.' They'd say it confidentially as if they'd been in on it themselves.

While I was with the Woodcocks I learnt something about myself that I wasn't able to fathom. When I first went there the butler was a man called Mr Boyd. He was a perfect butler, but also a perfect bugger. He worked me to the bone and never seemed satisfied. Even the housekeeper was astonished at the way I was treated.

'I don't know how you stand it, Charles,' she'd say, but I did and learnt a lot from him. When he left because of illness I breathed several sighs of relief, and looked forward to a happier future. The man who took his place was the exact opposite, slack, lazy, one of the don't botherers; I could have had it easy but I disliked him and his attitude more than I did Mr Boyd's. I didn't seem to know who or what I wanted. Eventually a few years later I found it in a butler called Edwin Lee, but I'm getting ahead of myself.

Finding that I couldn't come to terms with my position in the house I thought I'd make a change. I saw an advertisement for a second footman at Badminton House, the Duke of Beaufort's place, then and now the greatest sporting country house in Britain. I was interviewed by the butler, Mr Bevan, at Swindon. If he'd seen me at Badminton and I'd had a chance of observing what things were like I would probably not have taken the position, for the house was in some disarray. It had been allowed to run down as a result of the war and it was to be my job to help to get it back to its former glory, and that meant a lot of hard work; employers had a habit of expecting things to return to what they considered as normal very quickly, and couldn't seem to understand that in service as in anything else it wasn't easy to get a good team working together. Attitudes too had changed; there was a smell of socialism in the air, and it took some time for most of us to realise that the upper classes were determined that things should be as they had been, and to understand that with high unemployment we would be forced to dance to their tune.

The house lent itself to the hunting and sporting scene. It had been the Palladian mansion home of the Dukes of Beaufort since the seventeenth century, though there had been some alterations and additions made in 1740 by William Kent, who also laid out the grounds, which were later extended by the famous landscape artist Capability Brown. It was renowned for its international horse trials, though these had been suspended since the beginning of the war. The hunt kennels were still operating, and there were two packs of hounds, a bitch pack and a dog pack, and I believe occasionally they ran a mixed one. There were stables for about sixty horses and a stud farm. The place lived and breathed horses, so that as well as the indoor staff of six in each department three were the head huntsman, the first and second whipper in, six to eight huntsmen who combined this with their stable duties, grooms and strappers. The village of Badminton at that time housed the people who worked on the estate and all the farms around belonging to the old Duke.

During the season there was hunting five days a week, and coursing and shooting on the other days. The house was constantly full of guests and the size of the staff was sufficient to cope with them. The Duke and Duchess were, of course, the heads of the house, there was a son, the Marquess of Worcester, and two daughters, Lady Blanche and Lady Diana Somerset; it was the usual mix-up of names of people belonging to the same family. In a way I was a kind of lady's maid to Lady Diana for I had to clean and look after her hunting kit, and she spent a lot of time in it. I didn't of course dress her but often had to help her out of her boots when she came back spattered in mud.

It's a very unrewarding task caring for hunting clothes; everything has to be immaculate to put on and when they set out they sit there looking proud and haughty, like a fashion plate on their horses, and you're expected to beam in pride at them, though you know bloody well they're going to come back later in the day dirty and dishevelled and you've got several hours of work before you putting their clothes and boots to rights again. I used to feel particularly sorry for the first footman who looked after the Duchess; she was getting on in years and would only go out for about an hour. It hardly seemed worth the effort for so short a time. She was a game one though. Many's the time I've opened the door when she came back dripping from the rain and looking as though she'd fallen into a pond. 'I want a cup of tea immediately, Charles. I'm not wet, I'm not wet at all.'

Then she'd wander away murmuring and leaving a trail of rain behind her.

'She's piddled her way to the sitting-room,' I'd say to the stillroom maid when I went to deliver her orders.

His Grace the Duke was a great character, both mentally and physically; he weighed twenty-four stone (nearly 350 lb). His hunting days as an equestrian were of course over, but he followed the hunt in an old open Ford, a tin lizzy as we used to call them. It had had its seats removed, so that when the foot-men carried him in his Windsor chair we could hoist it into the back and lash it in. Off he would go, shouting and swearing at the chauffeur and giving the hunting cries, for all the world as if he was still part of it. Unsuspecting guests, who were not riding, would be invited to follow him in their Rolls and Daimler cars.

Now the old Ford had a high clearance and the chauffeur was experienced at driving over rough country, so he and the Duke would dash up the rough farm tracks, even across ploughed fields, leading the followers to their doom and leaving them with their cars bogged down to their axles. The Duke would then circle around them like a black crow, jeering or shouting advice at them. Sometimes he'd get hoist with his own petard, fall off his seat and return home grovelling on the floor and cursing his chauffeur for what was his own stupidity.

He had a most unfortunate complaint; he was incontinent. Of course opportunity would have been a great thing, because once strapped in the car he couldn't get out, and it wasn't pleasant for us men servants, when after a day's hunting he had to be carried upstairs; two poles were inserted in slots in the Windsor chair and he was lifted by four of us. Invariably I got the rear end, and the odour that went with it. I comforted myself with the thought that his valet had it worse than I did, he had to bath him. To do this he had to use a block and tackle to lift his grace in and out of the bath.

Edward, Prince of Wales, was a frequent visitor to Badminton. Although he generally travelled incognito, he was a bit of a nuisance to all of us. He wasn't a good rider, more off than on, and since he was heir to the throne everyone was scared for his life, except of course the Prince himself, who was a game young cove. A couple of riders would secretly be briefed to look after him, local doctors were alerted and of course there were the press men to be coped with, who despite the secrecy of the visits seemed able to smell a story and were always ready for the worst. There was a time later when parliament and the newspapers tried to stop him from hunting for nothing worse than a broken collar bone.

The discipline in the servants' hall was tight, very much in the old style. We all had to be in our places round the table at least five minutes before the senior staff came in in procession, and as they approached we stood smartly to attention. After the meat course there were three divisions instead of the normal two; the butler, housekeeper, valet and ladies' maids went to the pug's parlour, and the housemaids to their sitting-room. The meal was served and eaten in absolute silence. Many of the visiting servants remarked on the way we had to behave. 'It wouldn't suit us,' they said.

Butlers' attitudes towards chauffeurs have always been severe; there it was one of almost fanatical hatred. We lived by the horse, and the motor car was seen as a menace to our way of life, so chauffeurs were treated as lepers.

Jimmy Weedon, the under butler at Badminton, was one of the great characters in my life in service. His duties were ill defined, and he seemed to do a bit of everything. Perhaps this was because he had come to the house some forty years before as telegraph boy. It was of course in the days before the telephone, and he'd been sent from London to take and transmit messages in morse code. When the phone was installed Jimmy was out of a job, but as he didn't want to leave he was allowed to stay on as a general dog's body. He was lamp boy, odd man, steward's room boy, footman and butler rolled into one. He had no pride of office, but a deal of pride in his work. When I arrived he was three parts blind but had a fantastic sense of place and touch; to watch him carrying food on a butler's tray fitted to his stomach, from the kitchen to the dining-room, was a sight to wonder at. He'd leave the kitchen, pacing his way to the stairs, up eight, turn right, down four then to the green baize door, push it open, so many steps across the octagonal hall and into the servery, moving at one hell of a pace so that the food arrived hot. One day trying to be helpful I opened the baize door to let him through; he was lost. 'You stupid bugger, what did you do that for? Now I don't know where I am, guide me to the dining-room.'

I did this with him swearing at me all the way. Again it was fascinating to watch him lay the table for dinner. He would edge his way along the side of the table until he got somewhere near the middle, then he'd shake his head and from his reflection in the mirror on the sideboard he could gauge to half an inch where centre was; starting from there he could lay the

silver perfectly. When he was serving he always took the vegetables, since it didn't matter whether the guests had previously
been given meat or not.

He taught me a lot about silver cleaning. For him it was a
ritual. He had two lead sinks; in one he had a mixture of soft
soap and water and whisked it until it had a good froth; this he
made in the morning and it lay there all day being occasionally
replenished. In the other sink he rinsed the silver under the
hot tap, then transferred it to the soapy water, returned it and
rinsed it in cold. Then he would lay it on the draining board on
its side; it could stay there all day and not get smeary. When it
was required he would throw a jug of hot water over it, wipe
it and it was perfect.

Jimmy also did part duty as lamp boy. Although the lamps in
the drawing-room were supposed to be filled while the family
and guests were changing for dinner, Jimmy was allowed to
replenish them whenever he wished; indeed he became almost
a showpiece for the family. He would get up, collect the table
lamps, take them behind a screen and as he poured the oil in he
would tap the sides of the lamps. Often a guest would inquire
about this tapping and the Duchess would say,

'Oh, that's Jimmy, filling my lamps, he's blind you know but
he can tell exactly how much oil is in them from the sound they
make when he taps them.'

One of the difficulties in looking after the hunting set was
that they generally came back all at the same time, wanting
baths immediately, and if I was looking after two or three
gentlemen I had to move fast. They were very free with their
language and when they'd had a bad day they vented their
spleen on me. It was like water off a duck's back; one thing I
learned early in service was never to allow myself to get has-
sled. The bathing arrangements were, even for that time, a little

old-fashioned. The baths were contained in cupboards; when the doors were opened they came down on hinges. They weren't very large and if the gentlemen were careless much of the water would end up on the floor, so I was constantly having to mop up after them. Although they were free with their language they were also free with their cash and I did well with tips; I think they looked on it as conscience money.

We occasionally had time off, particularly in the summer. There were dances every fortnight and as I was nimble with my feet I enjoyed them and the pleasures that went with them; I mean of course the young ladies. I forged an arrangement with a little girl from Badminton village; I'd meet her on certain evenings at the post office, and guide her into the woods where we'd have a kiss and a cuddle. There was also a Scottish house-maid that took my fancy, a nervous lass who didn't like going down into the dark of the cellar to fetch her morning beer.

'It gives me the shudders,' she would say.

I was quick to volunteer to accompany her.

'You can come down with me if you'll be good,' was the answer.

I don't know in what way she meant me to be good but I got a sour look from the butler when she emerged one day screaming 'You'll have to marry me after that, Charles!'

We were very much watched over and well segregated from the women staff there. Only one old crone, a daily, was allowed in our rooms to clean and make our beds. One day she offended my manly pride. I hard her approaching my room and called out, 'Just a minute, Ma, I'm changing.'

She poked her head round the door and said, 'Don't take any notice of me, Charlie Boy, I've seen miles of them in my day, another inch won't hurt me!'

Although I enjoyed Badminton I couldn't see myself staying

there for the rest of my life and becoming another Jimmy Weedon, yet the idea of London frightened me. I'd been there once on a choir outing from Bisley and the noise and the people seemed to overwhelm me. I do recall however driving up Oxford Street in a horse tram and seeing Selfridges when it was only a tiny store. I was persuaded to try my luck there by a butler friend Tom Carey, whom I met at a dance near Badminton. He worked for a Mrs Strutt, a society figure of the time whose three daughters all married well – becoming the Countess Munster, Lady Stavordale and Mrs Phipps Formby. She was also, I discovered later, a close friend of Lady Astor's. I gave in my notice, which was graciously received. I don't think they wanted to see the back of me but appeared to understand that I wanted to take a look at London.

I was 'little boy lost' when I arrived at Paddington station. As the other passengers moved away I went up to a porter, put my situation to him and asked him where he thought I could get a bed for the night.

'Why move further?' he said. 'There's a Salvation Army hostel next to the station.'

So my first night in London fifty-five years ago cost me one shilling.

The next day I found Campbell and Hernes Agency. They had two jobs for under butlers on their books, one for Lord and Lady Astor, and the other for Lord and Lady Leigh of Fareham. Since St James's Square was near by I decided to have a crack there first.

I went up the steps to the front door and rang the bell. It was answered by a very smart young footman in livery. I asked for Mr Lee, the butler.

'You would be inquiring about the position as under butler I presume,' he said sweetly.

'Yes,' I replied.

'Then I suggest you take yourself round to the tradesmen's entrance down the area steps, and ring the bell there. This door is for the use of Lord and Lady Astor and their guests.'

I lost about a foot in height as I did what he had said. To my surprise the door was opened by the same chap, beaming all over his face.

'I've been waiting for that opportunity for a long time,' he said. 'When I first came here I did the same thing myself, and was given the same kind of welcome.'

He was, I discovered later, Gordon Grimmett, a man who was to become a lifetime friend.

My interview with Mr Lee proceeded happily. I think us both being country men made things easier. Eventually he told me I'd do.

'When can you start?' he asked.

'As soon as you like, sir, but I've got no clothes with me.'

'We can fix you up with those,' he said. 'I'd like you to begin straight away. We've got a dinner party tomorrow night for the royals with a reception afterwards for a thousand. The silver's in rather a bad shape I'm afraid, but I'm sure you'll get enough of it ready in time.'

Within the next fifteen minutes there I was in the pantry, cleaning and polishing away and thinking, 'Why the devil did I ring that ruddy bell.'

I was amazed how smoothly that dinner went. It was the night Gordon made his classic remark about Will Thorne's dress. I remember thinking he might well get the sack for it, particularly when the *Tatler* came out the following week with, 'We wonder if the staff of 4 St James's Square have got over the shock of Mr Will Thorne's idea of clothes that are fitting for a dinner party.'

Mr Lee I found impressive. He seemed to be everywhere at the right time, smoothing things over when they might well have gone wrong. He had eyes like a hawk. A temporary waiter I was working with fancied a peach and after he'd taken the dessert round he palmed one into the pocket of his tails. Mr Lee was on to him like a flash and he was out of the house in a matter of seconds. When the party was over and we'd cleaned up he held a sort of inquest, praising us for our work that evening but pointing out the few things that had gone wrong. He then opened a bottle of champagne, gave us a glass each and sent us off to bed. It was three in the morning when I eventually got my head down.

As I settled in to the job and got to know the other servants I was told the usual stories about Lady Astor, and soon discovered the truth of the saying 'Please Lady Astor, and you please everyone.' As under butler I was lucky in my dealings with her; I didn't have many. I was more of a loner. The care and cleaning of the silver was my main concern, and that meant that I was safely out of the way in my pantry for most of the day. I did only occasional door duty and waited at table for lunch or dinner parties. I found that Mr Lee's estimate on the state of the silver had been an understatement, and since it was one of the finest collections in the country it took me some time to get it into condition. It was now I had cause to bless the days that I'd spent at Badminton working with blind Jimmy Weedon.

It was weeks before I really met her ladyship and by then I'd settled down in the job and was unruffled by her darting tongue. Mr Lee I know was well pleased with my work; indeed when finally I asked him to inspect the silver safe he expressed his pleasure and ended by saying, 'I shall bring her ladyship down to see it.' He was as good as his word.

When she arrived she clapped her hands and jumped up and

down like a little girl. 'It's like Aladdin's cave, isn't it Lee,' she cried.

I thought to myself, 'That's you home and dry, Charlie Boy,' which showed I didn't yet know my Lady Astor. Some weeks later a dance was held for the servants, which of course Lord and Lady Astor attended for the first hour. I was uncertain about the etiquette, so I asked Mr Lee if it was considered right and proper to ask her ladyship to dance.

'She'll expect it, Charles,' he replied, so I waited for my opportunity. I'd taken her twice round the room when she stopped, and held me at arm's length. I thought, 'Now what the hell have I done', then she smiled at me and said, 'If you were half as good at your work as you are at dancing, you'd make an excellent under butler, Charles.' Then she whisked me off again. That was Lady Astor, no matter how well you did your job she wasn't going to let you know she thought so.

As under butler I now had a position in the servants' hall. After the senior staff had retired to the pug's parlour I was in charge. I also had to learn how to carve. It was an art which I enjoyed. The kitchen staff also appreciated my efforts, for Mr Lee was called down by the chef and shown a joint that had been returned from our table.

'That's the way my meat should be treated,' he said.

I stayed with Lady Astor for three years. They were years of experience, and it wasn't long before I discovered that I was working under a great man in Mr Lee. Up till now I'd been content to meander through life, living from day to day and giving no thought for the future. Through him I saw that there was more to life than just living. I got ambitious. I worked harder and watched more closely. The lavish scale of entertainment gave me the opportunity to practise, and Mr Lee was the model on which I could shape myself. I didn't try to look for promotion I just waited for the opportunity to come, and come it did in the form of another Astor lady.

Prince and Princess Obolensky came for a short stay to Cliveden. Now the Princess was Alice Astor, her ladyship's cousin by marriage and daughter of Colonel Astor, who went down on the *Titanic*. Her personal maid, Isabella Boyack (though why she was allowed to keep either of her names and not just be called something simple is beyond me), was chatting to me when she said,

'The Prince needs a butler/valet, do you know of anyone who would suit him?'

'Why not me?' I answered.

She said she would mention my name to her mistress.

'Swear to secrecy, or the sparks will fly,' I told her; no one liked their guests 'stealing' their servants, and for a member of the family to do it would be considered almost incestuous. It was a hurdle I might eventually have to meet, but not one I was anxious to set myself until I could see something on the other side. Negotiations went on secretly and surreptitiously until finally I was offered the job. I went to see Mr Lee for advice.

'Don't be a bloody fool, Charles, the prince is penniless,' was his comment.

Now no one could have possibly had a higher opinion of his judgement than I but in this instance I knew it to be faulty. The prince may have had no money, but Alice Astor had. It was common knowledge that she was one of the richest heiresses around, and that on her coming of age she'd inherited several millions of dollars. Again from my experience of the Astor family it was always the women who were in charge of the staff. In any case I had nothing much to lose if it didn't work out, my experience would soon find me another job. When I told Mr Lee of my decision he still wasn't happy. 'Who's going to tell her ladyship?'

When I said that I would, he became a little easier. He made an appointment for me, and very apprehensively I walked into the lioness's den. She took it calmly at first, then asked,

'How did you hear about the position being vacant?'

I knew I was on dangerous ground now, for she hated liars, so I said that in London there was a kind of servants' underground and that's how we learnt of any vacancies. She accepted it.

'But why do you want to leave me, Charles?'

This was another dicey question and she'd cleverly personalised it. Servants weren't expected to care about money, so I avoided that subject.

'To better myself and because I'm anxious to travel.'

'Oh, if it's travel you want I can see to it. I'll hire all the films you need and you can see the world in the comfort of your pantry.'

There was nothing I could say to that, so I grinned and stood there looking foolish.

'I shall miss you, Charles.'

This was the tack I wanted. 'But I shall still be in the family, my lady.'

She thought about this for a moment. 'Well I suppose I shall have to be satisfied with that. How long have you been with me?'

I told her nearly four years.

'I shall give you a present. It will not be money, I'll give you a pair of gold cuff links and I'll put your initials first, C.D. from N.A.' She handed them to me four weeks later when I went to say goodbye.

I must say I felt a bit of a heel when I left the room and

thought of some of the names I'd called her in the past. I'd always liked her but she had strained my affection to its limits. I knew I should miss her but I needn't have worried, we were to see very much of each other before my life in service was over.

Alice Astor was a very different kettle of fish from her ladyship. She was young, about twenty-two. She and her husband, Prince Obolensky, belonged to what was called 'the faster set', that group of young people who, when the war was over, set about forgetting it in their own particular way; parties, drinking, dancing, nightclubs – it was the era of gaiety and fun and lasted up to 1926, the year of the General Strike. I joined her just before her son Ivan was born, in the spring of 1925.

At first I found her pernickity and fussy about small things. Being a night bird she slept until eleven every morning, which put the work of the whole house back; there had to be no noise, so no cleaning was possible, and we couldn't move around easily till midday, which didn't suit the housekeeper. It took me some time to get accustomed to late nights; I began to have nightmares, reliving my job over and over again until I was on the verge of packing it in. I think she must have found a change in me because one day she said,

'I know I'm difficult, Dean, but please don't take any notice of me.'

After that I didn't; whatever she said I just got on with the job.

She had one quality that made her similar to Lady Astor, only worse. She had absolutely no sense of time. She was even late at parties that the royals were attending. Many's the night the prince would be sent on in advance, Miss Boyack, her lady's maid, would rush down to the car with her evening clothes and make-up and dress her while they drove to her destination.

She wasn't all frivolity, she was interested in the arts;

painting, theatre and ballet, and was quite an authority on antique furniture. Her mother, who'd married again after Vincent Astor's death, was now Lady Ribblesdale, a most doughty lady, an American turned Aristocratic English. She'd disapproved of her daughter's marriage, but had come to terms with it.

Prince Obolensky I liked as a man, and he was a pleasure to serve. I found him a blend of Russian aristocrat and English gentleman. As a result of the revolution he was penniless, but his education and training stood him in good stead, as did his looks and charm. He was suspected and accused of marrying Alice Astor for her money, but he mixed in circles where this was usual practice, so who can blame him if in some respect he allowed his head to rule his heart. He gave Alice Astor excellent value for what he cost her. He showed all the signs of being in love with her. He was for the most part gay and amusing, though he had periods of intense depression, an inheritance I suppose from his Russian ancestry. He was superstitious; he worried that Alice Astor had been one of the first inside Tutankhamen's tomb and seemed to suspect at times that the curse of the pharaohs was upon her.

They lived in Hanover Lodge, a large country house in Regent's Park, where it was my responsibility to provide the background to the fun. It was an ideal place, of medium size and with a delightful garden running down to the canal. It was sold to them by Admiral Beatty. Apparently there had been a bit of a mix-up; the Admiral thought his wife wanted to sell it, and she thought he did and put it on the market. When the transaction had gone through they both discovered they wanted to keep it, and tried to buy it back for a large premium; they failed.

The Regent Canal was a source of annoyance. One day I was called to the princess's bedroom.

'Dean,' she said, 'I can't sleep, someone is firing a gun at the bottom of the garden, I think you should call the police.'

'No, your highness,' I explained, 'it's the bargees cracking their whips at the horses.'

'Oh is that all, then please go down and tell them not to do it.' I quietly left the room, without committing myself.

We had a medium-sized staff; myself and two footmen, a housekeeper and two housemaids, Vassily Yourtchenko the chef (who'd escaped from Russia to follow the prince; one of the great culinary artists of his time), with two kitchen maids, Miss Boyack the princess's maid, Miss Spiller the nanny, Gilbert the chauffeur, and an odd man; there were also three or four in the garden.

Now I've complimented Vassily on his cooking, but he wasn't an easy man to work with, he was moody and had a fiery temper. Chefs are notoriously temperamental but occasionally he could behave like a madman. Over the years I got used to his ways, but others didn't and I lost an odd man because of him. When I found someone suitable to replace him he stipulated that if he came he would have to bring his parrot. This was a situation I'd never come across before, and I wondered whether I ought to interview the bird, but decided against it and just asked a few pertinent questions. I then said I would have to speak to the princess about it. She was quite happy. 'It'll be nice for the children' (by now she'd had a daughter).

Just as I was leaving the room she inquired, 'Does the bird talk, Dean?'

I told her that I understood that it was an excellent talker. 'Hm.'

I knew what she was thinking.

'I've been assured, your highness, that it could be taken anywhere and into any company with complete confidence.'

She was satisfied. John – that was the name of the odd man – kept the bird in its cage in his boot hole, which suited it well as it was heated by the warmth of the kitchen. It became a great favourite with the children and they would take it tit-bits and chatter to it. Some two months after John had joined us I was called for by the princess.

'Dean, I'm worried about the children, I understand from nanny that they've taken to using bad language. Have you any explanation?'

'No, your highness, it is not our habit to swear downstairs, and most certainly no one would do so in front of the children. Is it possible for you to give some indication of the sort of words they have been using?'

'No, Dean, I could not bring myself to repeat them.'

'You bloody hypocrite,' I thought, for I'd heard her use some ripe language in my time.

'But,' she went on, 'I've written one or two down.' She handed me the paper. 'I suggest you read them at your leisure and investigate the matter.'

The list contained one or two of the better-known expressions, then came 'Sod England' and 'Bugger Britain'. This gave me the clue I needed. I lingered between the coal hole and the kitchen for a few days. Eventually my patience was rewarded. I heard a cry of rage in the kitchen and Vassily came out screaming Russian curses and brandishing a carving knife.

'Allo Vass,' said the parrot.

The chef gave vent to his rage on the wretched bird. He thrust the knife through the bars of the cage.

'Bloody bird, I kill you. Sod England! Bugger Britain! Arsoles to Alice!'

This last expression of course hadn't been written down. I wanted to die with laughter but I had to deal with Vassily and get him back into the kitchen. I reported my findings to the princess; I knew what the outcome would be, John and his parrot had to go. Vassily stayed on.

Although Hanover Lodge was our base it couldn't be considered as our real home; indeed during my many years with Alice Astor nowhere really was. We lived like this; after the London Season in the midsummer we left for the States, staying first at Newport and then going to Rhinebeck in the autumn. We returned to London for Christmas and then in January left for St Moritz for the ski-ing, staying at the Palace, then to Paris, the Ritz, and to the South of France, the Carlton at Cannes, for the spring and back again to London as the new season began. Sometimes there would be various excursions around Europe and week-endings in England. I crossed the Atlantic twenty-eight times with the Obolenskys on ships like the *Majestic*, *Olympic*, *Berengaria*, *Mauritania*, *Aquitania* and the *Leviathan*, and I always travelled first class except once.

The family entourage included six servants, Vassily, a footman, Miss Boyack, Miss Irvine the nanny, and a nursery maid; I had to go and book the tickets, and it cost a tidy sum. This once that I referred to was when I told the princess how much the tickets would be; she blanched a bit and complained of the price. This was the opportunity I had been waiting for. Travelling first class and in such close proximity we were always kept busy; it was no holiday for us and it was made worse when we saw other people's servants having a good time in tourist.

'It would save money if Miss Boyack and I travelled tourist,' I said quickly, and this was agreed.

I had the time of my life for the first half of the voyage; the run of the bars and the run of the girls. Then one morning, when I was splicing the mainbrace, someone came in and said, 'Your lady's outside looking for you.'

I slipped out of the bar hurriedly, down the companion way, into the prince's room and began busying myself. The princess came in a few minutes later and said,

'I seem to have spent most of my time on this voyage looking for you, Dean.'

'I'm sorry about that, your highness,' I replied. 'I can't have been very far away though, can I?'

'I know where you've been. Even if I hadn't seen you there it would still be obvious,' and she made a little sniffing noise. 'You're travelling first class from now on.' She handed me a ticket with my cabin number. 'And here's another for Miss Boyack.'

There was no more high jinks for us on that voyage; we had to be at her beck and call from then onwards.

Packing now became a great art. Needing clothes and sporting gear for all seasons meant that we travelled with a huge quantity of luggage, ninety-nine pieces, most of which were trunks. Each piece was numbered and its contents catalogued, so by travelling with lengthy lists I was able to find anything at a few minutes' notice. I carried several bunches of keys and clinked along like a prison warder. On one journey when we'd arrived at our destination the prince, thinking he'd be helpful, said, 'Look, I'll see to the luggage and I'll meet you at the Customs. By the way how much is there?'

'Ninety-nine pieces, sir,' I replied.

'Christ! Then forget it, Dean, I'll see you at the hotel.'

Going through Customs could be difficult. I learnt that in some countries if you left a few bank notes on the luggage you went through quickly, but there were others where such a thing would have been fatal, and it was expedient to wait until everything was over before presenting a tip. Once we'd arrived at New York harbour and I had at last got everything around me when I was approached by a Customs official.

'Jeez, is all this yours?'

I explained exactly whose it was and who I was. He was not impressed.

'I don't care if you're butler to Antony and Cleopatra, you're going to have to open some of these. We'll start with that one.'

He pointed to a trunk containing the princess's riding clothes. I opened it, he rummaged around and came out with a pair of riding breeches.

'What are these, you lady's passion killers?'

I tried to explain. He then held up a shirt, some ties and a hacking jacket.

'And these?' he queried.

'They're her riding habits,' I spluttered.

'Riding habits,' he said scornfully, 'it seems to me your princess has some very nasty habits. You can pack up this trunk and then perhaps we'll have a look at your master's dresses!'

I shall never forget my first visit to America. I'd seen a fair bit of splendour in my life by then, but nothing to touch the richness of the Astors' homes there, and the style of their everyday living. The Astor mansion, 650 Fifth Avenue, was the last word in opulence. You entered into a great hall and passing through two huge bronze gates came to a reception room whose walls were panelled with painted canvases. Beyond it was the ballroom which was also an art gallery. It was here that Mrs Astor, the princess's grandmother, had held the great dances and receptions that had made her the leader of New York society. It was she and Ward McAlister who drew up the famous list of the four hundred who were to comprise New York society. There were statues and tapestries galore; marble stairs led to a heavily gilded drawing-room. Some people might say it was in bad taste but I'm glad to have seen it. Not long afterwards it was knocked down and a Jewish synagogue built in its place.

We went on to 'Beechwood', the princess's brother Vincent Astor's home, travelling there on his yacht. The house had a mixed staff, the butler was British as were one or two of the others, the rest American. There was no pug's parlour, or steward's room. As I was introduced around in the servants' hall I thought, 'This is a strange bunch' – they were so formal with their 'How do you do's, sir', the maids giving curtsies and then sitting around like stuffed dummies. What little conversation there was was stilted. I was getting a bit hot under the collar as it was a warm July day, so eventually I turned to Mr Brooks the butler and said, 'May I make a request?'

'Yes, Mr Dean, what is it?'

'Could I take my jacket off, it's so bloody hot in here.'

With that everyone relaxed. 'He's human after all,' they cried.

Apparently Mr Brooks had fed them with some sort of yarn about British butlers being super snobs. It wasn't long before they realised that I was only a simple country boy, though a bit later some of the maids didn't think I was as simple as all that!

During this first trip Vincent Astor gave ninety-nine acres at Rhinebeck to the princess so that she could build a house there. It caused a bit of a stir in the press, it was thought that it would be a huge monstrosity. People used to wander around while it was being built saying, 'Is this where the institooshun's gonna be?'

In fact it was a delightful Queen Anne style house, but the sightseers must have had some foresight because it's now an 'institooshun' for wayward girls.

It was fascinating seeing money being spent in the grand manner. Vincent Astor had a yacht built, the *Nourmahal*, in a

German shipyard. It was like a gun boat with three decks and eight guest cabins. It cost him a million dollars, which in those days of hard currency was a hell of a lot of money. Our house at Rhinebeck was furnished with priceless antiques sent from London. It had everything – or practically everything – but two days before the grand opening party we found there were no kitchen utensils and no bed linen – the bare necessities had been forgotten.

Another 'necessity' which was my responsibility was the booze. It was the time of prohibition. The prince asked me if I thought we could stock the cellar. 'Given enough money we could stock the house,' I replied.

'If anything goes wrong though, Dean, you'll have to take the rap but we'll get you a good lawyer and come and visit you in jail.' Not very comforting but since I was going to get a slice of the money I was able to shrug it off with a brave smile. Everything went according to plan, a car was arranged to bring the stuff from New York. It contained thousands of dollars worth of liquor yet when it drew up to the house there wasn't a bottle in sight.

Although on that occasion I took a bit of the action I was generally pretty scrupulous over their money. I carried a tidy sum of it around with me and always entered it up in a notebook as I spent it; 'The book' it came to be known as. Occasionally if I went out for an evening my companions would say, 'Come on, Charlie, let's have a drink on the book,' and I've been known to give way. I recall one night in Paris when I was out on the tiles with a couple of other men servants; we were drinking pernods at a table with three demi-mondaines, as tarts were called in France, and it was suggested that we went home with the girls. 'Not me,' I said, 'I've got to get back. In any case we haven't enough money with us.'

'We don't need it, Charles,' said my first footman, 'let's have it on the book!'

I enjoyed our travels around Europe. We British were treated handsomely at that time, not like poor relations as we are now. I was able to compare conditions of service in the various countries. It seemed to me that nowhere were the standards so high as they were in Britain. Nowhere, that is, until we went to stay with Count Potocki in Poland.

It was like going back a couple of hundred years in history. We were met at Warsaw station, where at least half a dozen servants descended on our luggage. Outside were three four-in-hand coaches, one for the prince and princess and the others for we servants. We drove off into the country led by horsemen. 'It's like the Lord Mayor's Show,' I said to Miss Boyack, who was not amused. She was busy pretending to be a queen, bestowing gracious smiles on the peasants. Eventually we turned into a long drive and watched as a distant palace grew nearer. One of the horses in front found it necessary to answer the call of nature and from nowhere a man appeared to clean away the offending pile.

The courtyard to the house was gravelled and as our coaches crossed it servants came from behind to smooth away marks of the wheels and the horses' hooves. Finally we drove through an archway where the carriages were halted and we were assisted from the coaches into the grand hall. The indoor staff seemed numberless and appeared to do everything to a drill, and in silence. It was impressive but a little frightening. During dinner that evening music was played by an orchestra made up from the ranks of the stable boys; Poland's answer I thought to our band of the Royal Horseguards. I was glad when we returned to civilisation.

We rented Byron's house in Venice for a few delightful

weeks. I loved the city for there was a surprise round every corner. Early on in our stay the prince's gondola bumped into that of Mr Michael Arlen, a fashionable writer of the time, and for the rest of our visit he was in and out of the house. Staying with us was Atlanta, the daughter of Count Mercati; she and Mr Arlen took a shine to each other and he later married her. Chips Channon, afterwards equerry to Edward, Prince of Wales, was also a member of our party.

The thing about being a butler/valet is that you're in very close contact with the family. With the Obolenskys, whom I'd joined at the beginning of their marriage, I was able to watch happiness turn into mutual acceptance, lovers' tiffs turn into wrangling, boredom lead to suspicion; things were said that couldn't be taken back and consolation was sought from others who were more than ready to offer it.

People are quick to criticise the morals of the rich and aristocratic, forgetting the temptations that are always there. Under stress and emotion employers sometimes forgot themselves and asked for opinions, and even advice, from their near servants. At the risk of giving offence I always, as politely and delicately as I could, declined to give either. It wasn't easy because one can feel flattered at being admitted to confidences and sharing intimacies. 'Hear no evil, see no evil, speak no evil', those three monkeys had a lot going for them as far as I was concerned. Always before me was the case of a valet whom I'd known, who agreed to give evidence in a famous divorce case and who ever after found it impossible to get employment because he couldn't keep his own council. I won't deny that I enjoyed a bit of gossip from time to time but the hanky-panky of the rich is much the same as that of the poor, so 'What the butler saw' is much the same as what everybody has seen.

It was my princess who in 1931 decided that she wanted

a divorce. She stopped travelling and we stayed in residence at Hanover Lodge with several people visiting us under the pretext of trying to bring about a reconciliation, but in reality wanting to hear the details. Tilly Loshe, the famous dancer, really did try to patch things up; she wasn't successful and it was a little ironic; she'd just married the brother-in-law of the wealthy Marshall Field and almost a year later to the day divorced him.

I was in a curious situation, fortunately one I was never called upon to resolve, for it was accepted by everyone, including myself, that I should remain in the service of Alice Astor. In December 1932 the divorce came through and early in 1933 my mistress married Raimund von Hofmannsthal, who'd been around in the background, as it were, for some time.

My new master was the son of the Austrian, Hugo, the librettist for Richard Strauss. He himself had also done a bit of writing for Max Rheinhart, the great Viennese impresario, who put on *The Miracle* at London's Lyceum Theatre, with Lady Diana Cooper playing the Madonna. Lady Diana shared Alice Astor's love of the ballet; they were both patrons of Sadler's Wells and I think to some extent were responsible for its survival in its early years.

I got on well with Mr von Hofmannsthal, although I was glad to surrender my valeting duties to an Austrian, Max, who acted as chauffeur/valet. Strangely the chef Vassily also stayed with us, I suppose because the prince had nothing to offer him. We now travelled between England, Austria and America, with of course occasional journeys to Paris, St Moritz, Biarritz and Cannes. We rented a house in Austria at Cammar, part of a castle owned by Count Yesanski. While we were there we travelled the senior servants, and the staff was augmented by Austrians. They were excellent servants who, although the house was run English style, were able to pick things up easily. By now, too, I think I can say without conceit, I was becoming international. Anyway I learnt enough of the language to make my orders understood; it was I suppose a sort of below-stairs pidgin Austrian.

One thing I learned from von Hofmannsthal which was of great value later, was about wines. Before I'd met him I thought I knew a thing or two, but it wasn't until I was with an expert that I realised how thin my knowledge was. He chose and superintended the drinks for every meal. Early on in his marriage he bought part of the Rothschild cellar when it was put up for auction. He took great pains in matching the wines with the food; together we would taste it and sometimes he would discard a bottle as not being quite right. Then of course it would make its way to the servants' hall. In London a frequent visitor to Hanover Lodge was André Simon, the connoisseur from the Wine and Food Society. They would spend hours together over dinner describing the merits of various vintages. I was able to listen to them closely. I was also able to extend my knowledge when I superintended at dinners given by the London Livery Companies, where I was often asked to assist.

Once again I watched a marriage decay. This time the process was quicker and by 1937 Alice Astor had obtained a divorce. I was naturally interested on whom her choice would fall on the next occasion. When eventually I heard, I realised that my time in service with her had to come to an end. I was not a snob, but the idea of being in the employ of even an ex-editor of the *Daily Worker*, the Communist newspaper now called the *Morning Star*, was not one that I was prepared to consider.

After twelve years I was looking for a job again. This time I didn't contemplate using an agency, I was now well enough known to put the word round the underground and wait for a response. I didn't wait long. I was offered and accepted the position of butler to Mrs James Field, the ex-wife of Marshall Field of Chicago. She was living at Holme House, Regent's Park, near to Hanover Lodge and in a similar style.

I'd previously met Mrs Field in America. She and her husband had a lovely home at Huntingdon, Long Island. It was the replica of an English country estate. I'd visited there with the Obolenskys for shooting and other parties. They had an English staff and Scots gamekeepers.

I discovered that she now had a gentleman friend, a Mr Peter Pleydell Bouverie, a brother of the Earl of Radnor, and that they were shortly to be married. She was also a close friend of the royals, her mother, Mrs Willie James, having been perhaps the most famous or notorious of Edward VII's mistresses. This may seem a strange reason for her having the entrée to Buckingham Palace but, as is said, blood is thicker than water, and I understand that in Victorian and Edwardian times children often took after the men that their mothers admired. Anyway taking it all in all it seemed a job that I would enjoy, so I arranged to be interviewed by Mrs Field, and accepted the post when it was offered.

I now gave in my notice to Alice Astor and really put the cat among the pigeons – feathers flew. If ever I could have got really big-headed it was then. Changing butlers it seemed was more upsetting than changing husbands. I was offered a deal more money than I was to get with Mrs Field; I refused it. Then Alice Astor's agent, Ketchin Kommer, sent for me; he tried flattery, said I was indispensable to him, then offered even more money; I wouldn't budge. Finally, and this I thought beat everything, von Hofmannsthal asked me to go and see him. 'Please stay with her, Dean,' he said, 'she'll need you more than ever now.'

'I'm sorry, sir,' I replied, 'I just can't face it.'

When finally I said goodbye to Alice Astor she shed a tear or two which didn't make things easy.

'Never mind, madam,' I said, 'I'm only moving down the road. If ever you need help I'll be pleased to give it.'

I've recorded this not to boast or show off but to demonstrate the dependence people had on servants who'd been with them for any length of time.

I'd no reason to regret my decision to move; Mrs Field was easy to work for and there was no noticeable change in her manner when she became Mrs Bouverie. She was a handsome lady of about forty, near the same age as Alice Astor, but she was less wild. She didn't often keep late hours, so the house was easier to run. She entertained rather after the style of Lady Astor but on a smaller scale. She went abroad frequently but I was not required to accompany her; this didn't worry me, I'd seen enough of the world for the time being.

Mr Peter Bouverie I found a typical English country gentleman with the interests which that implies: hunting, shooting and fishing. He had a position with the Calor Gas Company and tried to persuade his wife to put some money into it; I was tempted but since Mrs Bouverie insisted that it would never do well I followed her example, more's the pity!

He was easy to look after, and with his arrival in the house I combined the duties of butler and valet. I travelled regularly with him to Longford Castle, his brother's place near Salisbury, a similar house to Cliveden, only bigger. I was no stranger there, I'd been a number of times with Prince Obolensky. We had an excellent staff at Holme House and a good chef, an Italian called Salvatini, and I used the same tradespeople as I had done for the last thirteen years. The gardens were extensive, we had about seven acres which was an extraordinary size for a place in central London. We even had a bothy to house the seven gardeners.

I have mentioned that Mrs Bouverie was a great friend of the royals, particularly of the King and Queen and the Duke and Duchess of Kent. They were regular visitors to the house and of course the atmosphere was very much less formal than at the dinner parties Lady Astor gave; it was Christian-name terms and the servants' manner towards them was more relaxed.

By accident I became quite close to the Duke of Kent. One weekend early in my association with Mrs Bouverie, he arrived without his valet, John Hall, so I was called upon to take care of him. I must have suited because always after that he'd give John time off when he came to see us. This of course pleased his valet and when I went down to Coppins, the Duke's country home, we became good friends. It was therefore a personal tragedy for me when the Duke's plane crashed in August 1942, killing both John and himself. By that time I'd collected two mementoes, presents from the Duke; a set of cuff links and tie pin and a silver enamel cigarette case, both inscribed and engraved with his crest.

When the Second World War came we decided to sit it out in London, taking our cue of course from the royals. We were fortunate as there was a natural air raid shelter in the garden, a sort of cave which we had furnished and installed heat and light; there was a drinks cabinet and it was as good a place in a raid as any in London. It had to be because the King and Queen occasionally shared it with us and I don't think servants can get closer to the royal family than being in action with them. Eventually Holme House was hit and it was necessary for us to move. For a short time we had a temporary home at Reading, a furnished house belonging to the Duke of Bedford. Then Mrs Bouverie bought a property, Julians, near Baldock. It was a glorified farmhouse which proved useful at the time since we were able to augment our rations with milk, butter, poultry and anything that was shot on our land.

Again I watched another marriage break up. I began to think that perhaps I put a jinx on them, and again I stayed with the lady. As a flower seller I knew in New York once said to me, 'These ladies you serve seem to change husbands regularly, but never butlers.'

I wasn't to stay with her for long. In 1942 I had to go before a tribunal who directed me into war work. I was able to get a job near my home in Bisley as a security guard, a sort of human watchdog. I spent most of my time watching to make sure that my superiors didn't catch me smoking or drinking tea. I didn't distinguish myself in any way; as my superior officer said, 'You'll never make a security man.'

'No,' I replied, 'and you'll never make a butler.'

I think they were glad to see the back of me when the war ended and I got the chance to leave.

I wasn't in any hurry to go back into service. The war had seen great social changes and I thought I'd look around a bit before I committed myself to a full-time job. A temporary part-time position fell into my lap. Sir Robert and Lady Perkins of Rookwoods, he was our local member of parliament, needed a butler at weekends, so I worked there from Friday to Monday. We had a skeleton staff; a cook, a housemaid and myself. The atmosphere was family and friendly.

I watched as it were from the side-lines as the wealthy and aristocratic families settled themselves down after the war and tried to get back to the old order of things. They refused to accept that they could never be the same again. For some their wishful thinking almost succeeded through the efforts of people like Mr Lee. I had several offers of employment but preferred my life as a loner, contenting myself with a few extra days here and there organising the large parties that the new school of servants was untrained or unfitted to do.

Eventually after the Perkins decided to move from the area I got caught. I was asked to arrange a party for Mrs Nancy Lancaster, one time Mrs Ronald Tree and Mrs Marshall Field, at Hasley Court, near Oxford. On my arrival there I had a slight altercation with her odd man who refused to hand over the keys of the safe and cellar. I sorted him out but he then went and packed his bags and left. Mrs Lancaster now had me over a barrel, for although I was in no way responsible for his action I felt duty bound to stay on. Once again I was in an Astor household, for Mrs Lancaster was Lady Astor's niece. Not only were they related, they were great friends and her ladyship was a constant visitor, though – and this shows how times had changed – as a paying guest.

I was now able to renew an acquaintanceship of many years' standing with Miss Rosina Harrison, Lady Astor's personal maid. Our paths had crossed during our years in service. She had a great reputation below stairs and among her other qualities was said to have as sharp a tongue as her mistress, though a different accent; 'Yorkie' she was familiarly known as to many of us. Being two old-timers our friendship quickly developed into a deep affection. Like any woman she used this to put the pressure on me.

'Her ladyship wants a butler and it's our opinion that you're the man for the job. It'll be just like the old days again, we've got a trained and seasoned staff and it's high time you stopped being a country bumpkin; you're getting fat and running to seed.'

It was the kind of flattery I'd come to expect from her. Then Lady Astor started in. One evening just as they were sitting down to dinner and I was pushing Mrs Lancaster's chair in Lady Astor said, 'You know, Dean, you shouldn't be doing that, you belong to me.'

'No, my lady,' I said, 'I don't belong to anybody but at the moment Mrs Lancaster's paying me to work for her.'

'Yes, Dean, but she wouldn't be able to if I didn't pay to come here,' a nasty reference to her capacity as a paying guest. I didn't answer but she'd got the bit between her teeth. 'I understand your home is not far from here.'

'That is so, my lady.'

'And your mother lives there.'

'Yes, my lady.'

'Then tell Pover (her chauffeur) that I shall be driving over there to see her tomorrow morning.'

Off she went to Bisley the next day, bought my mother, who was now well into her eighties, a beautiful woollen shawl, and then started in on her.

'Mrs Dean,' she said, 'I want your son to come back and work for me.'

Mum replied that she thought that I was old enough by now to know my own mind.

'That's just where you're wrong, Mrs Dean. In my experience men are never old enough to know their own minds, they're just boys at heart.'

Then she went on buttering Mum up by saying what a nice lad I was and how this was due to the way Mum had brought me up. She must have spun a right old yarn because when I went home a couple of days later Mum was singing Lady Astor's praises and saying she thought I'd be making a big mistake if I didn't go and work for her. Then Mr Lee telephoned giving me the old flattery bit. This was the straw that broke the camel's back and a few weeks later I was with her ladyship at 100 Eaton Square. I didn't regret the decision that had been made for me, it was as if I was home again and the clock had been turned back twenty-five years, for the staff were all of the old school, Mrs Hawkins the housekeeper, Rosina Harrison lady's maid, old and trusted William the odd man, Pover the chauffeur and Otto Dangl the chef; even the servants were well trained; it was a great team.

Otto might well have been the odd man out, he came as a stranger to us but of all the chefs I've ever worked with he was the most congenial and one of the most talented. He had a kind of bubbling gaiety, cooking was fun for him and he suited all our palates; for we and her ladyship had a taste for American food. Otto during the war had been taken prisoner by the Americans who were quick to realise his quality and he was rapidly promoted until he was chef for five star generals like General Mark Clark. His genius had its disadvantages for he had difficulty in getting away and believes he was one of the last prisoners of war to be released.

Lady Astor, who'd lost none of her wit and sparkle, had matured well. She was now more reliant on us and therefore closer to us, she was a pleasure to serve, and I honestly believe we all did it with devotion. The family recognised this and gave us respect and trust, so for the next five years we reaped the rewards of our service.

One of our constant delights was what I can only call Rose-baiting. Miss Harrison had now been with her ladyship for nearly thirty years, yet they could still squabble and fight like Kilkenny cats. I think it was the thing that gave her ladyship the greatest pleasure; she would always be thinking up ways of putting a spanner into Rose's works. Arguments like this were daily events.

'Rose, will you come here.' There'd be silence. 'Rose, I'm talking to you, come here at once.'

'I know you're talking to me, so does the whole house, but I'm not coming until you apologise.'

'I'm not going to apologise to you, I engaged you, I pay you.'

'Yes, but you don't own me.' And so it would go on.

I remember a time when Rose had asked me to take her ladyship's hair drier into the bedroom. Lady Astor stopped me in the hall and said, 'Where are you going with that, Dean?' and she winked at me to take up my cue.

'Miss Harrison said ...'

'Anyone would think Miss Harrison was the mistress around here, take it back to where you found it.'

Then Rose came running with her hackles up and there was a glorious slanging match. Rose with her strident Yorkshire twang, and her ladyship waxing into her Southern American. I think Miss Harrison had her suspicion that these kinds of occasion were put-up jobs but she couldn't be quite sure so she reacted to them predictably as she had done over the years.

Lady Astor's hatred of the drink was well known if not notorious. She was a strict teetotaller all her life until the end, then she never knew it. When I was with Mrs Lancaster at Hasley she'd given her ladyship a little Dubonnet, pretending that it wasn't alcohol. It was noticeable that it perked her up and did her a bit of good. It was her ladyship's custom to drink a glass of Ribena, a blackcurrant essence, every morning at eleven and every afternoon at four, so if ever we thought she was a bit down in the dumps I'd put a small slug of Dubonnet in her glass; as it was the same colour she couldn't detect it.

So the years passed quietly and pleasantly. There was only one dark cloud that was slow to pass over, Lord Billie's involvement in the Profumo affair. Enough has already been written and said about it. Our own major concern was to prevent Lady Astor from hearing of it, and Rose has written about our success in this. For all the servants it was a time of great bitterness, not with Lord Billie but with the public for the way they condemned a gentleman without trial and on hearsay evidence. In contrast, a happy event was her ladyship's eightieth birthday when family, friends and servants united for a tribal celebration.

After Lady Astor's death I resumed my freelance way of life. I was determined never to return to full-time service. Few families now could afford to live in style, and trained servants were rare. In any case I was getting on in years and felt I'd qualified to live an easier life. I should by now have learnt never to make resolutions for from out of the blue came the one offer that I could not refuse; Mr Jakie, Lady Astor's youngest son, phoned saying that Lord Harlech, the British Ambassador to the United States, was staying with them, that he was in desperate need of a butler and would I please take on the job for six months, the remainder of his time of service in Washington. I didn't need to think, I gave an immediate 'Yes' for an answer. My reasons for accepting were all good ones. During my life in service I'd come to regard the States as my second home; I loved the country and the people; I hadn't had the chance of visiting there since the war and I was unlikely to have a similar opportunity; finally only in an Embassy in the United States could I now perform the skills I'd learned. Entertaining would be on the big scale and money (tax payers') would always be available. In any case six months wasn't a long time if things didn't come up to my expectations. But they did. I enjoyed the work, I renewed friendships and made others.

When the six months was up I was looking forward to returning home, but I'd reckoned without Sir Patrick Dean, the new Ambassador. It was part of my agreement that I should stay on for a fortnight after Lord Harlech had handed over. During that time I got to know Sir Patrick, one of the greatest gentlemen it had been my privilege to meet, so when he asked me to continue to serve him and his family I was unable to refuse. He and Lady Dean were a joy to work for, always appreciative, trusting and helpful. They charmed the rest of the staff as they charmed me.

Once again my training under Mr Lee was to prove useful. An occasion I particularly recall was when Princess Alexandra was visiting America. We were required to give a dinner party. The trouble about having royalty in the States is the number of people who expect to be invited to meet them, which is why generally they go in for buffet suppers and cocktail parties. Lady Dean felt that Her Royal Highness must be tired of these affairs and wanted to do it in the old style.

'How many could we seat in the ballroom?' she asked.

'It's no good guessing,' I replied, 'we'll have to try it and see.'

We did a mock layout and decided we could cope with a hundred and ten guests.

'How many footmen will you need?' she asked.

'That depends, my lady, on the menu.'

'On the menu?' she seemed surprised.

'Yes, you see if you have a simple menu we can manage with one man a table, but if we are serving sauces and side dishes, we shall need two.'

She went to the chef and it was decided it would be a complicated menu, so I needed twenty-two to serve and since with a large party of that kind I would only be able to supervise I engaged another four for the wines. I was only able to have a short rehearsal with them, as Mr Lee did. I told them to look to me for their cues to serve and to clear and, apart from one man who jittered with nerves and had to be removed quietly, the whole thing went off like clockwork. The following day Lady Dean asked me to go and see her and, unlike Lady Astor, who could never bring herself to do such a thing, congratulated me on the evening.

'How did you manage to control all those waiters?' she asked.

'That, my lady, was as a result of serving under "Lord Lee of Cliveden", Lady Astor's butler.'

Her ladyship always got some of Lee's credit. I suppose she deserved it.

Although mine was not an uncommon name it was in a way odd that I should be butler to Sir Patrick Dean. It was also occasionally embarrassing, particularly when I was answering the phone.

Mr George Brown when he was Foreign Secretary also found it a bit bewildering.

His Excellency, which was Sir Patrick's title, and Lady Dean with their two sons had been to meet Mr George Brown at the airport. When they arrived back at the door I opened it and said, 'Welcome to the Embassy', to sort of make him feel at home. Some Labour members I knew looked on us as a stuffy lot and seemed a bit ill at ease in our presence. Sir Patrick then introduced me.

'This is Dean, our butler.'

I was wrong to have worried about Mr Brown not feeling at home.

'Another bloody Dean! that makes five. What sort of place is this, Barchester bloody Towers?'

Everyone laughed of course, and I took to him straight away. He seemed to be able to get on with anyone and his visit was a great success.

When I agreed to stay on with Sir Patrick I had made one stipulation, that I should leave in time to return to England on the maiden voyage of the *Queen Elizabeth 2*. During my life-time I'd travelled on the best of boats, trains, aircraft, carriages and cars, and I thought I could now allow myself the luxury of returning home on the latest and best of her kind. Everything had worked out well, Sir Patrick was recalled just before I was due to leave, I was able to see Mr John Freeman in, and say goodbye to my friends before finally waving farewell to America from the deck of the *Q.E.2.*

If I had dreams of retirement they were not to be granted. Demands on my time were greater than my powers of supply. It seemed that butlers of the old school had retired, died or simply faded away. The shooting season was my busiest time. It was the one scene that hadn't changed over the years. It was still conducted on the same sort of military lines and the moors, of course, were as they always had been.

It was in the freedom of these Scottish moors that I now allowed myself time to reflect back over my life. How a simple country boy with no ambitions or qualifications had been able to lead so full and interesting a life; how through the good fortune of meeting one great man, Edwin Lee, my life had been given a purpose and a direction; how the riches of the Astors had enabled me to travel and to practise my craft in the grandest possible manner; how I had been privileged to be able to call two countries, Britain and America, home; how in the eyes of many I was despised as a domestic servant but in the eyes of kings, queens and princes I was a friend; how Sir Frederick Ashton when he met me in Washington had said, 'You know, Mr Dean, you used to terrify me, in fact I think I was more frightened of you than of any man in London when you were butler at Hanover Lodge'; how Lady Ancaster that very day had christened me 'The soft-hearted butler', meaning the man who always said yes to a job if he was asked in the right kind of way.

I suppose I must blame my hair for not allowing me to retire. It had remained jet black and therefore my advancing years went unnoticed, except by myself. When I protested that I was too old employers would dismiss it with the cliché, 'A man is as old as he feels', and if I replied that I was beginning to feel old, would say, 'A creaking gate lasts longest'. I must not, however, deny it was very good to feel I was still wanted. As I approached eighty I began to look in the mirror regularly. At last I saw what I wanted – my first grey hair. 'That's it,' I said to myself, 'I'm finished. Now I can tell them that the old grey mare ain't what she used to be.'

## Some Reflections on Charles's Story

Few men I think can have led fuller or longer working lives than my friend Charles Dean. As with Mr Lee I can vouch for the truth in his story for I've heard it many many times. His more recent experiences I have watched in wonderment. 'Whenever will Charles take a well-earned rest,' I have thought many times, since my own retirement. Now he is taking it, in a bungalow near his native village of Bisley. If you were to visit him you would almost find it impossible to believe that the person who greeted you was the Charles Dean of his story. He has reverted to type, back to the country boy of his youth. His garden is witness of the work he puts into it, and so are his rough hands. He has not given up looking after people, for he tends his invalid sister. Although he has over the years collected many treasures from his employers the bungalow shows little evidence of them, for living up to his reputation as 'The soft-hearted butler' he has given most of them away to his friends. His most precious possession is the noisiest and worst-behaved dog I've ever come across!

Charles's early life was in a way after the pattern of Gordon Grimmett's; both were fun-loving and easygoing until they worked under Mr Lee, who gave them a sense of purpose.

Charles's account of his life with Alice Astor I found fascinating. It is the other side of the coin of my life with Lady Nancy. They belonged to two different sets – or cliques as we used to call them. It was an echo of the late Victorian days when society was divided into the Queen's set and the Prince of Wales's set. The one political and respectable and the other fast and fun-seeking. Lady Astor might have been more wild if she hadn't in her early days been held on a tight rein by her husband, and later by her own political position and religion. Alice Astor had no such curbs, she rode free and pretty rough-shod, she looked for fun and gaiety and she found it in the flapper society of the post-war period and later in the world of ballet, theatre and art. It brought no lasting contentment. Charles feels with me that her happiest years were those spent with Prince Obolensky and that it was a pity that they couldn't have come together again in later life.

So it was that when Charles left Lady Astor it was to provide the glitter, the tinsel, the fairy lights to the dashing pleasure-seeking Obolenskys. He must have had fantastic stamina for when they were in London there would be supper parties almost every night. This meant that no sooner was dinner cleared, than the staff had to begin again preparing a buffet of cold salmon, turkey, chicken, ham and tongue, sweets and cheese as well as seeing an ample supply of champagne was on ice. Charles would seldom reckon on getting to bed before two in the morning, having to be up again no later than seven. I know about the pattern of behaviour at Hanover Lodge because my sister Olive went as kitchen maid there. She lasted six weeks. She simply couldn't take the hours of work. Then Charles had the business of travelling with so much luggage. To any ordinary mortal this would have been a nightmare; Charles was able to take it in his stride.

His love of travel, of America and the American people was something we both had in common and we were able to enjoy it the splendid way, sailing on the big ships.

Perhaps the most fascinating thing about his story is that it shows the dependancy of employers on their servants, one that was noticed by an American shopkeeper. It was around the time that Alice Astor's marriage with von Hofmannsthal was breaking up. 'Hello, Mr Dean,' she said, 'nice to have you back, I hear your lady's getting another divorce.'

'Is she?' responded Charles.

'Didn't you know?'

'British servants, ma'am, are like the three monkeys; they see no evil, they hear no evil, and they repeat no evil.'

'Is that so?' replied the shopkeeper, and then added slyly, 'Another thing about you Britishers that I've noticed is that while your ladies often change their husbands, they never change their butlers.'

# A FRIEND IN SERVICE

## George Washington

My first meeting with George Washington was one I shall always remember. Lady Astor had been away for the weekend and, finding herself near Dytchley, on impulse decided to visit her niece Mrs Tree. When we arrived at the house she jumped out of the car and sped up to the front door, leaving me to follow with her case containing her 'sparklers', as we both called her jewels. I saw her thumb pressing on the bell impatiently. It was answered by a new footman, who seemed to be barring the way to my lady. Suddenly she thrust out an arm, handing him off like a rugby player and throwing him back into the hall. Then she bounded into the house calling out 'Nancy, Nancy,' as she went.

As I made to go indoors the footman, now red-faced and angry, said, 'Who the hell does she think she is?'

'It's not who she thinks she is, it's who she is. That, my boy, is Lady Astor.'

He muttered something I shan't repeat, then made to take my case.

'You can take your hands off that,' I said, 'it never leaves my possession nor my sight.'

This put him back on his heels again.

'I'll make my own way to the servants' hall,' I called over my shoulder. As I left him I heard him mutter,

'What a bloody pair!'

It wasn't long before we became firm friends and the 'sparklers' were a joke between us. He would try every way to get that case from me. He never managed it.

He was a servant of a different mould from the others. Where they had a flair for the job, he succeeded by taking pains. He studied and learned his way up the ladder. His early deformity had left him uncertain and unsure. Confidence was something he had to find out and he soon discovered that the way to get it was through work well done. He was a man who when you knew him you had to like and to respect.

I introduce George Washington to you as the self-made butler.

# V

# THE HALL BOY'S STORY

## George Washington

Let me begin by saying that my name is not George; I was christened Eric but, with a surname like mine, it was inevitable that I should be rechristened by my fellows. When I first went into service as a hall boy and told the butler that I came from Westcott he said, 'Westcott, yes I've heard of it, it's that place between Bicester and Aylesbury; have they stopped eating the missionaries there yet?'

It was indeed an old-fashioned place, right off the map as they say, and the lives of its villagers, like those of the two nearby hamlets of Waddesdon and Winchingham, were dominated by Waddesdon Manor, 'The House on the Hill', home of Mr and Mrs James de Rothschild, since most of the men and some of the women worked on the estate and its surrounding farms. My father was one such, a farm worker and a forester, though when I was born in 1915 he was away in the army.

My mother should have gone into domestic service like her two sisters, but, because she was the youngest, it was considered to be her job to look after her father on her mother's death, and later to care for me.

I was nothing but a nuisance to her, for I was born with a twisted foot; it's on my medical records as infantile paralysis, but I have it on good authority that I was born the wrong way round, and if only I'd been able to delay coming into the world for a few years my limb would have been quite sound. As it was, as a child I was in and out of hospital, which interfered with my early education. My deformity made me a target of the other boys' derision; they were really no more cruel than most children, only they'd been born in the country among animals. Weakness was despised in the animal world so it was natural for them to apply the same philosophy to a child. Perhaps as that butler later implied they were little savages.

Eventually my treatment at their hands came to the notice of the authority and I was transferred to Waddesdon School, where I was put into the care of a teacher called Harris, a great boxer and football player with a gentle heart, who saw to it that when I left school I was able to meet the world as easily as my schoolmates. It was accepted that I would have to start work when I was fourteen; my father was earning only thirty-five shillings a week and so, following the general pattern, I went to the Rothschilds' as garden boy.

I suppose the gardens at Waddesdon Manor were among the finest in this country, if not in the world. I wish I were competent to describe them. In the summer, around the Knob – as those gardens which surrounded the house were called – there were masses of flowers in formal and informal beds. The roses rivalled those in Regent's Park and all the year round the greenhouses were a mass of colour and fruit. 'Paradise' was the name given to the greenhouses where fruit and fresh vegetables were grown to be available at all times of the year.

The showpiece was the 'Top Houses'. This was arranged so that you could walk from the house through to a vestibule into the Dome which was massed with palms and huge cacti. Leading from this dome were four houses, one for each point of the compass, each with the temperature and humidity for the kind of flowers they contained; to wander in it was to take a journey round the world. Later in my life in service I was to meet Frank Copcutt, then head gardener at Cliveden who had worked for several years at Waddesdon. He told me that when he first saw the Astors' gardens, good by most standards, he thought he was slumming!

I'm afraid my efforts added little to the beauty and style of the place. I assisted a gardener in the rose beds, sweeping, weeding and clearing up for him, and occasionally I did duty in the vegetable garden which meant my collecting whatever was required for the house. Orders were rung down from the kitchen, the fruit and vegetables cut and cleaned; then a small cart would arrive from the stables painted in the Rothschilds' colours of blue and yellow; its brass was burnished, the horse beautifully groomed and the driver in a coachman's uniform with a bowler hat and cockade. So the vegetables were transported in a truly regal fashion to the kitchens.

Another feature of the estate was the variety of trees in the park around. When I learned that the house had only been built during the years 1880 to 1889 I wondered how they could have grown so large. My grandfather enlightened me. He could remember them being dragged there fully grown on a specially made trailer drawn by twenty-two horses.

It didn't take me or my superiors long to realise that gardening was not my vocation. I was continually casting envious eyes on the indoor servants who would come sweeping down the drive on their beautiful bicycles; 'That,' I thought, 'looks like a job for me.' In 1930 my mind was made up for me; there was an economy drive over the country, which meant that the wealthy made big efforts and sacked junior staff whose absence was unlikely to affect their lives in any way.

My mother was upset when I left. I suppose she imagined that, having got my first foot on the Rothschild's ladder, I'd be employed by them for life, and of course my twelve shillings a week made a useful contribution to the running of the cottage. With those bicycles sweeping down the drive still in my mind's eye I studied the papers for a job in service, and eventually saw an advertisement for a hall boy at Little Missenden Abbey at a salary of ten shillings a week.

My family were not pleased, they felt service to be the lowest of the low but they agreed with me that beggars couldn't be choosers; there was little work around at the time and even menial work was better than none. And it was menial.

The house was owned by a Mr and Mrs Ronald, reasonably wealthy, but definitely not gentry. He was an Australian wool broker who'd made his pile during the First World War. His wife was middle class English trying her utmost to ape her betters. They kept a butler, cook and kitchen maid, housemaid, under housemaid and me. I was a sort of dog's body, at everyone's beck and call; no sooner would I settle down to do one thing than I would be told to do another – Cinderella couldn't have had it worse. The nickname that I was given, 'Washy', I think describes my condition and state of mind. One consolation was that I was within cycling distance of home and could see my family occasionally.

Another was Doris, the little housemaid whose life was nearly as wretched as mine. Her father ran a pub, the Black Horse, at nearby Lacy Green and whenever we could snatch an hour or two off we would cycle over there for tea. I suppose in an innocent way we became fond of each other, but our relationship was not allowed to blossom.

The head housemaid, whom I looked on as an old spinster though she was probably only about twenty-five, took a shine to me, only I didn't realise it at the time. I did think it a bit fishy when she kept calling me up to her bedroom to give me orders and that she always seemed to be in various stages of undress, pretending that she was changing. She also seemed to be pawing me when she talked to me. I took no notice; if I thought about it at all I put it down to a sort of motherly feeling for me, but I suppose she felt my growing friendship with Doris was putting her nose out of joint.

One morning I overslept and Doris, noticing my absence, ran up to my room to wake me. As she was leaving she bumped into the head housemaid who went up like a volcano and accused us of having spent the night together. Nothing we could say would quieten her and the long and short of it was that I was sent for by Mrs Ronald, called a filthy fornicator and told to pack my things and get out of the house immediately.

It wasn't pleasant for me to explain what had happened when I got home. I think it would have been simpler if I had been guilty, at least then I could have made a clean breast of it and started from there; as it was, although my word was accepted, it was done in a half-hearted sort of way as though there was no smoke without fire and I felt my behaviour was watched not only by my family but by the villagers who had girls of a seducible age, while friends of my own sex seemed uncertain whether to admire or despise me.

I decided that I would try and get away completely. I wrote for a job as a hall boy/footman to Lord and Lady Tweedmouth at 57 Seymour Street, London, and to my surprise I was accepted. I say surprised because I was given no reference by the Ronalds. Mr Gray the butler showed little interest in my character when he interviewed me. I wasn't there long before

I discovered why. He was thoroughly disreputable himself and expected me not just to turn a blind eye to his misdemeanours but to assist him in them.

It was a fair-sized staff for a house of its kind, three in each department. We entertained regularly and although Mr Gray was somewhat sleazy in his personal behaviour he was reasonably good at his job, so I learnt something by working under him.

To show how green I was at the time I have to tell a story against myself. Mr Gray and I were preparing the lunch table. 'Pop down and ask the cook if there's a fish course today,' he told me.

'No, they're having cheese omelette,' was her reply. I delivered it as I understood it.

'They're having cheese on the mitt.'

'What the hell's that?' demanded the butler.

'Well, cheese on the hand I suppose, sir.' He thought I was trying to be funny.

'You saucy little bugger, don't you try and be clever at my expense,' and he cuffed me across the room.

We learnt the hard way in those days.

We did other things the hard way, too. There were none of the sophisticated burglar alarms that there are today. It wasn't thought necessary when you could get a human alarm also performing household duties for twenty-six pounds a year.

I was that alarm. I didn't have a room, I slept in the pantry on a bed so arranged that it pulled down on hinges from a cupboard and fell across the safe door. This meant that any intending thief would have to slit my throat before he could get to the safe and it was hoped that I would be able to give some sort of warning before I was done to death.

I did in fact have many disturbed nights not because of burglars, but because of Mr Gray's nasty habits.

He had an arrangement with some of the Mayfair ladies of easy virtue who trod the nearby streets whereby, if trade or the weather was bad, he could have his way with them in exchange for a bite to eat or a glass or two of port. My involvement was that if one of these ladies knocked on the door when the house was asleep, I had to let her in and go up to his room and inform him of her presence. This in my opinion made me his ponce and I realised that, in the event of Mr Gray's indiscretions being discovered, others might think the same way and some of the blame would be laid at my door. In view of my previous experience with the Ronalds, if this happened I'd be in danger of being considered some sort of sexual maniac and my career in service could end before it had properly started. I decided therefore to look around for another position.

I was lucky, for shortly after I was appointed steward's room boy at Holland House, Kensington, the family home of the Earl and Countess of Ilchester.

Although when I went there I was ignorant of the history of Holland House, during my service I was instructed in bits of it. What I learned would take up more than my story. Let me just say that almost all the outstanding men and women of genius and talent of the early nineteenth century passed through its rooms or wandered along its many walks, and that for three hundred years the plotting and planning that went on there showed its results in the parliament of Westminster a couple of miles or so to the east.

I vividly remember my interview. I felt so small as I approached the huge black and gold gates which spanned the arched entrance. I made my way through and knocked at the side door of the lodge. It was opened by a man wearing a top hat with cockade, livery tailcoat and wasp waistcoat; he inquired my business and directed me from a map to the house.

It was three-quarters of a mile I found out later, but on that day it seemed four times as far.

It was strange, I thought, that I'd been told to go to the front door, since servants were normally expected to use the tradesmen's entrance, but according to the lodge keeper people like myself had been known to wander for days looking for it, so a concession was made for first visits. I had never seen a door like it. It was huge. In bygone days it was possible to drive a coach and four through it and pull up at the foot of the grand staircase; it was so vast that when Mr Pettit the butler opened the door to me he seemed like a dwarf, yet he was six feet three inches tall and weighed twenty-three stone.

Once again I stated my business and was taken to his office. He made the interview easy and I was appointed at a salary of twenty-six pounds a year, with a rise every twelve months if I proved satisfactory, and the promise that if I continued to work hard he would look after me in the usual manner, meaning that I would be promoted if a vacancy occurred. But this wasn't all. I was allowed three new suits annually. Having only ever had one in my life this seemed great riches to me. Mr Pettit was better than his word for though my first two suits were charcoal (duty suits that is) when he saw that I'd been taught to look after my things and that they were still presentable, he allowed me the pattern and colour of my choice.

When I look back over my three and a half years at Holland House I can see how there was something particularly sad, almost unreal about them. We were propping up something that belonged to another age, trying to pretend that what had passed still existed or even if it didn't that if we tried hard enough to keep the old order of things going, it might come back. The house was really run for Mary, the Dowager Countess of Ilchester, widow of the fifth earl. She was a very old lady, a semi-invalid, and had been widowed for many years before I joined the staff. Much of the time she spent in her bedroom and it was my job to take her meals up and hand them to her nurse or lady's maid. Her son, the sixth Earl of Ilchester, spent little time at Holland House even though it was entailed to him, just using it during the London season and on short occasional visits. He had two country homes, Melbury and Abbotsbury, where he preferred to spend his time.

So the purpose of the staff was largely one of appearance. We were there as a sign that every attempt was being made to maintain a traditional heritage. And there was a number of us, Mr Pettit the butler, a first footman, an odd man and myself; a housekeeper and four maids, a stillroom maid, a cook, two kitchen maids and two scullery maids, a chauffeur, Mr East; a head gardener, Mr Rintle, with eight gardeners, a lady's maid and day and night nurses. So what did we do with ourselves?

Speaking personally I don't think I've ever worked harder in my life; I think that there I learned almost everything I know about private service. My specific job as steward's room boy was to look after the steward's room and to valet the butler. I got up at five-thirty and woke Mr Pettit at six, with a mug of tea and a can of hot water. I would lay out his clothes and clean his boots. Then came the lighting of the fires. This in retrospect was a little ridiculous. I had to light the ones in the stillroom and the breakfast-room, while the stillroom maid lit those in Mr Pettit's bedroom and the housekeeper's sitting-room, and the under housemaid lit the one in the steward's room. There were two fireplaces in the breakfast-room with surrounds of steel. These I had to burnish with a leather pad lined with chain mail. I felt like a valet to a knight in shining armour and I expected he suffered in the same way I did for on heavy or misty days I could rub until my hands fell off trying in vain to get a shine. On a clear day it would look like a mirror and all my hard work would be worth while.

Generally the countess would have her breakfast in her bedroom. The procedure for preparing this was fascinating; I'd start by getting the cloth and napkin from the house-keeper, taking it on a tray to the pantry for the silver, then to the stillroom for the rolls, toast and croissants and finally to the kitchen for the eggs, bacon or whatever cooked food was required.

Unfortunately the odd man was an old retainer of some seventy years or more, only capable of pottering about, so that the heavy jobs that normally would have been his responsibility fell on me. Perhaps the hardest of these was carrying the coals, and since all the rooms, including some of the bedrooms, were heated by coal fires this meant climbing to the top of the house with two galvanised buckets of around 56 lb each. At the time I was only just tall enough to get them off the floor; they seemed to wrench my arms out of their sockets and it's my opinion that's the reason why I've got such long ape-like arms today.

Another soul-destroying task was scrubbing the passage which ran the whole length of the house below stairs. I would start at the back door and end up a hundred yards later at the butler's office. My journey was broken by small flights of stairs and here I had to take particular care as Mr Pettit's eyes were most likely to fall there and if he noticed the slightest bit of fluff he'd ring the bell for me, and I was for it. He was a cun-ning bugger; his office was near the front door and knowing we could hear him as he came from there to the pantry, he'd sometimes take his boots off and walk in his stockinged feet expecting, even I think hoping, to find that we were up to no good. I was able to sort him out for a time. There was a loose tile under the rug outside his room; I ran a wire there and connected it up to a bell in the pantry so that when he left we were given a timely warning. I can still feel the pain on my backside when I recall the day he discovered it.

When we speak of elevenses today it's in terms of tea or coffee; this wasn't the case in service – then we were given beer and that included both male and female staff, and if it wasn't provided we had beer money in lieu. At Holland House the drawing and carrying of the ale was my province. Every day I would take the jacks to the cellar, fill them, carry one to the butler's room for Mr Pettit, the footman, the head gardener and the chauffeur; another I would take to the housekeeper's room, another to the kitchen, another to the housemaid's sitting-room, and a small one to the stillroom. Jacks came in various sizes; they were copper jugs wide at the base coming to a small opening at the lip, and their shape and metal helped to keep the beer cool. Those we had measured from a quart to a gallon and a half. The largest one was for the butler and his cronies. They weren't great drinkers and would often leave at least half of it, which had to be poured down the sink. There were always eight barrels in the cellar, four on tap and four set up. The beer was excellently kept by the odd man, it was the one job he did really well. He was up and down the cellar all day like a yo-yo tasting it to make sure it was in good condition – to the detriment I thought of his own.

One of the traditions which had been discarded at Holland House was the drill at mealtimes in the servants' hall. The steward's room was used by the senior staff for all the courses, and I was there to serve it. It was under the eagle eye of Mr Pettit that I learnt the art of serving, how to move, the correct distances to stand, how to manipulate the spoons, how to carry and serve sauces, indeed the hundred and one things that go to make a good waiter. When I first went there he would carve the joints, but later, realising that I was anxious to learn, he would make me stand by him and instruct me, then watch while I worked alone at the sideboard. Today I would challenge any man to a contest in carving, any that is except those wizards at Simpson's-in-the-Strand, that great traditional English food restaurant, where style and service are still in the grand old manner.

The trouble with being in the steward's room was that for some time I was half starved, for while I was there the other servants were having their meal in the servants' hall, and by the time I went to get mine there was precious little left. In order to survive I would steal bread from the stillroom and lock myself in the lavatory while I ate it. One day while I was clearing a beautiful York ham from the steward's room I found myself drooling over it. I gave way to temptation, carved two slices and was putting them under the wooden cover of the sink outside when Mr Pettit came from the room and caught me in the act. He exploded, 'What the hell do you think you're doing, boy!' I then knew how Oliver Twist must have felt, but Mr Pettit was more merciful than Mr Bumble. He let me tell my story, said he would investigate the matter and then admonished me for stealing, whatever the circumstances might be. It worked the trick, for from then on my food was portioned out with the others and put into an oven to keep warm. Sometimes when I'd finished serving he'd tell me to cut myself a slice or two to augment mine. In that way I got the best of both worlds.

The duty that I most enjoyed brought me into close contact with the countess. Every afternoon if the weather was fair I'd push her round the grounds in a wheelchair. The gardens were her pride and joy, for in her younger days she had designed them. Her particular favourite was the Chinese garden, where there were Yokka trees that had a magnificent bloom. It's a plant that only flowers every seven years but fortunately these had been so arranged that each year at least one would be in flower. She also loved the birds and whenever I had time I would go out before our walk and put down food for them to make sure that they would be there later for her to see. A particular favourite was an old cock pheasant and from the amount I gave him I reckoned that there couldn't have been a better fed bird in the whole of the country.

She would chatter to me on our way round about the past; how her husband had loved the place and of the work he had done on it and on their two other country homes Melbury and Abbotsbury. Melbury with its deer park and beautiful trees, and Abbotsbury with its swannery and sub-tropical gardens. How for her first party as a hostess she'd given a masked ball in Holland House, how it had surprised the staid Victorian society at the time but how popular they were later to become. She had wonderful descriptive powers and made the house and the grounds come alive to me. I found it a little strange that she never inquired about my home life. It was as if she only wanted to hear about the past.

She was a Fellow of the Zoological Society and on Sundays the zoo was reserved for Fellows only, and I would push her round Regent's Park. It was a great education for me as we were always accompanied by one of the head keepers, so that I learnt about many of the animals and their habits. On these trips we would take a bag of fruit, stale cakes and buns from the stillrom. Stale! They used to make my mouth water. I hope the elephants forgot and forgave me if they saw me pocketing one or two.

If I thought I was hard done by over food I was shortly to have an experience that changed my attitude. Not long after I had joined at Holland House I became friendly with the stillroom maid, Maisy Withers. She was a little Welsh girl, with the most glorious ginger hair and a pert manner that went with it. Whenever possible we would go out and explore London together. We loved to get a bus to Kew Gardens where we could rid ourselves of the smell of the town, by running wild and then lying together on the grass and breathing in God's good air. Later we would have a fish-and-chip meal at one of the many Joe Lyons' restaurants that then used to offer such good food and service, afterwards going to the movies or if I'd got a bit of extra money to a theatre in the West End.

As hall boy I had my 'perks'. Mine were the empty wine bottles and corks that, whenever guests or the young Lord Ilchester were in residence, came down from the dining-room. These had a second-hand value and every so often a man would call to collect them, giving me twopence or threepence a dozen for the bottles. Corks could bring in much more. All the wines we served were vintage and had the year and origin stamped on the corks. An exceptional year for champagne, clarets and ports could fetch as much as five shillings, and a good year one and six to two shillings. They were resold to villains, who put them into cheap bottles with forged labels, or to wine waiters at expensive hotels and restaurants. Wine waiters were expected to put the corks of the bottles at the side of the table for the host to see; so a tipsy host paid vintage prices for cheap wines. I put the money I got from these sales aside so that when Maisy asked me to go home with her for a week's holiday I was able to say 'yes', and to take a tidy sum with me as spending money.

She lived in Brynmawr, a small Welsh mining town. We caught a train from Paddington to Newport where her father met us and together we went up the Welsh valleys, through Ebbw Vale to Brynmawr. Maisy had six young brothers and sisters and two grown-up sisters, all living in a small miner's cottage. The thing that struck me immediately was its austerity and cleanliness. We had toast Friday night for supper, bread and margarine for breakfast and when Saturday lunch was served it was a plate of chips and nothing else. When Maisy and I went for a walk over the pit tips in the afternoon she said, 'Are you hungry?'

'Not half,' I replied. Then she explained that her father had silicosis and had been laid off from the mine, and was living on relief money.

'We're no worse off than most people though,' she said, 'there's been no regular work round here for years.' This then, I thought, accounted for the look of hopelessness on the faces of the men and women that I'd noticed.

'Never mind, love,' I said, 'I've got quite a bit of money with me, we'll give them a treat, we'll buy them a joint for Sunday lunch.' They of course called it dinner. We went into the town to the butchers and I asked for a leg of lamb.

He looked at me incredulously. 'I haven't got a leg of lamb, in fact I haven't seen a leg of lamb for God knows how long.' But he added hastily, 'I can get you one by Monday.'

I ordered it. 'What can you let us have now,' I asked.

'I've only got some scrag-end of beef, how much do you want, a quarter of a pound?'

When I asked for 2 lb he nearly fainted. His reaction was nothing to the reception we got from Maisy's mother. When we put it on the kitchen table in front of her she sat down on the chair just looking at it, with tears pouring down her cheeks.

'What on earth will she do when she sees that leg of lamb?' I later asked Maisy.

She did the same, and when her father saw the joint on the table he went down on his knees and prayed, and we and the rest of the family joined him. Never since then have I complained of being hungry or under-fed.

Maisy and I had a wonderful week bringing joy and life back into a home. Regularly when we were back in London we'd send some food parcels. I felt no shame now from scrounging anything from the kitchen, and if the birds or the animals at the zoo got fewer cakes and buns than before I felt it was in a good cause.

Although the job suited me and my wages were raised annually so that I was earning forty pounds plus my three suits, after I'd been at Holland House three and a half years I could see no future there for me. The footman showed no signs of moving and I wondered what would happen when the countess died, since I was sure that Lord Ilchester had no intention of ever making his home there. I decided that I'd start looking for a job as a footman and hoping that I might get some help from Mr Pettit, told him of my intention. I got the usual encouragement. 'You, a footman, you'll never make a footman's arse.' So I went to an agency.

Hunt's Regina was the high-sounding name of the one I used this time. I suppose they put the Regina bit in to give the impression that they dealt with royalty. The treatment that I got at my next job with Sir Colin and Lady Campbell at 14 Lowndes Square was anything but royal.

I went as hall boy/footman. Mr Pettit was right, I wasn't recognised as being fully fledged yet. My discomfort was not caused by my employers or by the butler, Mr Brooker, who was a kind and gentle man, but by the housekeeper. It was one of those places where the duties were ill-defined and no sooner had I started on one thing than I was called for and put on another. In that kind of position it was impossible to do anything well.

I had however succeeded in one thing that had been my ambition, I was now in livery. It was the only compensation the job held. Feeling no end of a dog I wrote home and told my mother. She must have felt a flush of pride at her son's achievement and so decided to come and see me in my fine feathers. One day while I was doing the morning chores the butler came down and said, 'Young man, there's a lady to see you. She came to the front door but I have directed her to the back.'

I went to the door, there was Mum; she took one look at me and gasped. I quickly realised why – there was I dressed in an old boiler suit, with coal smuts all over my face, a dirty cap on my head, looking like any scruffy labourer and she was expecting to see a little Lord Fauntleroy. Sir Colin wasn't pleased about my livery for when, after a few miserable months, I decided to give in my notice he was quick to point out that it had cost him the equivalent of a year's wages.

I was right to have decided to change jobs for I now joined the staff of a great lady and became associated with a fine family, the Sassoons. Lady Edward Sassoon was a widow of about seventy-two, with four granddaughters, only one of whom was married, so the house – 17 Belgrave Square – was often a busy one. It was my first contact with Jewish people and I was very impressed, particularly with the strength of their family ties; Sir Philip, whose house in Park Lane was renowned for its beauty and its wonderful parties, and Sir Victor Sassoon were constant visitors. We had regular family lunches of up to twenty-two people.

There was a good staff, Mr Austin the butler, myself and another footman, a chauffeur, an odd man, a chef, and two kitchen maids and a lady's maid. The house was run in style and the atmosphere was one of culture. The food and wine were superb. There were three silver services there, Kings silver, Kings gilt and Rat Tail Kings. The china was beautiful and there were services to provide forty settings, which ran into many hundreds of pieces. There is an idea among the uninformed that china was washed by scullery or kitchen maids and that breakages were frequent. In fact it never entered the kitchen. It was the province and the pride and joy of the housekeeper, and was cleaned by either the stillroom maids or housemaids, who were carefully superintended. If anything was broken it was as though there was a death in the house.

I'd now won my spurs and was a proper footman. For the first and last time I did box work; this expression was a hangover from the days of horses and carriages; instead of sitting beside the coachman, I sat next to the chauffeur, in full livery covered by a large military-styled coat in the winter and a light alpaca one in the summer. Like the chauffeur I also wore a cap and white gloves. I tried always to have my cap at an angle, I thought it gave me a kind of sang-froid; her ladyship didn't agree, she'd tap on the glass partition of the Rolls and say, 'George, please adjust your cap, it's crooked.'

She was very much one for the arts, so visits to the theatres, concerts and the opera were frequent. I was always in on the tail end of these because, as she had bad sight, she made arrangements with the management so that I was allowed in to fetch her from her seat to the car. At Covent Garden I would stand outside her box, often for the whole of the last act. I particularly remember listening to Grace Moore's death scene in *La Bohème*. On our return home I would escort her to her room where sandwiches and coffee were left for her. Generally she wasn't hungry, but instead of saying, 'I shan't want this,' which would have meant that I would have to return the tray to the kitchen, she'd say, 'I expect you could do something with it,' which meant that I could eat them if I wished. I always wished.

Another first happened for me while I was with Lady Sassoon, a visit to Lady Malcolm's servants' ball, which was held each year at the Albert Hall. It was a sort of two-way charity, the proceeds from the sale of tickets to our employers were given to charity and charity was visited on us when we were presented with the tickets. It was always a splendid night, a fancy dress ball. As well as allowing us entrance, our tickets entitled us to a certain number of drinks; we danced to a famous band, renewed old friendships and made many others. I was asked by many maids to go with them, and always refused. There were girls a-plenty and I didn't want a hanger-on sitting sulking on the side-lines because I was dancing with someone else. Inhibitions went with the wind and with Hyde Park as a sort of garden where dances could be sat out there were a number of servant girls who a few months later were regretting their employers' generosity.

As well as 17 Belgrave Square, Lady Sassoon had a pleasant house, Keythorpe, on the cliffs at Bournemouth. This made a welcome change for the servants; I'd like to say holiday but I can't because there were always a few visitors staying so there was valeting to be done and this, combined with regular lunch and dinner parties, meant more, not less work. It was from one of the gentlmen that I looked after that I received a tip in crowns. I kept them for a time and would show them to my colleagues. Unfortunately when Mr Lee later saw them he was able to top me by producing a handful of sovereigns and half sovereigns.

I stayed with Lady Sassoon for two years. It may seem strange that since I was so happy there I should want to move, but now I was at an age and at a stage of experience that I was considering my future. I was getting satisfaction from a good job well done, I realised what I had gained through working in service, I'd made up my mind that I would make it my career, had become accustomed to the disciplines that it demanded and had decided that the advantages far outweighed those of any other life that I could make for myself.

I wanted to get the various kinds of experience that would see me up the ladder. Butlers who were likely to be my employers for the next few years liked a man with a variety of experience, so it was better to have had three different places in six years rather than one.

It so happened that a footman friend of mine had just been appointed to his first position as butler; he wanted someone he knew and could trust as a single-handed footman, so I joined him at the house of Mr Leo d'Erlanger, the banker. It was to be a temporary appointment for six months or so only and would give me time to look around for my next place which I hoped would follow the pattern of the life I planned for myself.

Although it was smaller, Mr Leo's house, 44 Upper Grosvenor Street, had the style and beauty of Lady Sassoon's, and he showed similar kindness and courtesy to his servants, so my time there passed happily and uneventfully. I did have one mishap, what might be called the servants' nightmare, which taught me a lesson.

I'd been there about five weeks and was still feeling my way around. Mr Leo had two Venetian candelabra whose beauty and value were obvious to me, and I handled them carefully and nervously. One day I was carrying them to be cleaned, holding them tightly against my chest, and as I put them down in the pantry one of the arms caught in my waistcoat. It snapped, fell and broke into three pieces. I suffered every kind of torture as I waited for Mr Leo to return. I think my consternation must have been written across my face because when I went to speak to him he looked up and said, 'My dear George, whatever is the matter?' He seemed almost relieved when I told him. 'In a house of this kind where beautiful and valuable things are in everyday use breakages are bound to happen. I accept that risk, otherwise they would all be locked up in the safe, out of sight and giving happiness to no one. Show me the damage.'

I did so and he said, 'It's better than I had hoped. I shall send it to Venice to be repaired and when it returns neither you nor anyone will be aware that it has been broken.'

At the risk of giving offence to the ladies I found that most gentlemen were more understanding in such matters than they were. The lesson I learnt from this incident was never to handle things too carefully, be bold with them, but not foolhardy. It's strange, too, how when you've been in a house for a length of time the pieces that you deal with you tend to regard almost as your personal possessions – you speak of 'my' silver, my table, my candelabra and so on, so any loss or breakage is as much a wound to you as to its real owner.

After I'd been with Mr Leo for the promised six months I found what I hoped and thought was the ideal position to take me up the next rung of the ladder; I went as first footman to Lady Hulton at 50 Upper Brook Street.

Lady Hulton was the widow of Sir Edward Hulton, the newspaper proprietor, who owned amongst other things the *Evening Standard* and the *Picture Post*, at one time the most popular weekly magazine in the country. She kept a full staff for the London house, a butler, a footman, odd man, a housekeeper, two housemaids, a cook and two others in the kitchen, a lady's maid and two chauffeurs. Two chauffeurs I thought was going it a bit, an unnecessary luxury, but she kept them coming and going constantly and her son, Mr Edward, also used them from time to time. He didn't live with us but was always in and out of the house.

The butler had the unlikely name of Kitcat; there was a club in London of the same name but never before or since have I come across it as a surname. It was because of him that my duties were almost doubled.

He had the butler's complaint and was tipsy for the most part of the day, and almost invariably blotto after we'd served dinner. He was a married man and though his wife didn't live in the house with him he'd visit her once or twice a week. Heaven knows what happened when he did, for the day after he'd be in a complete coma. Her ladyship knew of his habits but couldn't bring herself to sack him. It was fellow-feeling in a way I imagine, because she was no mean drinker herself; champagne was her tipple, she took it throughout the day and night, but never did I see her the worse for it. She used a special champagne glass, one of a set of a dozen; it held half a bottle, it was something I had never seen before, nor have I since.

While I was with her ladyship I learnt the merits and demerits of wine. She entertained regularly and there were always three kinds served. She would ask me to select it and taste it with her and though there wasn't a large cellar (for she bought it more or less as it was drunk) she knew her wines, and imparted some of her knowledge to me. I think that in the past she must have done the same to Mr Kitcat which could have accounted for his present condition and her easy acceptance of it.

By now although I had by no means set the Thames on fire I was beginning to get a local reputation in Mayfair as a useful footman and waiter, and was occasionally asked to assist at big parties. This meant arranging evenings off which wasn't too easy with Kitcat so constantly on the wobble; still I managed it. A friend of mine, Leslie Wright, was butler to Lady Cunard of 7 Grosvenor Square and as she played Tinkerbell throughout the London season, going here, there and everywhere and giving a succession of parties, I would help him as often as I could. He would put me in charge of the wines which again increased my knowledge, and kept me out of sight. This was important since employers didn't like to hear of their servants working for anyone else. At other places I'd try to act as plate man, receiving and feeding back the dishes, glasses and silver from the other side of the green baize door; a man who knew what was going on outside the door and was ready to collect or deliver was worth two good waiters.

Lady Hulton kept a parrot as a pet. When I first joined her it lived in her boudoir; then there was some scare about a disease they spread so she banished it to the servants' hall; apparently it didn't matter if the servants got it, we were expendable. However I enjoyed its company. It was a good talker and a quick learner. It stood in the semi-basement window of the servants' hall from where it could look up to the pavement, and a good pair of lady's legs would earn a loud whistle. The local tarts would sometimes walk backwards and forwards past the window thinking, I suppose, that its calls attracted attention to them. I trained it use a few foul expressions and one day thought of getting it to take the micky out of Mr Kitcat. 'Go away you red-faced bastard,' I repeated to it, but getting no response, after a few days I gave up. Some time later Lady Hulton took it into her head to come down to the kitchen with a visitor; as she entered the servants' hall she said, 'Oh, there's Polly. Hello Polly, how are you?'

Bang on cue came, 'Go away, you red-faced bastard!'

Give her her due her ladyship didn't bat an eyelid, and said nothing more about the incident.

I enjoyed my time with Lady Hulton, life was pleasant, the food excellent and I thought I'd been able to come to terms with Mr Kitcat. I might have stayed on and got into a rut if her ladyship hadn't decided to go to Baden Baden for the waters there.

From the moment she left the house Kitcat went berserk. He sent for me and said, 'Her ladyship wishes me to give you a month's notice as from today.' Since I was sure that if she'd wanted me to leave she was the kind of person who would have told me herself, I immediately wrote to her. She replied by return and told me to ignore what he had said, and that she would attend to the matter on her return.

I communicated this information to Kitcat who went into a drunken rage. He became so intolerable that I knew I couldn't see my lady's holiday out without hitting him, and I decided to pack the job in.

I went round to Hunt's Agency, told them that I was tired of London and that I wanted a country place. This I knew would delight them as country positions were now getting harder to fill with everyone wanting to be among the bright lights. The woman behind the counter there leant forward conspiratorially as if she was going to tell me where I could find the buried treasure and said, 'We've got a Mr Collins interviewing for first footman for the Trees of Dytchley Park, Oxfordshire. It's a position I can thoroughly recommend.'

'All right,' I said, 'I'll see him.' She was right in her recommendation, it was an excellent position in a fine house, and I stayed there for five years. It was the beginning of my association with the Astors, for Mrs Tree was Lady Astor's niece, and I was to stay with the Astor family for the rest of my life in service.

I find it hard to know where to begin in describing Dytchley and the life and atmosphere there. Let me start by saying that the five years I spent there from 1935 to 1940 were the happiest of my life. Many things combined to make them so. We had an experienced and well-trained staff; Mr Collins the butler, a valet, two footmen (myself and another both equal first), a pantry man, an odd man and a hall boy.

Perhaps it's worth explaining here that a pantry man was engaged to make the lives of the footmen easier. He cleaned the silver, washed up the china and was responsible both to the butler and the housekeeper. He was seldom seen outside his pantry, but was invaluable since we were constantly entertaining.

Then there was a housekeeper, a head housemaid, with five others; a chef, two kitchen maids and a scullery man; a lady's maid; a head groom, Jack Boneham, and four under grooms, two chauffeurs and a house driver for the luggage bus; a head gardener, Mr Williams, and five or six others. The Trees also had a small London house at 28 Queen Anne's Gate, where there was a resident housekeeper.

As I've said it was a well-trained staff and a happy one, due in part to the butler. He had, as we say in service, started half way up the ladder; he'd been a batman to a Captain Jenkinson of the Life Guards, continued to valet for him when he left the service and eventually made his way to the top. He was smart, a good disciplinarian in the army manner, not afraid to take his coat off and help when it was needed. Mrs Hayes the housekeeper also played her part. She was a wonderful woman, full of fun but like any good mother would check our faults. She enjoyed a good laugh but would play hell with us if our antics got out of hand.

The person though who breathed her spirit into the house was Mrs Nancy Tree, who had been Mrs Marshall Field, wife of the president of the American chain store. Everyone adored her, perhaps the men more than the women. The picture of her sitting sidesaddle on her horse before a hunt, immaculate in her top hat and veil and wearing a blue coat and long skirt, is one I shall take to the grave with me, and if afterwards I see her looking the same I shall know I'm in heaven. Her beauty though wasn't just skin deep, she was wonderful to be with, she had superb taste, had been a professional interior decorator and the house gave evidence of her skill; the right things were put together in the right places. She had a perfect sense of period and in the blending of colours. The gardens were an expression of her personality.

She didn't confine her interest in the house just to herself and her friends. I remember when I first arrived at Dytchley and was shown my bedroom, I thought I had been put temporarily into one of the guest rooms. It had a fitted Wilton carpet, a comfortable bed with a matching chintz valance, bedspread and curtains, an antique chest, fitted wardrobe and wash basin, and of course central heating, an untold luxury for any servant's room at that time.

She commanded us all, but in such a charming way that made it impossible to refuse her anything that she asked. It was, 'Could you spare a moment', or 'Would you be so kind as'. She hardly ever rang a bell, she would telephone or try to find you. She really didn't give orders, only asked favours. But she was sharp. We used to say she was blessed with two brains not one, and that you needed roller skates to keep up with her. Her reputation as a hostess was reflected in the kind of guests that were entertained.

Well I've never written a reference for an employer before, and looking back over what I have said it would be hard to give a better one, yet I mean every word of it.

Mr Ronald Tree was to my mind the perfect partner for her, yet sadly the marriage was to end in divorce; it was after I had left them. He was a member of parliament who took his duties seriously. He gave many political parties which were attended by the highest in the land. What time he had to spare was given to hunting and shooting. When previously he had lived at Kelmarsh in Northamptonshire, he had been master of the famous Pytchley Hunt, but now owing to the pressure of his duties he contented himself with occasional appearances with the Heythrop. We kept fourteen hunters and a pair of high steppers, which Mrs Tree would drive in her phaeton. It was now that I began to learn how to clean hunting gear.

My first customer as it were was Mr Roach, the Trees' agent. He wore black with whipcord breeches. It was when I graduated to pink that my worries started, for one slip and a coat can be ruined, since it's about the most expensive garment that a gentleman wears; a ruined coat leads to an unpopular servant. On a wet day or with the going heavy spots of dirt speckle the back of a coat. This causes the pink to go black when it's cleaned, as a result I believe of the kind of dye that is used, so that after the spots on a coat have been scrubbed in soft water and every bit of mud removed it has to be treated with a renovator, a pink liquid which is bought at a saddlers. It sounds easy enough but if the coat got the slightest bit damp before it was on the rider's back the spots went black again. Many's the sleepless night I've had worrying whether a coat was going to be pink or measly the next morning. On occasions I've got up and sneaked down to have a look.

If a coat came back filthy dirty I'd put it on a clothes hanger with two largish stones in the pockets, plunge it into a rainwater butt, leave it to soak for a couple of minutes, then hang it above the butt and brush it down with a large dandy brush. The process would be repeated several times until the dirt was completely removed and the water was running away clean from the jacket. I'd then remove the stones, hang it outside until it had drained sufficiently, and put it in the drying room where it would drip and slowly dry. It had to be examined every so often because if it became the slightest bit creased it would stay like it for ever. The jacket couldn't be worn the next day of course but those gentlemen who hunted regularly would bring two sets. White breeches I would wash in Lux soapflakes. The chamois would be treated with a cloth ball or, if they were white, sprinkled with a yellow powder and then beaten with a little stick until the surplus dust was removed, for otherwise it would fall on to the boots.

Boots were cleaned in the way that soldiers have done them over the centuries, by spit and polish. First I would put blacking over the boot, then polish it. After, with a finger in a cloth, I'd begin again this time mixing spit with the polish rubbing it in a circular manner until there was an even shine all over the boot. With a bone from the foreleg of a deer, the shin bone, I would then rub them all over and give a final polish with a cloth. It took time, particularly with a new pair of boots, but it was a job which, like the others I have described, gave a deal of satisfaction when on the following day I saw my gentlman mounted on a horse that had been as carefully groomed as himself, looking as handsome a picture as he could be made to look. People will laugh at me I know, and find it impossible to understand my feelings, but we did in those days get pleasure out of a job well done however menial it might seem, and it was appreciated.

After I'd been with the Trees for three years I was promoted to valet. It was the appointment I had wanted, for by now I had the urge to travel and I particularly wanted to see the United States. It was an ambition that I was not to realise, for in 1938 war clouds were gathering and Mr Tree's parliamentary duties now kept him in Britain; so my journeys with him were confined to frequent visits up and down to our house in London.

I now saw more of my master, and I liked what I saw. We were friendly without being intimate. I think some servants like to pretend that they knew their employers' innermost thoughts and were their confidants and advisers as well as their valets. This was never my experience, nor would I have wanted it to be. It's my belief that the less personally involved you are the better you do your job. Of course I got to know certain details about both Mr and Mrs Tree's lives, but it didn't affect my attitude towards them. It only takes a look into one's own life to realise that none of us is anywhere near perfect. There's a saying that no man is a hero to his valet; of course it's true but it would be bloody dreary serving a hero all the time. You get a mutual understanding and trust between you and if you're sensible you leave it there.

When the Second World War came it brought changes; some immediate, some slow. I was exempt from military service because of my twisted foot, and others of the inside staff were not required for the first two or three years. Those maids that went into industry were replaced with dailies. One wing of the house was taken over by a nursery school, but it moved after about a year. It was in November 1940 that a top-level decision was made in London that was to affect all our lives.

The facts that later emerged were these; that German reconnaissance planes had flown over Chequers, the Prime Minister's, Mr Winston Churchill, weekend home and political headquarters. Some bombs had already fallen near by and it was feared that a heavy air attack might be launched on it. It was also thought that these would only be possible when the moon was full and visibility was good. It had been suggested by the Prime Minister's advisers that it would be sensible to have alternative accommodation at this time and Dytchley, which was not too far from London, was thought to be the right place.

We weren't given much warning. I think it was on a Tuesday that a dispatch rider came to the door and handed a message to Mrs Tree. That must have been the first she knew about it for immediately the house was all bustle. The servants were assembled, sworn to secrecy – I think it was on pain of death – and then given their details. The great man was to arrive on Friday and by then everything had to be ready, not just for Mr and Mrs Churchill but for his personal staff and any visitors that might be called over the weekend. As well as this there was to be a contingent of soldiers from the Oxfordshire and Buckinghamshire Light Infantry to act as a guard, but they were not to know who or what they were guarding. I later discovered they were taken out in buses with blinds fitted and drawn, driven for miles around the countryside before they were finally delivered to Dytchley, so that they would be completely baffled as to where they were.

Workmen descended on the house; telephones were installed, the kitchen went mad, and the rest of the staff were on their knees by the time Friday came. We had to get up and dust them off at teatime when Mr Churchill arrived, and we must have found some hidden strength for we were kept on our toes until he left.

The visits, sometimes fortnightly, sometimes monthly, developed into a routine. Often it was my job to valet for the Prime Minister. He would arrive, generally with Mrs Churchill and sometimes with his daughter, Mary, at around five o'clock, have a cup of tea or a whisky while chatting to the family and those guests who had already arrived. Then he'd go to his bedroom, get undressed and into a nightgown, the long sort that came down around his ankles, and sleep until eight when it was time for me to dress him for dinner. He wasn't a fastidious eater, indeed I sometimes would wonder how he managed to get anything down for he could be a constant talker, and of course he held court. If the news was particularly bad, and there wasn't a lot that was good in those days, it was reflected in his moods, and at times he would sit staring in front of him making no attempts to be sociable. During dinner he would generally drink champagne and afterwards a brandy or a whisky. Whisky was his main tipple. The house smelt of his cigars, but I think he used them more as a symbol than as a smoke, for often they would be unlit or put to one side when he'd had no more than a few puffs.

After dinner when the men joined the ladies, they assembled in the library where they would talk the night away. The ladies would gradually disappear and eventually The Man himself would go to his room at around one or two in the morning.

There were several C.I.D. people around the place and although I suppose they were only doing their job they seemed an officious lot to me. I had a brush one morning with their controller, a chap called Thompson. I was taking breakfast up to Mr Churchill's bedroom – he liked a hearty early-morning meal, bacon and eggs or a cold partridge, something substantial – and as I was going through his door, Thompson made towards me and lifted the silver cover from the dish. This riled me as he knew well what and who I was. 'What did you expect to find under there, a bloody bomb?' I asked in a stage whisper. He gave me one of those nasty looks that all coppers have which means 'You wait till I get you inside', then he let me pass. I thought I'd only spoken quietly but there was Mr Churchill sitting up in bed grinning from ear to ear. He'd heard what I had said but he winked at me and under his breath he said, 'I wish I could have said that.'

Tradition or rumour has it that Churchill drank continuously. I didn't notice it; he liked his whisky but there wasn't a glass in his hand permanently as many people think. Heavy drinkers liked to believe that he did so as to excuse their own habits, just as dunces like to say that he was a poor scholar at Harrow.

Although his visits meant a deal of hard work the staff looked forward to them because of the films that were shown while he was with us – he was movie mad. Two projectors were rigged up in the big front hall and every Saturday evening, and sometimes on Sundays, they would be in action. It was in his company that I saw *Gone with the Wind*, all four hours of it straight through.

We were visited by the top brass of the services and the Cabinet. It was good to see these very important people looking quite ordinary as they hung about waiting for an audience, with the most important person. Guests that were staying in the house generally included Brendon Bracken, Anthony Eden, Duff Cooper, Oliver Lyttleton and later Averil Harriman – Roosevelt's special representative in London. Another American visitor was Harry Hopkins and rumour has it that he paved the way for Lend-Lease whereby Britain was able to get war supplies without actually paying for them.

General Sikorsky, the then Prime Minister of Poland, was another who came to Dytchley. Apparently he and Churchill hit it off for it was decided that the guard should be turned out in his honour. The officer in charge was sent for but couldn't be found (poor bugger!), so Mr Churchill rushed out of the house, into the men's quarters and called them out himself. This sent the C.I.D. chaps sky high and hopping mad; there they'd been taking all possible precautions to see that the troops didn't know who or what they were guarding and he just walked straight in on them and showed himself. I understand one private fainted when he saw him, apparently he'd been drinking the night before and thought he'd got the D.T.s.

Despite the fact that we were kept running by the C.I.D. chaps, I and some of the other servants could have learned something about future events. For my part I heard as little as

I could on the principle that the less you know the less you are likely to tell by mistake. We were, as I've said, sworn to secrecy for life and I wouldn't now be telling my tale if Mr Tree hadn't written about it recently. Since that time it has come up in conversation with my friends and always they ask, 'What was he like?' and my answer is, and will always always be the same, 'Just like Winston Churchill.'

I've made little mention of my social life. I did of course have occasional skirmishes with the ladies but any idea of a permanent relationship had always to be quickly dispelled because of my work. It was not possible to be married as a footman, nor as a valet, but the time was approaching when I knew I could be considered for a butler's appointment and this permitted a wife, and in a country house a cottage on the estate. I wasn't looking for trouble but it was satisfying to know that if I did fall in love I could allow a relationship to grow.

It was a year or so before the war that my eye fell on someone to whom I was immediately attracted. It wasn't love at first sight or anything so romantic as that, but I met a lady whom I noticed straight away, and found my thoughts turning to. Mrs Tree had advertised for a new lady's maid and when I opened the door to an applicant I found it was Freda Rampton, whom I'd met and 'noticed' when she was working for Mrs Tree's sister, Mrs Reggie Winn. She was appointed and we became better acquainted. I use the word acquainted for it was a long time before I could pluck up courage to convey my feelings towards her. I was attentive and went out of my way to do little things for her. When I was appointed valet to Mr Tree we were on an equal social footing so I was able to relax in my attitude and leave it to time to ripen our friendship. She was six years older than I was which, while it didn't lessen my affection for her, I found made for a slight barrier between us.

I remember the day when I knew she was the only one for me. She was accompanying Mrs Tree to America and I'd wangled it so that I took her and the luggage to Victoria station. As I put her on the train for Southampton I thought, 'This is the moment for you to declare yourself', but I hadn't the courage and I cursed myself for a fool as the train drew out. The moment I got back to Dytchley I wrote her a letter. I couldn't express my feelings, I simply said that I hoped she'd had a pleasant trip, had arrived safely and that if she had a moment to spare I would be glad to know how she was getting on and the things she was doing.

She kept my letter, and I have it to this day. I watched every post and eventually my patience was rewarded. Her letter like mine was written in a formal sort of style. It was a long time after she had returned from the States before I asked her if she would marry me. 'No,' she said, 'if I did I should be accused of baby snatching.' Nothing I could say would budge her.

'Is there no hope for me then?'

'If you ask me again in five years' time, then I will say yes.'

I made a note of the date. Five years later to the day I telephoned her at Dytchley, for by then I had left, and asked, 'Do you know what day it is today?'

'Yes, Thursday,' she replied.

I then enlightened her. 'Five years ago today I asked you to marry me. You said then that if I felt the same way in five years' time I was to ask you again and you would say "yes". I am asking you. Can you keep your promise?'

And back came the word I'd been hoping for. I had of course seen her from time to time, not very frequently, but never referred to the bond we'd made. Shortly after our conversation she left Dytchley and joined me in Oxford. We're still together and speaking for myself in absolute sincerity, and not for the sake of my story, it was the best thing I ever did in my life.

I have said that within those five years I'd left Dytchley. It was because of the war. Somehow the sight of servants in uniform returning on leave to pay their respects to Mr and Mrs Tree made me conscious of the fact that I was doing little to further the war effort. In retrospect I'm inclined to think differently but at the time I wanted a closer involvement. So in 1942 I applied to and was accepted into a factory in Oxford that was making ammunitions of every kind. I thought of it as a way of getting out of domestic service because if I could succeed in industry I could say goodbye to it for ever. I was still conscious that being in service was almost a slur on my masculinity. Again if I could get away from it I would be in a better position to ask Freda to marry me. I still believe that my motives were right. It was the events that followed it that were not.

I passed my preliminary training period with flying colours and did well on the factory floor. It was in my relationship with my fellow workers that I experienced difficulty. They were good men but I had little in common with them. Unconsciously perhaps I'd developed a cultural approach to life. I'd been surrounded by fine things and in the company of people who appreciated them, and I found that these things had no place in the lives of the people I was now mixing with. If I was to succeed in industry my next step up the ladder would have been to the job of foreman; to be a good foreman meant having a complete understanding and identity with the men under you and this I knew I could never have. It wasn't a realisation that came to me straight away, of course, it developed over the months and years. The excitement and thrill of marriage kept my thoughts occupied for some time, but eventually it returned stronger than ever, because in order the better to make ends meet I returned to Dytchley at weekends to help out with parties.

With the end of the war and things returning to a kind

of normal, requests for these weekend services became more frequent. I was a constant visitor to Bletchington Park in Oxfordshire, the home of Mr William Astor, Lord and Lady Waldorf's son and heir. I was also invited to Cowdray Park, Lord Cowdray's place in Midhurst, Sussex, the great polo playing centre. It was there I met Mr Mountbatten, a young lieutenant in the navy, who was later to marry Princess Elizabeth, and later still to become the Queen's consort.

These glimpses of the old life added fuel to the fire of my dissatisfaction with my present situation, but like the stubborn fellow that I still often am I refused to admit defeat. There were three things that eventually changed my mulish attitude. First the trades union. During the war I'd been graded as a skilled worker but, as the men returned from the forces, I found myself down-graded to semi-skilled, yet there I was having to teach those who were designated as my superiors how to do their jobs. Then there was our landlady, who realising that she could get more money for our flat, did everything in her power to make life as miserable as possible for us in the hope that we would move. Then thirdly, as if in answer to my unspoken prayers, came a letter from Mr William Astor's London butler, Mr Coller, asking if I would go as butler/valet to Bletchington.

I accepted by return of post and on 26th October 1950 I started work and spent two happy years there with a small but efficient staff and in our own home – a flat on the estate. It was during this time that young William Astor was born who was eventually to become the fourth viscount.

On Lord Waldorf Astor's death in 1952, my Mr Billie, as I now familiarly referred to him, succeeded to the title and the estates. My position now became somewhat difficult because with everything else he inherited Mr Lee – 'Lord Lee of Cliveden'. I had of course by now met him several times and respected and admired him. Some sort of verbal arrangement was come to whereby he and I shared command. He had, I know, wanted to retire but it was almost as if he had become an institution, as if the Astor family felt that if he left, the walls of Cliveden would fall down and the tribal feeling which they had would disappear, so he was persuaded to stay.

Mr Lee and I are now great friends and have discussed the past together after his eventful retirement, so I know he will understand when I say that for much of the time our relationship wasn't easy. To some extent it was the old versus the new, but not entirely for I was able to learn much from him. Nevertheless no ship can have two captains, so on occasions we did clash. The house however was well run, for one thing he and I had very much in common was our respect for Lord Billie. It was a pleasure to work for him and to work in the old tradition. I, of course, now came into frequent contact with one whom I found a great old battle axe, Lady Astor, and her by now equally famous and hard-hitting maid and companion, Rosina Harrison. I add the word companion because their relationship bore no resemblance to that of lady's maid and mistress. Indeed at times it was difficult to tell who was what, except for Rose's strident Yorkshire accent.

I now also got to know other renowned servants, like Gordon Grimmett, who was often willing to come to Cliveden and help with dinner parties, Charles Dean, now Lady Astor's butler, and Arthur Bushall, who'd been valet to Lord Waldorf and was now residing with Mr David Cerbor in a semi-retired capacity.

It was Arthur who came nearer to creating absolute havoc at a dinner party than any footman I have ever known. He was serving the vegetables. On his way round a lady looked at them and said, 'What kind of beans are those?'

'Farting beans, madam,' replied Arthur, without batting an eyelid.

'Aow,' she went on, 'where do they come from?'

'Down under, madam.'

'Aow,' she said, 'I'll have some of them.'

Then she addressed her husband in a loud voice across the table, 'Harry, dahling, you must try these, they're fahtin' beans, they come from Australia,' and she held one up on a fork.

All the waiters and footmen, including myself, rushed to the servery and curled up. According to Mr Lee, who was the only one to stand at his post, there was a deathly hush at the table with people staring in disbelief at the wretched lady. Then someone made a half-hearted funny remark apropos of nothing and the table dissolved into laughter, as if it had been the joke of the season. With a younger servant Mr Lee would probably have sacked him there and then, but as it was Arthur he was just reprimanded. 'It's pointless me saying anything,' Lee said to me later, 'Arthur is Arthur and he'd do the same thing again tomorrow if he was given the opportunity.'

I was with Lord Billie for fifteen years, and three wives. With this branch of the Astor family butlers stayed with the house. Unlike the older servants the changes and decay in standards of service came as no shock to me, and I was able to accept, even anticipate, them. With so many other opportunities in the world outside men and women were unlikely, indeed unable, to accept the disciplines and the hours of work. Mr Lee and I managed to keep a fair team but we couldn't rely on people and it was pathetic to see someone of Mr Lee's stature, a man accustomed to commanding an army of servants, having to roll up his sleeves and do menial jobs which he felt had to be done, and which no one else would do. Employers changed too, they became more easy-going, tolerant, friendly and approachable. The attitude of visitors was also different, many were unaccustomed to the ways of trained servants and were unsure in their manner towards us.

In 1962 Mr Lee finally retired and I was now completely in control. Despite the decline in standards I've spoken about I looked forward to many more happy years at Cliveden, but my hopes were not to be fulfilled.

In the following year the Profumo affair, as it's come to be known, broke on a salacious British public. Lord Billie it was that had introduced Mr Profumo to Christine Keeler, so, because he was a peer and possibly because Cliveden brought back memories of the 'Cliveden set', which according to one sensational news sheet, *The Week*, and taken up by other papers, had been active in encouraging a policy of appeasement towards Hitler, he was branded a ponce.

He was tried and sentenced by the public on no evidence at all. The good he had done, for he'd supported many causes personally and financially, was forgotten. He became a broken man, a sick man. From that time onward until his death he was an invalid in mind and body. Stephen Ward, one of the central figures in the case, killed himself. My Lord Billie became infected by it and died in March 1966.

It didn't do my health any good either, for while the scandal was at its height I was bombarded by newsmen, most of whom offered bribes for my story. One opened a case full of notes and said that, if I would give him the full low-down, and signed that whatever he printed was the truth, the money was mine. For the first time since I was a boy I hit someone.

The three years after the event were sad, sad times that I do not wish to recall. The year following Lord Billie's death was an empty one. Cliveden was entailed to the National Trust, but the furniture and the contents of the house were put up for auction. I was in the position of caretaker, and a wretched job it was, watching the things I, and many of my kind before me, had lived with and grown to love over the years being treated as 'lots' and given numbers. When the first day of the sale came the press descended on us again. This time one of them got the story right; 'The Broken Hearted Butler' was his headline.

I was now at a crossroads, where was I to go next? I naturally helped the third Lady Astor to arrange her domestic affairs but I knew she would not require my services. I think many people thought I would take a pub; I'd often spoken of it, but I decided on reflection against it.

I had a number of offers to go as butler to other houses; I considered these but thinking of myself almost as one of the Astor family, one of the tribe, there was a person I had to consult; the new Lord William. He was still at school at Eton, though nearing the end of his time there. I telephoned his house master, Mr Gardener, and asked permission to take his young lordship out to tea as I wanted to discuss a private matter with him. This was granted and I put the direct question, 'Do you want me to serve you?'

His immediate reply was 'Yes.'

I moved to Ginge Manor, Wantage, to look after William and his mother, who was by now the Honourable Mrs Baring. When the time came for Lord William to take over his own house I stayed with him at Ginge, still as butler, but not a very exalted one, for now I have to set my hand to everything and anything. Never mind, I am still a member of the tribe.

## Some Reflections on George's Story

George I might have described as a middle period servant, but his experience at Holland House puts him rather into an earlier category and gives him a place among his peers. In a sense it was a macabre kind of a job, working for work's sake, digging a hole and filling it in again, for there was no end result to be seen. This clinging to the old world was, and perhaps still is, something that is typical of English society, and not just high society. Trade unions behave similarly when they insist that a job should be manned by a certain number of men, even though they know that half of them will have nothing to do. There is of course a slight difference, for the money that such an arrangement costs is not theirs – it belongs to their wretched employers.

George's experience with Churchill I heard for the first time just as I was starting on this book. I find this extraordinary because Mrs Tree, or Mrs Lancaster as she became by her subsequent marriage, and Lady Astor were constant friends and companions until my lady's death. If she knew at that time, or later, it has proved something that I would never have believed, that Lady Astor could keep a secret.

George's almost hero-worship for Mrs Tree was in my experience justified, though I as a woman might have qualified it a bit. She was in many ways a younger version of my lady, though more predictable, less demanding and grateful for good service. She had not however quite the strength of character, the mercurial wit or the bite of Lady Astor.

To these people that believe servants only stayed in service under sufferance, George's anxiety during the war to get away from it will come as a justification of their opinion. His is not a fair example. Almost any man worth his salt was fired at the time by a sense of patriotism and a hatred of fascism, and wanted to be seen to be doing everything in their power to overthrow Hitler. George had in addition a deep-seated resentment of his physical disability, and I believe was anxious to prove to himself and the world that he could conquer it. He succeeded in part for some years but full success was denied him by circumstances and union rules.

It was when George went to Cliveden on Lord Waldorf's death that I got to know him well, for although Lady Astor and I were no longer in residence we were frequent visitors. That he and Mr Lee were able to share command there for so many years is a tribute to them both. I know it wasn't easy but it was interesting for me to compare their methods and their skills.

The mention of skills brings to mind a particular trick of George's. He made use of the two pockets that there are in the tails of a dress jacket. I've seen him slip two or three bottles of wine in them and despite his game foot carry them around unnoticed, slipping them out like a conjurer when they were required. He could even carry a jug of cream in a livery coat pocket without ever spilling a drop.

As trained servants became more rare, and 'anyone will have to do' the order of things, George became impatient. He says he was able to accept change more easily than Mr Lee. I'm not sure that he is right. 'Father's' attitude was more one of sorrow than of anger, a kind of resignation. George, who'd risen to his position by diligence and hard work, reacted strongly to anything he considered as laziness. On the other hand, to those who wanted to learn he showed great patience. There was a young Italian who came as a footman, who was raw to the English way of doing things, but was keen. George trained him to the highest of his own standards. About three years after the boy had left, George received an invitation to the opening of a new restaurant from him, shortly after followed another for a second restaurant, and later yet another, for the opening of an hotel. In each case this Italian laid his success at George's door.

After Cliveden was broken up and sold he showed great

loyalty to the family. When he moved to Ginge Manor with the young Lord Billie, the wheel had turned full circle. George had only dailies to do the cleaning of the house so he was back as hall boy, odd man, footman, butler, and chef all rolled into one.

# A FRIEND IN SERVICE

*Peter Whiteley*

I now come to the last of my friends who have contributed to this book. Peter Whiteley is definitely one of what my other colleagues and I call the 'new lot'. It sounds disparaging, in some cases it is meant to, but not in his.

I met him first when he was comparatively new in service at Michael Astor's home, Bruern Abbey. I must admit I didn't notice him very much at that time. It was later when I was visiting Cliveden and Mr Lee spoke about an excellent young footman he'd acquired that I pricked up my ears, for that sort of remark from 'Father' at that time was rare indeed. With my Yorkshire caution I watched Peter's behaviour in the servants' hall before getting into conversation with him. He seemed to enjoy people; he was a bit of an extrovert, but it wasn't long before his stories and impersonations had me in stitches.

When we talked together he told me of his ambitions and hopes for the future, and he listened as I related something of my past life. 'It's no use beating about the bush, Miss Harrison,' he said, 'the age of elegance is past, I shall have to settle for something else. When I've gained the necessary experience I shall cram as much variety into my life as I can. Servants are no longer two a penny so if I don't like a place, or find it dull, I shall move on.' That's what he's done. He has only related part of his life in service to me, skipping jobs here and there.

I saw him from time to time on his visits to Mr Lee, for their friendship has lasted and whenever Peter finds himself near Eastbourne he goes to see 'The Master' as he calls him.

I also remember when I was at Grimsthorpe Castle (I'd come out of retirement to help my Miss Wissie (Lady Ancaster)) he told me of a final ambition of his – to write his autobiography. I hope therefore that my story of parts of his life may be a taste of better things to come.

# VI

# THE ODD MAN'S STORY
## Peter Whiteley

I was born on 17th August 1930, the same day as Princess Margaret. I don't know what that makes me but apart from 1066 it's the only historical date I can remember. I arrived at a cottage in the village of Syston in Leicestershire.

At the time my father worked as a clerk in the town of Leicester, but his early life had been spent in service as a footman in one of the many country houses around, and later in London where he was carriage footman to Lady Playfair, a famous figure of the time. She was of great height, the hostess with the mostest, a pillar of society, with a mania for big hats. Dad said that it was pointless him standing on the back of the carriage when they went driving because he was almost completely hidden; as his fellow footmen unkindly said, his best-known feature was his backside.

Mum, who had met my father when she was in service in Leicestershire, joined him in London and was parlour maid and occasionally cook to Lady Playfair, whom she found difficult to serve – the sort of woman who went around the house picking up things to see if they had been cleaned underneath. Life must have been hell for her lady's maid, for when she travelled she couldn't make up her mind what to take with her; Mum kept getting letters asking her to send things that she later found she required, but since her handwriting was as illegible as a doctor's prescription these generally went unanswered and unattended.

When Dad enlisted during the First World War Mum returned to Syston, where she has been ever since. I was a late arrival. According to her I was born with an apron on for I always enjoyed working around the house doing the cleaning, making the beds and washing up. I went to the local village school and then to the secondary school for the area. I wasn't much good as a scholar but I came into my own whenever we put on a concert or school play. I took piano lessons for six years, quickly reaching a mediocre standard and then staying there. Handel's Largo was my piece. Whenever a list was being made out for the school concert a teacher would end by saying, 'Then we'll have Peter playing Handel's Largo.' I was what they called a useful fill-in.

I loved the drama and my happiest moments were spent in the theatre or cinema. Long before I left school I decided I was going to be an actor; I hadn't any training and couldn't afford it, so when I was fifteen I hung around the stage door of the Theatre Royal of Leicester. Eventually I got a foot in and was engaged as a temporary stage hand – it proved very temporary. I lasted a fortnight, the run of *Rebecca of Sunnybrook Farm*.

It was necessary for me to earn money, so with the smell of grease paint still in my nostrils, I joined as an assistant in the stores of a pram factory, and spent my days carrying prams down a narrow staircase to load on lorries. Not very inspiring work but I made the best of it, joking around and camping it up to the amusement of my mates, but not of the foreman. I must have made some sort of impression because one day a girl in the packing department came to me and said,

'Have you ever done any acting?'

'A little,' I said guardedly. 'Why?'

'Well, we're doing a pantomime, *Cinderella*, this Christmas, and one of the ugly sisters has gone ill.'

'You saucy little cow,' I broke in.

'Well, what did you expect, Cinder bleeding ella?' She was one of those quick ones. 'No seriously,' she went on, 'it's a good part and I'm sure you'd enjoy it. Why don't you come along and see the producer tonight?'

I went, accepted it and though I say it myself I was a near riot, so much so that I got a female impersonation act together and made quite a name for myself in the village halls around Leicester as a sort of local Danny La Rue. I found however that there's a lot of jealousy, even in the amateur world, so I decided to retire, gave my definitely final public appearance, and disappeared from the theatre for ever.

Meantime I'd moved jobs. I was now working in a cardboard box factory. It was all the stairs of the pram place that decided me. 'I must go somewhere where there's a lift,' I declared one day when I'd bruised my knuckles for the umpteenth time trying to avoid a nasty fall. I was soon to regret the reason for my decision to leave. One afternoon at the box factory we had a power cut, and there I was in the lift caught between two floors. I went hot and cold all over.

'Get me out of here,' I screamed. Someone tried to wind me down but the gears jammed. I was really sweating now and getting claustrophobia. A number of women who should have been making boxes clustered around giving unhelpful and vulgar suggestions. They compared me with various animals in the zoo, to my detriment. In retrospect I suppose it was a bit of a riot but it put me off lifts for life.

The women factory hands became the bane of my life. Talk about the fair sex. I found that carrying boxes was more hazardous than carrying prams; prams I could hoist on my back and so see where I was going and what other people were doing; boxes however were piled on to my arms, often covering my face, and as I moved off down the factory floor my body became a target for the women. No part of my anatomy was sacred and I had thought that pinching was something that dirty old men did. I'd arrive home black and blue. So, since I couldn't see myself making a career there I soon packed it in; my spirit might have been willing but my flesh was weak.

It was now that I decided to try domestic service, rough work, I thought, would be better than rough treatment, so I dressed up in my glad rags and took a day off and a trip to London. I decided to try and start a little way up the ladder as a footman, so I tried to look the part. I went to an agency I'd written to in South Audley Street in Mayfair, run by a Mrs Sandiman. I was inquiring from the girl in the outer office about vacancies when she came through. Not a very prepossessing person – of uncertain age, with a mop of tinted red hair, she was mutton dressed up as lamb. She looked me up and down,

'What on earth does he want?' she said to the assistant.

I felt my blood rising,

'He's come to see if there's a post as a footman,' said the receptionist. Madam Sandiman started to giggle,

'He looks like something that's stepped out of the eighteenth century.' That did it. I blew my top.

'Madam,' I said, 'I'm no more out of the eighteenth century than the hennaed hair of yours is red at the roots. Good day to you.' As I slammed the door the glass shivered, I thought it would shatter. 'That,' I thought to myself, 'is the nearest you will get to life in service, Peter.'

I was wrong. Mrs Sandiman must have been a bigger woman than I had taken her for; about a week later I received a letter from her agency offering me the job of odd man to a Mr and Mrs Coriat, at a house near Malmesbury in Wiltshire, at a salary of seven pounds a week. It wasn't what I'd hoped for but it was a start, and I accepted.

Mrs Coriat was aged between thirty and thirty-five when I joined. By a previous marriage she had been Lady Curzon, 'of the Keddleston Hall lot' I was told in the servants' hall. Lord Curzon was a motor racing driver, better remembered today by his later title, the Earl of Howe. Mrs Coriat's father, Sir Archibald Weigall, lived in a lodge at the end of the drive. He was to do with Maples the furniture store in Tottenham Court Road, and had previously lived at Englemere, the grand country house near Ascot. If ever Mrs Coriat got a bit uppity with the servants we would say,

'Definitely the wrong end of Tottenham Court Road this morning, my dear.'

Some of the servants were as well connected as the family. Mr Reginald Clement, the butler, had been a footman with Princess Marina, Duchess of Kent, at Belgrave Square, and the nanny, Valerie Smith, had brought up Princess Alexandra and the young princes at Coppins. We also had a parlour maid, kitchen maid and a lady's maid, Miss Donovan. 'Slippers' we called her because she was never out of them. There were dailies to do the cleaning and myself to do the rough work, the boots and shoes, the coals and logs, the scrubbing of passages, the dirtier washing up; you name it I did it.

Then of course there was the cook, or cooks I should say because we had an endless procession of them. There must have been fifty or so passing in and out of that kitchen in the four years that I was there. Cooks were definitely Mrs Coriat's blind spot. She got on well with the rest of the staff and heaven knows she tried her best with the cooks. They came in all sorts and sizes, Scottish, Irish, German, French, tall, short, fat and thin. They had one almost universal complaint, they suffered with bad legs; 'It's me legs', was their excuse to get me running around for them. One Scottish woman arrived dressed in a long black frock, looking like Queen Victoria. When Mrs Coriat came down to see her she stopped a bit short in her tracks.

'I know what you're looking at, madam, but I have to wear it because of my present from Hitler.' And she pulled her skirt up to her drawers to show us how parts of her legs had been blown away by a bomb. 'I had two hundred stitches in them,' she went on proudly.

'Quite a little needle woman your doctor,' I thought, as I moved away feeling slightly sick.

Another arrived in the kitchen with a wooden box under her arm; she put it by the table and stood on it, which was just as well for without it she couldn't see over the top! Yet another arrived with seven trunks, all dead weight – I should know I had to carry them up to her room. My first impression of her was that she was a merry old soul with sparkling bright eyes. It wasn't surprising, as I shortly found out, since she could lower a bottle of gin before lunch. The trunks contained the booty she had made off with from her last job. It didn't last all that long because soon when Mrs Coriat queried the grocer's bill she found that she had been paying for enough gin to keep a ship's company happy on a three-month tour of duty.

Another came with her own set of knives, one of which she tried to use on 'Slippers', the lady's maid, whom she'd taken against one Christmas Day. We managed to lock her in her room, from the window of which she threw her Christmas presents, all removables and some foul oaths. The family doctor arrived and it was obvious that he'd been enjoying his Christmas. He sobered up fast when he saw what he was expected to deal with. He tried putting the needle in her, got bitten for his pains and sent for an ambulance with a crew of three, who arrived looking as people feel when they're called out on a public holiday. Eventually they succeeded in getting her into a strait-jacket and away to hospital. As they left I started singing, 'I wish you a merry Christmas', then the butler kicked me up the backside.

Another cook had a mania for breaking china. If a dish crashed to the floor her face would light up with smiles. 'They comes in at the front,' she would say as she picked up the pieces, 'and they goes out at the back,' and she'd sling the lot through the door causing another crash and me a lot of trouble picking up the bits. She did it once too often, just as the butler was coming in and a piece hit him above the eye. It was another stitching job, and another packing job for the cook.

It seemed poor Mrs Coriat was fated, for when the next cook arrived, nanny was in the kitchen.

'Good afternoon,' she said, 'I'm Miss Smith, the children's nanny.'

'Oh,' said the cook, 'are you. Then what are you doing in here? This is my domain. Your place is the other side of that hatch and if you keep there you and I will get on all right.'

That put the cat among the pigeons, the two of them went at it, shortly to be joined by Mrs Coriat. It seemed to Miss Smith that madam was taking the cook's side, so she waded in to her with a few well-chosen words,

'Don't you speak to me like that,' said Mrs Coriat.

'I've spoken to a princess like it, she had to listen and so will you,' was the reply.

Losing a cook was one thing, losing a nanny another. This was an occasion when a cook left without so much as making a cup of tea, or unpacking her trunk. There was of course a succession of temporaries, some of them foreign, which was of advantage to the staff since there was never any monotony in the food we ate.

I have hesitated in mentioning the name of the house, it caused me considerable embarrassment. 'Twatley Hall' it was called, and if you had to give that address to people when they asked you where you lived, you'd feel pretty uncomfortable under the collar. Some whom I told looked quite nastily at me, as though I was having them on, others suggested another name for the place, and others were downright rude and said, 'Yes, you look as though you do,' or words to that effect. I blush to the roots even now when I think of it.

The main activity of the house was hunting. The family and their four children all rode and we kept a number of horses and ponies which were looked after by stable girls. Hunting meant a lot of work for me, brushing and cleaning their gear. I'm glad to say the valet looked after the master's hunting pink. Most of the entertaining we did was of horsey people who looked like their mounts and neighed as they talked and laughed. I did a few impersonations which were enjoyed below stairs.

After I'd been there three years I got a touch of the 'Folies de Grandeur'. I saw an advertisement for a nursery footman at Buckingham Palace. It was shortly after the Coronation of Queen Elizabeth in 1953. I took a look at myself in the mirror and said, 'That, Peter, is you,' and my mind went back to the ballroom scene of *Cinderella*, with all the flunkies to-ing and fro-ing. I told Mr Clement of my new-found ambition; he didn't laugh at me, but helped me with my letter of application.

In a few days' time I got a reply from the Palace telling me to report for interview, and enclosing a railway warrant for the return journey to Swindon. I dolled myself up a little more discreetly this time, I didn't want them to think I was looking for a job with the Prince Regent! When I arrived at Paddington station there was a chauffeur to meet me who took me to a back door of the Palace and put me into the hands of a footman. He looked me up and down, as if he was making sure my flies were done up, and took me to an office where I was introduced to the sergeant footman and the deputy sergeant footman who also inspected me, asked a few questions, then led me to the master of the household's floor where I was seen by Mr Ainsley, the steward. By now I was reckoning that at the rate I was going through the chain of command I'd see the Queen about Tuesday week. When Mr Ainsley had finished with me it was decided that I had better have some lunch, so another footman took me down to what I supposed was the servants' hall. It was like the description a friend of mine gave me of the beaches of Dunkirk during the evacuation. 'My dear, the noise, the people!' I remarked on it to the footman who was guarding me.

'This is just the first sitting,' he commented.

The lunch was lousy, cold meat with hot gravy and potatoes, sour rhubarb and junket. They weren't serving coffee and liquors that day so with my teeth feeling as though they didn't belong to my face, I was taken to see a Major Millbank (I think that was his name), who questioned me about my family, going back to my grannies and grandfathers.

'They'll want to know about my great Uncle Charlie, who went inside for poaching,' I thought.

Eventually this Major Millbank seemed satisfied that I didn't come from a long line of bachelor forefathers, and I was taken to see Lord Plunkett, the master of the Queen's household. He quickly told me what I would be expected to do, and then took three times as long telling me what I was expected not to do; finally he dismissed me.

I left the office and found myself looking into the waistcoat of the tallest man I'd ever seen, and I'm no dwarf myself. I looked towards the ceiling and was told that I was now to be taken to see the doctor. I was feeling dazed but not poorly and I nearly told him so before he added, 'For a medical inspection.' He showed me to a car, ushered me in, doubled himself up and somehow got in beside me.

After about a quarter of an hour's study of my manly form the doctor told me to put my clothes on and get out. In the waiting-room I looked for Atlas, the footman. He was nowhere to be seen. I questioned the receptionist who thought that he'd left because they'd done with me for the present, so I made my own way back to Paddington station.

On the journey home I cursed myself for a fool for ever having put myself in this position, and determined never to believe what I saw in pantomimes again.

'You can always turn the job down,' was the butler's comment when I told him my story and of my predicament.

'Yes, and get put in the Tower for treason,' I answered.

I need not have worried; a few days later I received a letter informing me that Her Majesty would not be requiring my services. I now became quite indignant. 'Who does she think she is under her tiara? In any case she doesn't know what I'm like, she didn't even take the trouble to interview me.'

Although I was anxious by now to better myself, as they say, it was some time before I could pluck up courage to apply for another job. Eventually, having watched a few more cooks come and go, I applied for the position of footman to the Honourable Michael Astor, and was appointed. So began an association that has continued during my whole life in service. It's not just that I have served with members of the family, but that I came under the influence and guidance of Mr Lee, and made friends with other Astor servants, Charles Dean, George Washington, Rosina Harrison and Bill Silver, with all of whom I've kept in touch over the years. Again members of the Astor family were visitors to a number of the houses in which I served and whenever we met they were friendly and quick to greet me.

Mr Michael Astor was the third son of Nancy, Lady Astor, and his home was at Bruern Abbey, Churchill, near Oxford. The Abbey was, as it sounds, a restored ruin, but now both a thing of beauty and a comfortable home. When I arrived it was still being made habitable, the family were living in a cottage near by and Mr Silver the butler was continually threatening to put in a bill for the shoes he'd worn out traipsing to and from there.

There was a good staff; the butler and myself, an odd man, Miss Tamms the housekeeper and a housemaid, Maurice the French chef, and Ron, the kitchen man; there were also a lady's maid, a nanny, Miss Coyle, and two chauffeurs. Not a bad lot for 1954, and quite costly if you consider that I was getting eight pounds a week. We all got on very well together, which was fortunate as we were miles from the nearest habitation. Mr Michael was a literary type, fond of the arts. Mrs Astor was very pleasant and kept herself busy with the house and her four children, two girls and two boys. It was another Astor marriage that didn't last though, for she later became Lady Ward of Witney. She was wealthy in her own right; her father was a Dewar of Dewar's Whisky.

The children gave life to the house, sometimes too much for the servants. Their sliding across the hall or their rushing around upstairs would upset Miss Tamms, and she made it plain. The children retaliated in the delightful, charming way upper class children have. 'How do you spell Tamms?' one would ask. 'B-I-T-C-H,' the others would chant, and then they would scream the place down laughing at their childish wit.

Mind you Miss Tamms asked for it, for she was a little eccentric. There was a nude painting on the first landing; she christened it the lady 'Cora Corby' (I never did discover why), and would chat to it as she went by, with remarks like: 'Good morning, Cora, we're dressed for the weather this morning I see', or, 'All ready for your bath, darling'. At other times she would take against her: 'You're a dirty little slut, Cora, go and get some clothes on this instant', and other little pleasantries of a similar, if coarser, nature.

Miss Tamms also used to complain about the amount of entertaining the family did, sometimes justifiably. Once Princess Margaret was coming for the weekend with a party, and there were still guests in the house at lunch time, occupying the room the Princess was to use. 'The royals will be coming up the front drive while the others are driving down the back, with the royal bed still hot from their common bodies.'

In my modesty I have omitted to tell of the talent I had acquired over the last few years. I was by now a fair performer on the accordion, and was frequently called upon to lighten the darkness below stairs. Miss Tamms's favourite number was 'I've got a lovely bunch of coconuts', which she would scream out at the top of her voice. It was not their favourite number upstairs, as Mr Silver was frequently required to point out to us. For most of the time, though, they suffered my playing in silence.

Ron, the chef's assistant in the kitchen, also had his

peculiarities. After dinner had been served he would set off on his bicycle, scouring the surrounding countryside. I seldom heard him return. It was our opinion that he gave the local girls French lessons. I once met him in a pub in Oxford with two of his pupils. 'Ah, Peter,' he cried across the bar, 'I've been telling these ladies about your instrument. Come over and give them a bit of your "Love's old sweet song".'

It was while I was at Bruern Abbey that I first met Lady Astor and the redoubtable Rosina Harrison. It came as a bit of a shock. I'd met a few mistresses and maids but never two such strong contrasting characters. Unconsciously Rose took over in the servants' hall just as Lady Astor did upstairs. My first reaction to her was not in her favour, but by the time she left I had changed. 'She's one that will be the better for knowing,' I thought, an early verdict that time has proved to be true. Lady Astor I never did come to terms with and gave up trying, for she was a personality outside my experience. During the time I was at Bruern my contact with her was confined to the telephone. 'It's Lady Astor, here, "His" mother.'

Mrs Dewar was another with a strong personality. The difference between her and Lady Astor was that while her ladyship and Miss Harrison had been together for nearly thirty years, Mrs Dewar couldn't keep a maid for thirty minutes. She was constantly changing, and I never saw the same one twice. Years later when I was with the Fitzwilliams at Milton Hall she arrived with a maid who was seeing out her notice. 'If she thinks I'm going to wait up till four in the morning to unzip her, she's got another think coming,' was her terse comment that spoke volumes.

Although life at the Abbey was pleasant enough it didn't suit me; the place was too remote and I felt I was being buried alive. When I told Mr Silver of my feelings, and that I would have to give in my notice, he was completely understanding, and so was Mrs Astor. Apparently I must have given satisfactory service for they said they wanted to keep me in the family and would I consider a similar appointment with Lord William Astor at Cliveden. It seemed a good idea; I was interviewed by Mr Lee, and accepted as a member of his staff.

It was a job that gave me confidence and competence for a lifetime. Mr Lee was a legend in service, everybody knew of him; such was his reputation that at first I was almost afraid of him. He had a great presence, it was as if he and not Lord William was master of the house. It was not long, though, before I found that behind this façade there was kindliness and patience. From the moment I arrived he began teaching me and he did it by showing me how things should be done. It was fortunate in a way that I had to valet him, as a steward's room boy would have had to have done years before; it brought us closer, and gave him a greater opportunity of passing on his knowledge and experience. George Washington, who shared Mr Lee's command, though also valeting his lordship, was very considerate too, though in a different way. The under butler, Mr Fowler, at seventy-three years of age, was even older than Mr Lee. When I told him my name was Peter, he said, 'Ah, we've had all the disciples here, five times over. It don't do them any good, not at this time of the year. Next week's the fourth of June, and the house gets invaded by half of Eton College, no sooner have we recovered from that than it's Ascot Week. You'd better make yourself comfortable now for you won't have time to go to the loo for three weeks.'

Fowler was the greatest silver cleaner I've ever known. His methods were old-fashioned, but so were the results. He was also what was considered at that time to be a dirty old man. On one day every week, bright and early, looking as polished as his silver in his blue suit, he'd catch a train to London and make straight for the Windmill Theatre where he would join the queue, with others of his age and type, to watch what in those days passed for a strip show. It was, by present-day standards, almost respectable, and some of our greatest comedians have had their training there; but Fowler and his like didn't go there to laugh, they went to goggle at the naked models who were draped around the stage. I must say this weekly orgy didn't seem to do him any harm, and the following day he'd be rubbing away at his silver just as vigorously as ever.

Fowler was right about the fourth of June and Ascot Week. There were fifty to lunch on the fourth, heaven knows how many teas we served on the terrace; and there was another crowd in for dinner. As for Ascot Week, I spent it in a haze. It wasn't who was there, it was who wasn't. I particularly remember Douglas Fairbanks and his wife, and Prince Aly Khan with Kim Novak – I naturally would because of my earlier theatrical ambitions. Lady Lambton I remember for a different reason; she didn't stop pressing her bell from the moment she arrived; she made us mad and her maid demented. I don't know how the poor girl had the strength to tolerate it, for no sooner did she sit down to a meal than her lady was ringing for her. To my knowledge she never finished a course.

Ascot Week at Cliveden was a great experience, but one I am glad I never repeated. Miss Harrison has told me how exhausted she used to get, but as I was able to point out in her day Lady Astor deplored the drink and kept respectable hours, while in mine champagne flowed like water, there were supper parties and carousing well into the morning, and we had less staff to cope with it all.

There was another exciting and work-provoking event; shortly after I got there Lord William's Lady Astor had a baby girl (I think it must have been arranged so that she arrived a few weeks before Ascot). Cliveden was turned into a sort of nursing home, and a wet nurse was flown in from Ireland. She was the first and only one of her kind I saw; I thought they'd been dispensed with years ago. Mrs O'Gorman was her name; she dressed the part – a long black dress, a nurse's cap and a veil draped down her back. She was a merry soul, particularly in the evening when she had a nip or two, for that baby's milk was well laced with whisky.

I've never been much good with babies; you'll not see me leaning over a pram tickling one under the chin and gurgling at it; they strike me dumb. I wasn't too pleased therefore when shortly after a feed, and Emily (that was the baby's name) was being carried along the corridor by Mrs O'Gorman, she stopped to show me the child.

'You've not met this gentleman, yet, come salute him me darlin',' she said in her broad Irish brogue.

I gazed tongue-tied at it. At that moment it smiled; this cheered me. 'It's laughing at me,' I said.

'Is it, be Jesus,' said Mrs O'Gorman, 'that means it's got the wind. Come along me darlin',' and she made to move off. She was too late, the wretched baby was sick all over its clothes.

'Not only an actor but a critic,' I thought, remembering the old saying.

I stayed about nine months at Cliveden. I felt I'd learnt a lot and was anxious to practise what I'd learned on another house.

I applied for a job with a Colonel and Mrs Harrison as a one and only footman – staffs by now had thinned down – and worked under a strict butler, a Mr Shaw. There was a cook/ housekeeper, a Mrs Key, who was so old she could hardly put one foot in front of the other. (Her name suited, for she carried a bunch of keys round her waist and every time she moved she rattled.) The housemaid was even older than Mrs Key, but a better mover. There was also a young daily cleaner which was just as well. Mrs Harrison had a ladies' maid, with another name to fit the job, Christmas – she was always 'coming'. The chauffeur, Wheeler, was yet another old retainer; this was easy to see as his uniform was green with age. Mrs Harrison used to say, 'Wheeler would never leave me, would you, Wheeler?'

It's my opinion that if ever he did he would have to be chiselled out of that uniform.

The house was at Kings Waldenbury, near Hitchin in Hertfordshire. It was old but well appointed, most of the bedrooms having dressing-rooms and bathrooms. They also had names which were shown on an old-fashioned bell board – Pearl, Diamond, Amethyst, Ruby and Sapphire, and were decorated in the colours of the gems. We tended to call the guests after their rooms! 'That bloody Sapphire's jingling again', or, 'Pearl wants his breakfast'.

The Harrisons were pleasant people to work for, even though the butler was a tartar. The snag was that they had eight daughters. They were nice enough girls, but they invaded us at weekends, bringing their husbands or boyfriends with them. It was bedlam. 'Who's for tennis?' rings in my ears as I recall that summer, and no self-respecting cucumber sandwich will ever look me in the eye again.

Colonel Harrison, whom I suppose was to blame for all those daughters, was a quiet gentleman – someone had to be. I think he must have wanted sons. He was a great knitter and sweaters and socks for the navy were his big thing; there was always something blue in his needles. 'Hello sailor' I used to murmur to myself as I passed him.

I was happy enough with the Harrisons but the style of the job was not what I was used to, so I told the butler I would be leaving. He took it badly and gave me a month of the sulks. Why do employers, when you give in notice, look on it as they would the break up of a marriage and make the last weeks the same kind of purgatory as the time must be before a final separation is arranged?

'You don't love me any more, do you, darling' seems to be their attitude. My answer to that to all my employers is, 'No, and I never bloody well did.'

My next position in 1955 was as footman to Sir Richard and Lady Fairey, the aircraft people, at Bossington House, near Stockbridge in Hampshire. This was a pleasant episode though tinged with sadness, since for much of the time Sir Richard was a sick man. He had heart trouble but wouldn't allow it to get him down. Shortly after any attacks he would be up again and down on the river taking it out on the trout and the salmon. He was a keen and successful fisherman; they even smoked their own salmon.

Lady Fairey was his third wife and was kind and attentive towards her husband, the children and the servants. Sir Richard's eldest son had lost his legs as a result of the war. He was a great friend of the legless pilot Douglas Bader, and showed the same kind of courage in his infirmity. He was very active and often would fly over in his helicopter for breakfast, on his way to work, brightening the scene whenever he came. Any cooks I met later who complained about 'me legs' got a back hander from me. 'You thank your lucky stars you've got any,' I said, and then I'd hold Mr Richard up to them as an example.

A Mr and Mrs Harris were butler and ladies' maid respectively, a delightful couple who had both been in very good service for years. The cook was a native of the village, but none the worse for that. The general cleaning was done by a daily.

Most of the entertaining was for those in the aircraft industry, many of them war-time pilots or boffins, a pleasure to valet and open-handed with their tips.

We got a bit of the mod scene there from time to time, for Sir Richard's daughter, Jane, 'came out' while I was with them, so during the season debs and their beaux were around the house. Sir Richard gave her a dance, the full treatment, champagne, a band, a large marquee, fairy lights, midnight bathing, the frocks, the jewels, the tiaras, the lot. Fortunately the food and drinks side of it was organised by outside caterers, but we were kept busy with an earlier dinner party and helping to clear up the debris. Watching people smothered in diamonds, half pissed, skirts hoist, eating bacon and eggs on the stairs at five o'clock in the morning is a quaint if jaundice-making sight.

I staggered up to bed, picking my way through recumbent couples, thinking how unattractive second-hand love can be. I opened the door of my room, switched on the light to find my bed was getting it first hand! There were a couple on it going at it like knives. My presence didn't seem to disturb them. A brazen little cow turned her head on the pillow and looked at me with what normally I would have taken for innocent eyes.

'Oh,' she murmured, cool as you like, 'is the party over then?'

'This one is for you two darlings,' I said haughtily. 'Now get yourselves out before I call the butler.'

Telling the story the next day in the servants' hall it seemed more amusing than it was at the time. It became one of my party pieces, 'What the footman saw'.

Just after Christmas we left for a holiday in Bermuda. Sir Richard took a house over there and as the butler and his wife had no wish to travel I went with them to run the place. Instead of a ladies' maid we took a nurse as the master's health had deteriorated. The sea trip did him good and so did life on the island. All looked set fair until one evening after dinner there came a fearful scream from the nurse's room. She had been attacked and robbed by some native. Sir Richard rushed out of the sitting-room in time to see the intruder running from the front door. Foolishly he gave chase, only to collapse in the garden. From that time on he was more or less a permanent invalid. We continued the holiday, ending with a visit to New York, but he was carried aboard the *Queen Elizabeth* on a stretcher, and our journey home was not the fun and games I had hoped it would be. He never regained his health and died some six months later.

I suppose my next job was the nearest I ever got to the old style of things that Rose's other friends have described. I was appointed as footman at Luton Hoo, home of Sir Harold and Lady Zia Wernher.

It was a great mansion of a place. Outside it was imposing but modern; it had been rebuilt after a fire in 1843. It was its contents that mattered. The collection of pictures, tapestries, mediaeval ivories, Renaissance jewels, Fabergé and English porcelain and china are among the greatest in the world. Fortunately I didn't have to clean or look after any of those things; they formed part of the museum, for the main house was open to the public. The family occupied one of the wings which was big enough in all conscience, and contained sufficient treasures of its own.

Sir Harold was the third baronet, having succeeded his brother in 1948. His mother had been Alice S. Mankeivicz, and later Lady Ludlow, and it was through her that he had inherited the famous Ludlow collection of porcelain. He was chairman of Electrolux, the vacuum cleaner people, and of the Ericsson Telephone Company, so he wasn't short of a shilling or two.

Lady Zia was the daughter of the Grand Duke Michael of

Russia, a relation of the late Tsar, and many of the treasures of the house belonged to her through her ancestors. She had two daughters; her only son had been killed in action during the Second World war. The family's main interests, apart from their collection, were shooting, and horse riding and breeding; Brown Jack and the filly Meld are themselves internationally famous.

The Wernhers kept what was to me a large staff, a butler/valet, under butler, a footman, an odd man, a housekeeper and two housemaids, a chef and three in the kitchen, a lady's maid, plus a host of dailies who descended on the place every morning, many of them of course employed in the museum. After I'd been there for a time the butler died, the under butler took his place and I moved into his.

It was a pleasant job and the staff got on well together, but there were two slight snags. One was that when visitors to the museum tired of looking at beautiful things they would wander round outside the house, and since we worked in a semi-basement they got pleasure watching we treasures going about our tasks. They weren't above making personal comments either. I was no sensitive flower but when one day I looked up and saw a party of schoolchildren sticking out their tongues at me it gave me a nasty turn. I made a V sign and shouted a few well-chosen words at them, to which they responded by throwing peanuts in through the window, cheeky little sods! Eventually they went away. A couple of minutes later the butler came down and tore me off a strip; a teacher had complained about the words she said that I had taught her children!

Lady Zia had a habit I couldn't abide. At meal times she'd sit with a pad and pencil by her side and whenever she noticed any mistake or fault she would make a note, and whoever had slipped up was in trouble. It's the sort of thing which can make even the most perfect servant blunder, for the sight of her, pencil poised, affected the concentration; I was never able to get used to it. Still no employer is ever quite perfect and it's just as certain that no servant is either.

For the first time in my life in service I had to wear livery. The idea fascinated me; it was part of the theatre that I hankered after, and with the smell of grease paint again in my nostrils I went to be measured at a tailors in Conduit Street in Mayfair. I'm told that in the old days tailors treated servants with every courtesy in the knowledge that a new footman might one day become a butler who could put trade in their way. Not this lot; I suppose they realised that I was one of the last of the Mohicans. They put the tape measure round my body like streak lightning and left me doubled up after they had taken my inside leg measurements. Then they took the gilt off the gingerbread by comparing our livery to the porter's uniform at the Dorchester Hotel. It was made up of a green tailed coat, green trousers piped with gold, and a gold and black striped waistcoat; with it we wore a white stiff shirt, white bow tie and black shoes. I don't know whether it was as a result of the rushed measuring job but when I put it on it was like being in a strait-jacket. I began to look forward to the summer when we were allowed to wear a thinner jacket of cream linen, piped with green and gold round the collar and sleeves.

We entertained regularly – generally the racing set, but also in the winter there would be shooting parties. The Wernhers were very popular with the royals. The Queen and Prince Philip came three times while I was there, always for a weekend on their wedding anniversary. In fact the only member of the royal family who I didn't meet at that time was the Queen Mother. Foreign royalty also came, people like King Gustav and Queen Louise of Sweden, Prince and Princess Paul of

Jugoslavia, the Grand Duchess Xenia of Russia; you name them we had them.

The Queen's visits used to cause the most flutterings in the dovecotes. They were 'quite informal'; heaven knows what we would have had to do if they had been formal.

Preparations started weeks before; the drives were gone over, gardens tarted up, painters all over the place, the kitchen staff were more edgy than usual, and Lady Zia's notepad got filled up. The extraordinary thing was that when Her Majesty arrived it did become informal. She seemed to breathe her spirit into the house and everyone immediately relaxed. She was friendly to all without being patronising. I remember on one occasion when the wife of a member of the staff was expecting a baby during the weekend; Her Majesty's interest made it an excitement for everyone, and the delight she showed when it was born was an expression of almost personal involvement.

I think she would have enjoyed as much as I did an event that occurred on her first visit while I was there. It was a foggy afternoon so her arrival was delayed. There were look-outs down the drive whose job it was to keep the house informed so that the Royal Standard could be struck at the moment her car came into sight. We were all standing ready at our posts. I felt a thrill of anticipation as the flag went up. There was a few seconds' pause, and then the Luton laundry van appeared out of the mist!

The serving at dinner was little different from normal, except that there was a double service for the Queen and Prince Philip; that meant that two waiters served them instantaneously with meat and vegetables while other servants looked after the rest of the table. The food was simple and the Queen and the Prince seemed to be very fond of melon starters. She drank sparingly, a glass of sherry before a meal, very little wine – and of only one kind – with it. The china was of course of the best and the Russian crystal glasses were always used. Both the royals had finger bowls by them whatever they were eating. Her Majesty's favourite flowers were carnations and the table decorations were a delight, though it seemed a shame that they had to be changed for each meal.

After dinner there was either a film or some other entertainment. While I was there Winifred Atwell the honky-tonk pianist appeared; she didn't quite come off – it spoilt her style playing on a newly tuned grand piano.

The royal couple were given a suite, a main bedroom, dressing-room and bathroom. None of the house servants were allowed in it. The Queen took breakfast in her room and always ate a cooked meal. On the Saturday there was a shooting party and the men left the house early; the ladies followed later. Her Majesty showed the kind of consideration one expected of her. When she returned for lunch, her lady's maid would meet her at the door with a pair of slippers into which she changed on the rough matting. After lunch the ladies would again join the shooting party and return with them. Afternoon tea was served in the dining-room, which made sense, saved a lot of work and avoided accidents.

On Sunday morning the royal party would go to church locally. I remember once one of the chauffeurs being detailed to drive the Queen and the Prince. He had been a racing driver at one time and I heard Lady Zia giving her instructions, 'Remember who you are driving. You will proceed very slowly, people like to look at Her Majesty. We want none of your race track antics today.'

Below stairs the servants' hall was all bustle during the day and well into the night. Lunch was served in the old style, with places allotted in order of seniority. It was more formal than the dining-room upstairs. During the years I was there the Queen's maid was the famous Miss Macdonald, 'Boo Boo', and the Prince's valet, Mr McNair, though one year he brought his late father-in-law's servant, Mr Macdonald. It was most confusing having the two with the same name. The place hummed with secretaries, officials and C.I.D. men who were augmented by the local police.

I'd always heard that the royal family never tipped. This is wrong. After each visit I was handed an envelope containing a pound. From the other servants I heard that the amount varied according to status. My name was written in the Queen's hand; I checked this by comparing it with the visitors' book.

Then one day Mrs Pallett, the housekeeper, said to me, 'Isn't it about time you got a butler's job, Peter?'

I hadn't considered moving, but it got me thinking. So in 1960, when I saw an advertisement for a butler in *The Times*, I decided to apply. I didn't much like the look of it, it was under a box number which, as many of my colleagues had told me, covered a multitude of sins. They were wrong.

A reply came from Lord Boyd, better known in political circles as Lennox Boyd, one time Colonial Secretary. He interviewed me at his London house in Eaton Close, Belgravia; we both liked what we saw, and I stayed with the family for three years.

We were a small staff in London: a housekeeper who'd been with the Boyds since they got married, and who also looked after Lady Patricia; a cook; a daily maid, and myself as butler/valet. His lordship also had a secretary who came daily.

The main family home was Ince Castle, Saltash in Cornwall, a large place, which Lady Boyd had had renovated, and which was an expression of her excellent taste. Although they had a resident staff there, I often travelled to Ince.

Apart from his political duties, his lordship was also a director of Guinness the brewers of Park Royal, and her ladyship was the daughter of the second Earl of Iveagh, son of the founder of the firm. The Boyds had three sons, but it was the youngest, Mark, whom I saw most of.

Lord Boyd was the busiest man I'd ever served. I would call him at seven fifteen in the morning and often find him working away with piles of papers surrounding him on his bed. He was never still. Every day I was given a list of his meetings and appointments, so that I knew exactly what clothes he would be wearing, and when. Generally he left the house for Park Royal at nine each morning, in a large Rolls, with a deep red carnation in his buttonhole. If by any chance he was unable to go the house would be invaded by secretaries and would rattle to the sound of their typewriters. On many occasions he was so pressed for time that I would have to pack his clothes, rush to wherever he was in a taxi, jump into the Rolls, help him change and see that he looked like a bandbox when he reached his destination. Once I had to get him into court clothes for a Lord Mayor's Banquet. We got to the Mansion House just as he was putting on his scarlet and white ermine-lined coat. As we drew up he called to his chauffeur, 'Hurry up, Price, get me out of here,' and as we did he shouted, 'Three cheers for Father Christmas,' to the astonished crowd who were lined up around the steps.

He collected walking sticks of every age and nationality and a corridor at Ince Castle was lined with them. Another feature at Ince was the white peacocks. Lovely though they looked, they could be a menace if afternoon tea was being served on the lawn. They would stand around and the moment attention was diverted from them would move in on the food; they could demolish a plate of cakes in seconds.

The major event during my time with the Boyds was a visit to Windsor Castle for Ascot Week. It was my turn to be entertained by the Queen. One morning in 1964 Mr Mark came down to my pantry and asked me if I would do him a very great favour. Guardedly I replied I would if it was within my power. 'If I can get my father's permission, would you consider coming to Windsor Castle with me for Ascot Week, and looking after me during my stay there?'

Would I? He didn't need an answer, my face showed it. To have the opportunity to attend what was probably the greatest social event of the year was every servant's ambition. Lord Boyd duly agreed to my going, and he and her ladyship took themselves off to Cornwall, leaving the coast clear for both of us to get ready.

We were to arrive in Windsor on the Monday, in time for afternoon tea; so after lunch I made my way to Waterloo to catch the train; Mr Mark was travelling by car. The platform was packed with servants, valets and ladies' maids and the guard's van was bulging with luggage.

Windsor station was like Southampton docks 'You'll never get through Customs with that lot,' I said to Lady Harlech's maid, who was standing looking pathetic by a mountain of trunks. There was a fleet of shooting brakes to take us and our stuff; she had to make two journeys, which didn't please her or the driver.

As we got into the town we were held up because the Garter ceremony was just ending. It was as Miss Tamms had said at Michael Astor's, in by one drive and out by the other, and the castle servants looked the way she did when she said it.

I was driven to an inner courtyard between the Lancaster Tower and the Edward I Tower, where our rooms were; there I was deposited with the luggage and told to wait for the housekeeper, Mrs Holmes. She was a charming lady, extremely helpful and understanding. She showed me Mr Mark's room, then directed me to mine, telling me that I would be sharing with another valet.

I sat on one of the beds and took stock of my surroundings; I was not impressed, neither was the bed! It had a hard uneven mattress all in waves like the English Channel, which was contained inside a black iron bedstead. I tried the other. It was no better. Apart from the two beds there was an old-fashioned wash-stand with basin and jug, an antiquated patchy mirror, tatty curtains, a wooden bar to hang our things on, one cane chair, a linoed floor and worn rug. Since it was in a tower the room was circular; even so I thought they could have done us a bit better than that. After all Mr Mark's room was delightfully decorated with fitted wardrobes, a divan bed, easy chairs, the lot. I was sitting feeling a bit disillusioned, when in came my companion for the week, Richard Wood. He looked around the room. 'Ah,' he said, 'the usual regal furnishings, brother prince of the bloody tower.' He started chatting away about how the royals housed visiting servants.

'You seem to know a lot about it,' I remarked. 'I should do, I am valet to Lord Snowdon; palaces are my speciality.' He proceeded to send everything and everybody up rotten; my spirits brightened and I could see I was in for an amusing and entertaining week.

Eventually we went down to supper, and if I hadn't been with Richard this was a meal I should have missed. We wandered down spiral staircases, along vast corridors, across courtyards, with Richard being continually stopped and asked for directions.

'I can only do my best,' he said to me. 'On our return we shall meet the same people trying to find their way. History has it there was one valet who only found his master in time to pack for him on the day of their return.'

When we finally reached our dining-room I found it in a way similar to the servants' hall I'd eaten in at Buckingham Palace. This time however the meal was properly laid out on a long table with linen tablecloths and napkins. The food was excellent and well served on good china. We were waited on by men in battle-dress and pretty waitresses. When I commented on this I was told that a special effort was made for Ascot Week. It was good to know that the Queen treated her guests in the same way that we treated her.

Next to the dining-room was the brushing-room where we took our charges' clothes to be sponged and ironed; it was like a vast dry cleaners; and all bustle first thing in the morning and in the early evening.

After supper Richard led me back to our room and I then attended to Mr Mark, who seemed to have settled in quite easily. It was white tie and tails for him every night. He was given a seating plan for dinner that evening, and each morning when I woke him with his orange juice I handed him a similar one for the day, which gave his place for lunch and dinner, and the coach he was to be driven in to the races. It must have been a great experience for him, going to the racecourse in a carriage down the long mile. On one of the days he went with Elizabeth, the Queen Mum. I think I was more excited than he was. 'I'd give a year's wages to be in your place,' I said, and told him that she was the greatest and the most gracious of them all as far as I was concerned. Though familiarity may have taken the gilt off the gentry's gingerbread I've never lost my respect for any of the royals.

Mr Mark wore casual clothes first thing in the morning, changing into morning suit and cravat around midday; a carnation would be brought in by one of the castle's liveried servants and he was then ready for the off. I would go down into the courtyard to watch them leave. The police didn't care for me very much, one of them saying to me, 'Stop pushing, you, I should have thought you'd have known every wrinkle on her face by now.'

I wasn't going to let him get away with that. 'It's because I know every wrinkle in the back of your neck that I'm trying to look at something more attractive for a change.'

Another put an elbow in my stomach. 'Get back, you,' he said, 'she's not taking any hitch-hikers today.' I couldn't think of anything to reply to that, so I gave him one of my looks.

The evenings were the best time, with everyone done up in their finery. That first night Richard told me they would be going to the Theatre Royal at Windsor, for a special command performance. So after we had finished our duties we rushed down there. There were floodlights everywhere and the cars were lit up inside. I got my first perfect view of the Queen Mum. She was wearing a pink crinoline dress, all tulle and organdie, and her hair was sparkling under her tiara.

Friday night was the ultimate in everything – it was the day of the Royal Ascot Ball. This was usually held in the Waterloo Chamber, but this time it was taking place in Windsor barracks, while dinner was served in the chamber. The visiting servants were allowed to go and see the preparations that were being made for the banquet. The room was laid out for hundreds of guests, the chandeliers giving a wonderful shimmer to the gold plate, silver and crystal. The sideboards were already laid out and, like the tables, were decorated with mauve and white sweet peas; their scent was everywhere. Men were standing on the tables in stockinged feet to lift the heavy table ornaments into place. While we were watching about a dozen chefs came in to have a look; they were smiling with pleasure at the sight, and twelve smiling chefs before a dinner party is a sight that is worth special mention. I'm afraid my powers of description do scant justice to the magnificent scene.

While we were standing there, Mrs Holmes the housekeeper came to tell us that anyone who wished could assemble around the grand staircase to see their Majesties and their guests pass down on their way to dinner. With no police to worry about this time I was one of the first there. I was joined by maids from the castle in their black dresses and white frills, then the visiting ladies' maids gathered and started rehearsing their curtsies. I found myself bowing in return. Eventually I was joined by Richard, who brought with him Lord Rupert Nevill's butler, Mr Field. We got chatting and I told him about my feelings for the Queen Mum. 'Oh,' he said, 'then I suggest you stand next to me, she visits us regularly and if she sees me she'll stop and have a word.' I took that with a pinch of salt. Still, thinking nothing ventured nothing won, I did as he suggested.

There was a hush as we learned They were approaching, then a gasp as the Queen and Prince Philip appeared. It was indeed a breath-taking sight. The Prince in his naval uniform, and the Queen glittering like the chandelier above her; then Princess Margaret and Lord Snowdon. Then lo-and-behold there she was, the Queen Mother, with a white ermine fur wrap, looking for all the world like the sugar plum fairy; the red band of the garter over her shoulder and meeting at her waist, wearing another beautiful tiara, pearls and diamonds from head to fingertips, for like the others she wore her rings over white gloves. What a sight she was. She couldn't have got another pin on her.

Then my great moment came as Mr Field had said it might; as she reached us she turned her head, recognised him and came over and asked how he was, saying how good it was to see him again, and how much she'd enjoyed her last visit to the Nevills', and while they were talking she was smiling at me. I could have swooned. Then she moved on. I held my breath as she came to the polished stairs. How would she manoeuvre them in that crinoline frock and her high-heeled silver shoes? But she did and she was able to wave to us all as well. Others followed, but to me now they were second and third best.

That evening was a gala night in the servants' dining-room, with a special buffet supper and wine. A band of Scottish pipers ate with us, dressed up in their kilts and sporrans – they were later going to play at the ball. We got pretty merry, we could afford to, after all we'd got our masters through the week successfully. There was one hiatus; Leslie McCloud, the Duke of Gloucester's butler, saw a dog's paw appear on the table. 'Good God,' he said, 'what's that thing?'

Miss Suckling, the Queen Mother's maid, trying to look more regal than her mistress, said, 'Thing! Thing! Be careful of your language, it belongs to this royal dog, here,' and she lifted up a corgi she was looking after for the Queen Mum.

The following day it was all rush and bustle to get away. When we arrived home Mr Mark expressed his satisfaction and thanks to me. He was very effusive, but I was surprised that there wasn't a tip on the end of it. I needn't have worried, a couple of weeks later I answered the door to a messenger from Aspreys, the Bond Street jewellers, and was handed a small parcel which to my surprise was addressed to me. It contained a gold tie pin, inscribed with my name and the dates of our visit. I only wear it on high days and holidays, but it is a wonderful memento of the most memorable week of my life in service.

I have to explain here that earlier I have interrupted the chronological order of jobs. I did this because for the

Fitzwilliams of Milton and Wentworth I served two separate periods; two years as footman in 1961 and 1962 and two years as butler in 1971 and 1972.

Lord and Lady Fitzwilliam were members of an old family, the first Baron Fitzwilliam having been created in 1620; they were Catholics like the Norfolks. It was, I thought, extraordinary that her ladyship had been married previously and that her first husband, Viscount Fitz Allan Howard, was still alive. I later learned that there had been some special Papal dispensation for her.

His lordship succeeded to the title indirectly, one of the previous heirs had been Lord (Peter) Milton, who was engaged to be married to Kathleen Kennedy, President Kennedy's sister, when both were killed in an air crash.

That I found both Lord and Lady Fitzwilliam delightful to work for must be apparent since I returned for a second helping, as it were.

When I first went there things were not easy among the staff. Mr Needs, the butler, had come with her ladyship when she remarried, his wife was her lady's maid and his niece was cook; quite a family affair. The housekeeper, Mrs Gregg had been with his lordship when he was a bachelor; she was very grand – grander than the people she was serving; she considered she knew the way things should be done and they weren't the way the butler and his lot were doing them, so sparks flew continually. I was in no-man's-land, constantly having to duck to keep out of trouble. My sympathies lay with Mr Needs; he was a highly trained butler of the old school, his wife was also well versed and well travelled. The only thing I had against them was that they not only coined but continually repeated the phrase, 'What fits us, Fitzwilliam.'

The family gave their name to a local hunt, and a pack of

hounds was kept at Milton. Both had given up riding but the first meet of the season would be at the Hall, and every Sunday the hounds were brought by the huntsmen to the front of the house for the guests to see. The butler and I would distribute the stirrup cups and fruit cake for the riders. It was a pleasant, friendly duty, the sort of scene shown on calendars or Christmas cards; but it could be hazardous.

One morning I was weaving in and out of the riders when a young lady's mount raised its tail. I jumped backwards, nearly losing my tray, but only just in time as with inches to spare its load fell at my feet. The other riders thought it funny. I expect they would have thought it funnier still if the horse had deposited on my tray. I unconsciously caused them further amusement.

'I'm ever so sorry,' the lady rider apologised.

'It's quite all right, miss,' I replied, 'I could see it wasn't your fault.' At this they all guffawed; a coarse lot hunting people could be.

A feature at Milton was their Jacobs flock, chocolate and cream coloured sheep, which were supposedly descended from the Biblical ones. They made excellent eating, and their coats wonderful hearth rugs.

The shooting season was their busiest time. The family would go to Wentwood Woodhouse in Yorkshire, for the grouse, then back to Milton for the pheasant – the two seasons ran into each other as it were. Wentworth was not so much a country house, more a palace. Its frontage was one of the longest of any house in Europe. It had three hundred and sixty-five bedrooms, which in my reckoning worked out at one for every day of the year. The family only occupied one wing, the main part of the house was used as a college. There was a small resident staff, and I didn't visit there until after I had returned as butler. It took an emergency to get me there then. At the beginning of the grouse season the butler there had some altercation with the other servants, and left. I was sent for and rushed up to take over. I was, of course, unaccustomed to their ways but was able to sort something out. Then I had a brain wave. If Charles Dean was free he, with his knowledge and experience of organising shooting parties, was the man to give help. He was free, and he came. With his unassuming efficiency he got things going, and kept them going. It was one of the most successful seasons that they had had. It was the Astor household to the rescue once again.

Now I come to the part of my story of which I am not very proud, though not to tell it would be like living a lie. As butler, sometimes now to two very big houses, running them with untrained or half-trained staff, many of whom were foreigners unused to our way, and with idiosyncrasies of their own, I began to come under considerable strain. I took what I thought was an easy way out. When I felt particularly tired I would pour a nip of spirits to get me through the next part of the day. It helped, but as with many before me, one nip led to two and so on, until my tiredness and irritation were a result of my drinking. Things moved fast after that and though I knew what was happening to me, I was unable to get myself under control.

Inevitably it came to the notice of my employers and one morning Lady Fitzwilliam sent for me. Few could have been more fastidious than she. She set herself very high standards, and expected others to do the same. I knew why she wanted to see me, I knew my behaviour had been disgraceful and I deserved and expected to be dismissed. No one could have been more fortunate in his employer. She listened to my story, then asked whether, if she was prepared to help me, I would try to help myself and make the efforts necessary if I was to be cured.

She took part of the blame on herself, and then said, 'It's only a sickness, Peter, and we'll see it through together.'

She paid for me to be treated by the highest doctor of his kind in the land. It meant many visits and subsequent weeks of torture for me; my work suffered but she didn't mind, and when I was pronounced as cured she was as happy as a mother would be for her child. I haven't had a drink since, nor do I think it likely that I ever will.

I continued in service with the Fitzwilliams for several months, but the reasons for my fall from grace were still there. I found it increasingly difficult to come to terms with my job employing the kind of servants that were now available. When I told her ladyship of my problem she was understanding, and accepted my notice in the nicest possible way. She then made her last great gesture. 'Peter, I've heard you admiring the four-poster beds we have in the house, I have one to spare and would like you to accept it as your leaving present.' My cup was full, so were my eyes. My room now boasts a Chippendale four-poster. I won't accept a job without it; take me, take my bed!

My experience with the servants at Milton was one that was repeated in successive jobs. If they were experienced, they were old, and trying to run a house with old retainers is neither exciting nor rewarding, particularly when employers expected the old standards. I worked for a time for yet another of the Astor children, Lady Ancaster, at Grimsthorpe Castle, but life was all bells.

I finally took stock of the situation. It seemed to me that the days of the old country houses were over, even if some were not prepared to admit it. I knew there were gentry who had seen what was happening and had cut their cloth accordingly, moving into smaller houses which could be well run by a butler, cook/housekeeper, and local daily women. I was fortunate to find such a place, a beautiful old house, carefully and tastefully furnished, Passenham Manor, Stony Stratford, in Buckinghamshire. I went there in 1970, to look after a Commander and Mrs Lawson. Unhappily Mrs Lawson died shortly after I had joined them, but the house is still evidence of her excellent taste. I have my own sitting-room and a bedroom; and of course my four-poster bed, lying on which I can dream of the glories of the past.

## Some Reflections on Peter's Story

There's no doubt that Peter Whiteley went into service with the image of the past in his mind. His father had been a box footman and his mother a parlour maid before the First World War. They must have told him of their memories and the discipline and conditions they expected he would find. He accepted these, but he didn't get the glamour, the style, the manner that two world wars had eroded from English society. It was the unsatisfied actor in Peter that pushed him into service; he was able to speak some of the lines, make some of the gestures, do some of the business, but the 'theatres' were closing down, or else becoming shabby, so he had to be satisfied with occasional glimpses of 'the old days'.

I believe that he was lucky, as all my friends were, to meet and serve the Astors. As children they had grown up, possibly in the shadow of their mother, but in the company, both social and political, of the guests of the most famous hostess of her time. They didn't attempt to copy their mother's style, but it gave them a background to work from. They also had money and they inherited the sense of service that the possession of riches and position used to require. Peter was also fortunate, which he admits, that because of the Astors he was able to work under Mr Lee, and meet Charles Dean and George Washington.

The thing I think which we all like and enjoy about Peter is his sense of fun, his extravagance of manner, his inability to be serious about anything for very long, and the way in which he is able to laugh at himself.

His affection and enthusiasm for the royals demonstrates this, for though he revels in talking about his experiences with them, he is to some extent 'sending himself up' as he would put it, at the same time.

The part of his story which I most admire is his open and honest admission to having been a victim of 'The Butler's Complaint'. In itself it is a courageous statement, but though he doesn't give us the details, the way he was able to pull himself back shows a courage and a will-power not given to many. His tribute to the help and kindness given to him by Lady Fitzwilliam does not in any way belittle his own strength of character.

Peter's life in service, at the age of forty-six, is by no means over, but it must be difficult for him to have any idea of the direction it is likely to take in the future. I can only wish him luck.

# THE EPILOGUE

So my pilgrimage has come to an end. It has been for me a fascinating journey, starting from the recollections of the nineteenth century and the halcyon days of the early twentieth, through the years between two wars – which were my own era, to the end of the means and meaning of service.

As my mother would have said, 'It's no good moaning, it's gone and will never come back.' I think though it's been worth recalling. In a way it has traced the decline of the British Empire, either leading or following that decay.

What have we lost? The great families of Britain have lost their power, which some will say is a good thing since it was an inherited power. I think we, as a result, have lost their example and influence and exchanged it for the example and influence of politicians and trade union leaders – lesser men. We have lost the spirit of country house life, with its style and grace; we have retained some of the buildings as museums, mausoleums, lifeless hollow things. As Sotheby's and Christie's auction sales have shown, we have lost many of the treasures that filled the houses, and we're going to lose a great many more.

On the other side of the coin we have lost the giving of service for the sake of a job well done and the satisfaction of having pleased.